The title — *Why We (Still) Believe* — connotes a team of seasoned advocates for the faith, with a wealth of experience and published insights. And that is what you find. Their occupational backgrounds vary (the academy, politics, medicine, the church and parachurch), as do their homelands (British/Scottish, Scandinavian, Middle Eastern), so there's a rich mix of illustration, citation, and style. And though the book bears the testimony of veterans, the work doesn't bog down in reminiscence. Rather, it offers pointed and argumentative counsel: theoretical and practical, pastoral and apologetical. I filled my copy with underlines and marginal notes, grateful for the 'conversation' and the prompts for further reading and writing.

Mark Coppenger
Professor of Christian Apologetics,
Southern Baptist Theological Seminary, Louisville, Kentucky

This volume is a rich, varied and accessible read: confident without being bumptious or triumphalist, and well-argued without being overly intellectual. The authors engage effectively with the many challenges to Christian beliefs and ethics that are found in contemporary society. The book will encourage and equip believers and challenge open-minded unbelievers.

Alistair Donald
Chaplain, Heriot-Watt University, Edinburgh

From its first chapter by Andy Bannister (whose doctorate is in Islamic Studies) to the concluding essay by the late Gordon Wilson (sometime MP and Leader of the Scottish National Party), *Why We (Still)Believe* is a clarion call to confidence in the truth and transforming power of the Christian gospel. Here a well-assembled team of fourteen Christian authors from various fields of expertise, give contemporary relevance to the psalmist's wise belief that 'In your light we see light'. Instructive, illuminating, challenging, and encouraging, these pages will motivate every reader to a clearer and more confident Christian worldview and lifestyle.

Sinclair B. Ferguson
Chancellor's Professor of Systematic Theology, Reformed Theological Seminary

D0302163

In a confused culture and an uncertain church, we urgently need this brave and confident clarion call. In a wide-ranging defence of the Christian faith, the contributors demolish contemporary secular arguments and strongly affirm the foundation truths of the gospel, demonstrating their essential relevance to today's world. Confronting the increasingly strident challenges to faith, this is a stimulating, robust and timely response.

Jonathan Lamb

Minister-at-large for Keswick Ministries,
IFES Vice President

Why We (Still) Believe is an insightful, informative compendium of extremely well written essays on contemporary hot-button issues. It will prove a helpful resource for thoughtful Christians seeking to respond in a gospel way in an increasingly secular West. Well played, Solas!

Jim Turrent

Lead Pastor, Central Baptist Church, Dundee

Apologetics needs to defend the biblical truth, as well as graciously attacking false accounts of reality. This twofold task is an on-going responsibility for all Christians although it is tough and at times intimidating. This book focuses on positively and freshly presenting arguments and reasons why evangelical Christians believe what they believe in the context of present-day Western scientific materialism and cultural relativism. The content is solid and the style is accessible. Apart from encouraging those who are already Christian, offering them tools to use in their evangelism, the book may stimulate non-Christians too in assessing the claims of the Christian faith. I welcome this collection of short essays that passionately and intelligently present a coherent and cogent case for biblical Christianity in our secular world.

Leonardo De Chirico

Director of the Reformanda Iniatitive,
Lecturer in Church history at IFED, Padova, Italy

The authors and contributors of this book write with incisive clarity, make use of their personal experience (including their mistakes) to bring together an invaluable resource for Christian students today seeking to share the gospel on campus. These chapters will give Christians courage, strengthen biblical convictions, develop vital listening skills in evangelism and potentially open many doors to speak of Jesus with winsome credibility, relational integrity and intelligent discussion that reaches the target audience.

Peter Dickson

Regional Team Leader in Scotland, UCCF: The Christian Unions

This book presents a compelling, cogent and elegantly expressed case for continued belief in Christianity. The book's strength is derived from the varied character and roles of its contributors. It is a must-read for Christians grappling with the challenges of a secularist society. It is also a good read for people not yet persuaded by the Bible but who may wonder why so many people believe its claims.

James M Fraser

Former Principal and Vice-Chancellor
of the University of the Highlands and Islands

I came to this book expecting to find the occasional nugget of gold. Instead I found a treasure trove overflowing with hugely valuable insights, thoughts, and truths. While in one sense challenges facing Christian belief are nothing new, they still need to be addressed in a contemporarily relevant way. This priceless collection does precisely that and leaves the reader immeasurably richer with lots of gems to share with others too.

Frank Sellar

Former Moderator of the Presbyterian Church in Ireland

WHY WE

STANDING FIRM ON BIBLICAL CHRISTIANITY

(STILL)

BELIEVE

EDITED BY DAVID J. RANDALL

SOLAS
CENTRE FOR PUBLIC CHRISTIANITY

CHRISTIAN
FOCUS

Copyright © David J. Randall 2017

paperback ISBN 978-1-5271-0088-6
epub ISBN 978-1-5271-0137-1
mobi ISBN 978-1-5271-0138-8

10 9 8 7 6 5 4 3 2 1

Published in 2017
by
Christian Focus Publications Ltd,
Geanies House, Fearn,
Ross-shire, IV20 1TW, Scotland.
www.christianfocus.com

with
Solas – CPC
Dundee, Scotland.
www.solas-cpc.org

Cover design by MOOSE77

Printed by Bell and Bain, Glasgow.

MIX
Paper from
responsible sources
FSC® C007785

CONTENTS

NOTES ON CONTRIBUTORS

ANDY BANNISTER is the Director of Solas (Centre for Public Christianity). He was formerly Canadian Director of Ravi Zacharias International Ministries and continues to work with RZIM as an adjunct speaker. He has a Ph.D. in Islamic Studies and has written *An Oral-Formulaic Study of the Qur'an,* and also the more popular level book, *The Atheist Who Didn't Exist (or: The Terrible Consequences of Bad Arguments)*. Andy has spoken in many settings, including universities across Canada, America and Europe, in business and parliamentary settings, in churches and on TV and radio. He has also been involved in numerous interfaith dialogue events, especially with the Muslim community. He is married to Astrid and they have two children.

IVER MARTIN was born in Inverness-shire but brought up in Paisley where his father was a minister. After studying electronics and electrical engineering, his first career was in the microelectronics industry in which he spent twelve years as an engineer. In 1992 he studied at the then Free Church College (now Edinburgh Theological Seminary) and thereafter spent twenty years in pastoral ministry in Scotland. In 2015 Iver was appointed as full-time Principal of Edinburgh Theological Seminary. He is married to Mairi and they have six adult children and eight grandchildren.

JOHN ELLIS is a consultant ophthalmologist working in the National Health Service in Dundee. He describes himself as terribly indecisive: after studying for five years to become a doctor, he spent the next five becoming a Mister again (surgical exams), and the five after that becoming a doctor again (Ph.D.). He thinks he'll probably stop there. He is married to Betty and they have two adult children (and an obnoxious cat). He enjoys cycling, reading, listening to music and flies a home-built single-seat micro-light whenever he can.

VINCE VITALE is the Director of the Zacharias Institute, and previously Team Director and Senior Tutor of the Oxford Centre for Christian Apologetics. He has taught in the Faculty of Theology and Religion at the University of Oxford and in the Department of Philosophy at Princeton University. His doctoral research centred on 'the problem of evil', and he and Ravi Zacharias have co-authored the books *Why Suffering?: Finding Meaning and Comfort When Life Doesn't Make Sense* and *Jesus Among Secular Gods: The Countercultural Claims of Christ*. Vince became a Christian as an undergraduate philosophy student, and – along with his wife, Jo – he regularly speaks and takes Q&A about the Christian faith on university campuses.

MAHER SAMUEL is an Egyptian Christian. He is a graduate of the Faculty of Medicine of Alexandria University and worked as a psychiatrist in governmental hospitals. He then obtained a Master's Degree in Philosophy & Religion from Trinity International University, Illinois, USA, and is currently an Arabic apologist and the Middle East Director for Ravi Zacharias International Ministries. He teaches in the Evangelical Theological School in Cairo and is the presenter of many television programmes on Arabic Christian channels. He is married to Magda and they have two sons.

JOHN BLANCHARD is an internationally known Christian preacher, teacher, apologist and author. He has written thirty books, including two of Britain's most widely used evangelistic presentations, *Right With God* and the booklet *Ultimate Questions*. The latter has over fourteen million copies in print in about sixty languages. His major book *Does God believe in Atheists?*, published in 2000, was voted 'Best Christian Book' in the 2001 UK Christian Book Awards. He is now heavily committed to Popular Christian Apologetics, a project involving writing, speaking, teaching and broadcasting in defence of the Christian faith. After the death of his first wife, Joyce, in 2010, he married Pam in 2015.

JOE BARNARD is a minister of the Free Church of Scotland and for eight years pastored a church in the village of Kiltarlity in Inverness-shire. He was a University Scholar at Baylor University in Texas and holds an M.Litt. in the Theological Interpretation of Scripture from the University of Saint Andrews. His passions are preaching the gospel to a secular audience and disciple-making. He is married to Anna and they have four young children. He is currently developing a men's discipleship ministry in his home state of Louisiana.

DAVID J. RANDALL studied in Edinburgh and Princeton before ministering in Macduff, Aberdeenshire, for almost forty years. He served as convenor of 'Why Believe?' and edited the previous Solas publication, *Why I Am Not An Atheist*. He has also written *Believe it or Not*, *Grace Sufficient* (missionary biography), *A Sad Departure,* and *Messages From Grandad* (teen apologetic). He is married to Nan and they have two surviving sons (who are also pastors), one daughter and six grandchildren.

STEFAN GUSTAVSSON is General Secretary of the Swedish Evangelical Alliance. He regularly debates and writes for different Swedish newspapers on issues such as religion, pluralism, freedom of expression, and theology. He also serves as the Director of

11

Centrum för Kristen Apologetik (Centre for Christian Apologetics), a Christian study centre in Stockholm, which focuses on cultural analysis, world view studies, apologetics and evangelism. He is also associate professor at the NLA University College, Kristiansand, Norway. He is the author of several books on Christian apologetics and the Christian mind. Stefan is married to Ingrid and they have three adult children.

RICHARD LUCAS is a teacher of mathematics in an independent boarding school. As a Christian apologist, he has engaged in many public debates with politicians and others, spoken at the Edinburgh International Science Festival, and been a guest on BBC1's *The Big Questions* as well as several other television and radio programmes. He is a prolific letter-writer with over a hundred letters published every year in newspapers. He is married to Mairi and they have two sons.

DAVID ROBERTSON is the minister of St Peter's Free Church of Scotland, Dundee, and a chaplain at Dundee University. He is the founder and Associate Director of Solas-Centre for Public Christianity. His 2007 book, *The Dawkins Letters*, resulted in invitations to debate throughout the United Kingdom and Europe in cafes, bars, libraries, universities, pubs, restaurants, village halls – and even churches! Since then David has had a large public profile in broadcasting, speaking and writing; he has also written *Awakening* (the life of R. M. McCheyne), *Magnificent Obsession,* and *Engaging with Atheists*. He is married to Annabel and they have three children.

NOLA LEACH was for many years Head of Religious Education and then a Year Head at a large comprehensive school; she also worked in the senior leadership team of a hospital in Suffolk. She joined CARE in 1999 as Director of the Caring Services Department, and in 2004 became CARE's Chief Executive. As well as being Director of CARE's Leadership Programme and Head of Public

Affairs, she oversees offices in Scotland and Northern Ireland. She is a speaker, writer and broadcaster, and has recently become co-leader of the Politics and Society Network at the annual European Leadership Forum in Poland. She is married to Tony and they have two sons and three grandchildren.

GORDON MACDONALD has an M.Th. in Christian Ethics and a Ph.D. in Political Economy. He has an interest in political theology and has conducted research on the Christian understanding of marriage and its interface with equality and human rights law. He has worked in political advocacy for seventeen years and has a wealth of experience in engaging with government, politicians and the media on social and moral issues. Gordon has served in local government as a Councillor and is a Board member of the Solas Centre for Public Christianity.

The late **GORDON WILSON** was the joint founder and first chairman of Solas-CPC. He was a lawyer and politician who served as Secretary of the Scottish National Party from 1963 to 1971 and became its Leader in 1979. He was elected Member of Parliament for Dundee East in 1974 and held the constituency until 1987. Among his writings are *SNP: The Turbulent Years* and *Scotland: The Battle for Independence*. He was Rector of Dundee University from 1983 to 1986, and has served on the boards of various voluntary bodies. He died on 25th June 2017, leaving his wife, Edith, two daughters, and five grandchildren.

PREFACE

Several years ago Solas published *Why I am Not an Atheist,*[1] in which various members and friends of Solas gave their reasons for their Christian faith and commitment. Interestingly, the German spin-off was subtitled, *9 Personnen erklären, warum sie noch anders können, als an Gott zu glauben* (*9 people explain why they couldn't do anything other than believe in God*).

Although that book included many positive points, it emphasised reasons for *not* believing in atheism. In *Why We (Still) Believe,* another group of writers gives a more positive account of why they believe in Jesus and hold to certain aspects of Christian belief.

The word 'still' indicates that they give answers to the various contemporary attacks on particular items of belief. Such attacks are not new, but perhaps the openness, belligerence and un-deferential nature of such attacks in the Western world is characteristic of our secularised culture that doesn't 'do' God.

Our writers are varied in nationality, background and experience, and they all hope that their words will (a) strengthen believers who may be tempted to buckle under the weight of current secular

---

1.   Christian Focus Publications, 2013.

attitudes, (b) equip them to 'give a reason' for the hope and faith they have (1 Pet. 3:15), and (c) prove persuasive to people who as yet do not believe. Our writers have approached the task in different ways, but they all deal with the question of whether it is reasonable to 'still' believe today.

We are not the first generation to face such pressure. A bishop wrote, 'It has come to be taken for granted that Christianity is no longer a subject of enquiry, but that it is now at length discovered to be fictitious. And accordingly it is treated as if, in the present age, this was an agreed point among all persons of discernment and nothing remained but to set it up as a principal subject for mirth and ridicule'.[2] That was written in 1736!

Long before that, the apostle Paul found that when he sought to present the gospel to one of the Roman governors examining him, he was met with, 'Paul, you are out of your mind; your great learning is driving you out of your mind' (Acts 26:24). Paul's response was, 'I am not out of my mind, most excellent Festus, but I am speaking true and rational words' (v. 25). The writers of this book share that view. Solas' ministry is one of 'persuasive church-based evangelism' and, while we know that no one is argued into the kingdom of God, we also believe that Christianity is, in Paul's words, 'true and rational'.

If we are asked why we believe at all, why we are Christians, the first and basic answer is that we believe God called us and led us to put our trust in Jesus Christ as our Saviour. In terms of an old hymn, we do not know 'how the Spirit moves, convincing men of sin, revealing Jesus through the Word, creating faith in Him', but we would wholeheartedly echo the sentiment of the hymn's chorus: 'But I know Whom I have believed and am persuaded'.[3]

Centuries before Paul's time, there was a crisis in the reign of King Hezekiah of Judah (727–698 B.C.). Sennacherib, King of Assyria, was threatening the people of Jerusalem with slaughter and he sent his field commander to call out to the people of Jerusalem,

---

2.   Quoted in Iain Murray, *The Puritan Hope* (Banner of Truth, 1971), 109f.

3.   Hymn by Daniel Webster Whittle, 1840–1901.

'Thus says the king: "Do not let Hezekiah deceive you, for he will not be able to deliver you out of my hand. Do not let Hezekiah make you trust in the LORD by saying, 'The LORD will surely deliver us...' Do not listen to Hezekiah"' (2 Kings 18:29–31). It's the same voice that says to us today, 'You don't mean to say that you still believe all that stuff!' That word 'still' carries the implication that if you still believe it all you must be some kind of old-fashioned throwback to the past, an ideological dinosaur.

The truth is, however, that other theories, ideas and world views come and go, while God's truth stands firm and outlives all passing fads and fancies. In G. K. Chesterton's epic epigram, 'At least five times in history the faith has to all appearances gone to the dogs; in each of these five cases it was the dog that died.'[4] Or, in the words of another hymn, God's throne 'will never, like earth's proud empires, pass away; His Kingdom stands and grows forever'.[5]

Christians find their security not in our holding fast to Christ but in His holding us fast (John 10:28; Phil. 1:6; Jude 24). But there is also the biblical call to stand firm:

• 'the people who know their God shall stand firm' (Dan. 11:32)
• 'take up the whole armour of God that you may be able to ... stand firm' (Eph. 6:13)
• 'continue in the faith, stable and steadfast, not shifting from the hope of the gospel' (Col. 1:23)
• 'we must pay much closer attention to what we have heard, lest we drift away from it' (Heb. 2:1)
• '... this is the true grace of God. Stand firm in it' (1 Pet. 5:12)
• 'be faithful unto death, and I will give you the crown of life' (Rev. 2:10)

---

4. Quoted by Os Guinness in *The Gospel in the Modern World*, ed. M. Eden & D. Wells (IVP, 1991), 105. Guinness writes, 'Like an eternal jack-in-the-box, Christian truth will always spring back. No power on earth can finally keep it down, not even modernity's power of Babylonian confusion and captivity.... To write these things is not to whistle in the dark, but to grapple with modernity with hope and direction. Our reliance from beginning to end must be on God's Word and Spirit and on their grave-opening, jail-breaking power in preaching, revival, reformation and mission'.

5. Hymn, *The Day Thou gavest, Lord, is ended* by John Ellerton, 1826–93.

The Solas website describes the organisation as 'a media and training ministry dedicated to resourcing and encouraging Christians and churches to communicate the gospel of the Lord Jesus Christ in the public square'. This outward-looking concern for evangelism is reflected in the first chapter of this book, in which our Director explains why he (still) believes in evangelism in a time when many want us to keep quiet — *believe if you must but don't try to convert other people.* After that, different aspects of Christian belief and commitment are considered — but perhaps the best introduction comes from the following C. S. Lewis-type communiqué which has come to light. In it the various subjects discussed in this book are highlighted.

~~~~~~~~~~~~~~~~

My dear Wormwood,

Many years ago I wrote to you about your attempts — pathetic as they turned out to be — to rescue one of these wretched humans from the clutches of the Enemy. Your failure caused much consternation down here, and matters were made worse when my letters to you were leaked, but the upside is that your story has been used in our seminars down here as a case study, so that other young devils have learned from your failure.

Since then I've been keeping a watchful eye on you and I am glad to see your progress in the intervening years (whatever they *are). You have made good use of your undeserved reprieve. I especially want to congratulate you on your success with that little word 'still'. You have managed to get so many of these miserable humans thinking that nobody can 'still' believe in God in this 'enlightened age' (not what we'd call it). In the minds of many people, belief in the Enemy has come to be regarded as old-fashioned and outmoded.*

You have made excellent use of the concept of tolerance, so that your patients are liable to be suspicious of 'evangelism' (excuse my language) and notions of trying to persuade or convert people. Work hard on getting religion privatised and kept out of public life.

Among our great successes has been our Bible Project. It was a massive forward stride to persuade the world to relegate the Bible to the museum, but our master-stroke has been to get doubt about the Bible into the church, so that many people only believe it where it backs up what they already think.

We can hardly believe that you've even convinced many people that the Enemy doesn't exist. You've used all the debates about science/religion, alongside all the old 'How can you believe in a good God when so many evil things happen?' arguments. You've had commendable success in getting people to think of God as a horrible sadist rather than a loving Father, and also to see the Enemy's 'Son' as a good man (again, not an assessment we'd second) who left them some fine teaching, and his Spirit as just a vague idea or even something to argue about.

Sometimes the church has been one of our best assets. You can easily get people criticising the church's history, its traditions, its music and the hypocritical lives of those who attend its services; how we love it! An unexpected success has been the downplaying of preaching. If you can persuade more of them to substitute talk-shops and other things for sermons, that will be good — anything to get people away from serious attention to that book.

I noticed your success with 'If God knows, why should we pray?' and other ways of undermining that strange activity they call prayer. Whenever your patients think of praying, remind them of a thousand-and-one 'more practical' things they need to be doing; it can be something as simple as checking their texts or tweets — whatever you like, so long as you just stop them praying.

Try to convince people that following the Enemy's way ('discipleship', as they call it) is an unrealistic notion in today's world, and when it comes to education, you must continue to pour resources into seeing that the young are protected from the Enemy's propaganda; do all you can to bury the idea that it was Christianity that led to universal education and to get religion out of schools altogether.

Recent attacks on the whole idea of 'fixed gender' have also greatly pleased our father below. We are delighted to know that you haven't fallen for the idea that marriage 're-definition' was a terminus — on with the work and do all you can to capture the young. 'The family' used to be a barrier to our work but we've managed to almost sweep it aside. Even I have been amazed at the rapidity of your advances in these areas. Congratulations also on your fruitful attacks on the so-called sanctity of life. Roll on the day when abortion, suicide and euthanasia are commonplace.

We hadn't really expected you to do so well. Before long Christians will be a tiny sect, hidden away from all possibility of doing any harm. Keep them out of public life; if they must have their stupid beliefs, persuade them to leave them behind whenever they leave the privacy of their own quarters. Do encourage every attempt to frame and use new laws to silence the Enemy's followers and to punish them if they raise their heads above the parapet.

You have made considerable progress, but we don't want you to rest on your laurels. There's much work still to be done and our successes have been so great that we must expect a backlash sometime. Vigilance is the price of success.

So, Wormwood, on with the good work!

Your forgiving uncle,

Screwtape.

1

WHY I (STILL) BELIEVE IN EVANGELISM

Andy Bannister

A couple of years ago I gave an open forum at one of Canada's leading universities on the theme, 'Is Christianity Irrational?' The topic drew a huge crowd — every seat was filled and students were even perched on stairs and crammed in at the rear. (I was later informed that the back row of seats was full of members of one of the LGBT groups on campus, ready to blow whistles and wave banners if I said anything too startlingly unprogressive, whilst the two rows in front of them were full of members of the Secular Alliance, preloaded with objections in case I said anything — well, too irrational, I guess.)

Despite the somewhat mixed audience, the event went amazingly well — I had an incredible opportunity not just to respond to the 'irrational' question but also to present the gospel and share why accepting what Jesus has done for us on the Cross is in fact the *only* rational response if Christianity is true. I even felt the Lord nudge me to end the lecture with a prayer for those who wanted to respond — something I don't always do at every university event. At the end of the evening, many sceptics and seekers hung around to talk further.

But my strongest memory of the night is neither the incredible way that God moved nor the many honest questions from those who weren't Christians, but a conversation with a campus ministry leader who waylaid me as I was leaving. 'How did you just do what you did?' he asked. 'Do what?' I asked, innocently. 'You preached, offered an invitation, and prayed. On *campus*.' He sounded incredulous, adding, 'In ten years of campus ministry I've never heard anybody end a lecture with a prayer like that. I didn't think it was possible'.

WHO'S AFRAID OF EVANGELISM?

Although it was the first time I'd heard it put quite that starkly, the sentiments which that campus ministry leader expressed to me that night are not unusual. I've been involved in public evangelistic ministry in various forms for some twenty years now and I regularly run into precisely this objection from Christians, whether it's in the UK, Canada or the USA. Evangelism isn't really *possible* anymore in today's postmodern world. We know we *should* be doing it, we feel guilty we're *not* doing it, we're incredibly grateful that God has given us SOLAS, or RZIM,[1] or J. John, or the Alpha Course, so that we don't have to do it.

Now I must stress that I sympathise with some of those sentiments because I used to hold them too. I remember doing all I could to avoid the 'e' word, not because I didn't *want* to do evangelism, but because if I was honest, I had a deep primordial *fear* of evangelism. And I suspect this goes for many Christians — most pastors I speak to mutter that it's easier to find volunteers to dredge the church drains by hand than to do street evangelism in the local shopping mall on Saturday afternoon. 'I'll do anything, pastor — just, please, not evangelism.'

So, what gives? Why are so many of us, if we're honest with ourselves, *afraid* of evangelism? After all, if the gospel is true — not merely a nice suggestion, but deeply, profoundly, life-alteringly,

---

1. Ravi Zacharias International Ministries.

world-shakingly *true* — then sharing the story of who God is and what He has done in Christ should be the most exciting, the most rewarding activity we can engage in. What a privilege to share the news of Jesus with those we care about. If that's the case, where does the fear come from?

FEAR OF OFFENCE

I think the first fear that many of us have when it comes to evangelism is a fear of causing offence. Most of us have a deep desire to be liked, to have our friends, colleagues and neighbours consider us decent, pleasant human beings and thus we have this fear that, were we to bring up the subject of religion, we'd immediately alienate our friends. And so we zip our lips, say nothing, and never allow the conversation to go any deeper than last night's football match or the latest amusing thing our three-year-old came out with. I suspect one reason we struggle with this is that many of us have got it into our heads that sharing Jesus is a little like a religious telephone sales script: we say X, our friend is supposed to ask Y, then we can share Z, and *whammo!* This feels forced and it feels false — for a very good reason: that's *precisely* what it is. The gospel is not a sales pitch.

But there's a deeper issue going on here, namely the deep discomfort many of us have with the idea of telling somebody else that they're wrong. Because that's what evangelism entails, right? If you want to share the gospel with an atheist, or a Muslim, or a Buddhist, or a worshipper of the Flying Spaghetti Monster, you are at some point going to have to tackle the fact that if the gospel is *true*, then what your friend believes is *false*. There's no way to beat around that particular bush and that's a problem, because, although we live in a culture in which almost anything goes, the one thing that doesn't is telling somebody else that they're *wrong*. We live in a culture very mixed up about the question of truth and that can make evangelism difficult.

Now 'truth' is one of those words we use every day but don't often stop to think about.[2] Truth used to be considered foundational, important, something that one must submit to, however uncomfortable it might be. Philosophers wrestled with it, theologians preached about it, scientists pursued it, poets wrote odes to it and politicians tried to ignore it. The universities, those great seats of learning in our culture, were the places *par excellence* where truth was pursued at great costs, both in the sciences and the humanities. Many universities enshrined the pursuit of truth into their mottoes: for example, the University of Lancaster's is *Patet omnibus veritas* ('truth lies open to all').

But this once-solid view of truth has been steadily eroding in our culture. Many people no longer believe in Truth with a capital 'T'; rather truth is seen as something woollier, softer, more pliable.

For example, many people think that truth is *socially constructed*. The reason you believe what you believe is because of where you were raised. I hear this from university students all the time: 'The reason you're a Christian, Andy, is because you were born in Europe. And that's great for you. But if you'd been born in Nepal, you'd be a Hindu. If you'd been born in Pakistan, you'd be a Muslim'.

Of course, the problem with saying that truth is just culturally conditioned is that you saw off the branch on which you're sitting; presumably the only reason somebody believes that truth is culturally conditioned is because they were born in a liberal, Western culture, and thus raised to believe that truth is culturally conditioned. This is one of the curious things about truth: the more you try and redefine it, the more it nips you on the nose like an angry ferret.

Other people see truth as *personally relative*. What's true for you is true for you, but not true for me. I hear this all the time, especially when it comes to ethical or religious issues. In fact, this view of truth has run riot in the Western world today. Huge numbers of people no

---

2.   See Os Guinness, *A Time for Truth: Living Free in a World of Lies, Hype, and Spin* (Baker, 2000).

longer believe in moral absolutes, but personal preferences. Believe whatever you want, just don't tell me that I'm wrong and you're right, because that would be distasteful, intolerant, disrespectful of my safe space and so forth.

I was recently talking to a high school student who explained she was having difficulty trying to have a conversation about faith with a classmate. 'My friend is a complete relativist', she complained. 'No matter what subject I raise, she always responds: "True for you, not true for me". I even tried using the Holocaust as an example, just to get a reaction, yet she replied: "I may not *like* what Hitler did, but I can't say that he was *wrong*." Nothing gets through to my friend. What should I do?'

We talked for a while and I suggested to the student: 'Next time you're chatting to your friend, lean across, mid-conversation, grab her iPhone and pocket it. When your friend asks: "What did you just do?" reply "Oh, I like your phone, so I thought I'd steal it." Your friend will probably demand you return the phone, at which point you say, "You've persuaded me that morals are just personal preferences so I've concluded that stealing phones is okay for me." Your friend will probably begin bouncing up and down saying "Give me back my phone!" You then look at her, smile sweetly and say, "It rather seems to me that you've discovered a universal moral truth: stealing phones is wrong. Why don't we start from there and see what else we can discover?"'

Our culture is deeply confused about truth and at times we've bought into it too. One place I frequently see this is when it comes to the question of the uniqueness of Christ in a world of other religions. Many of our major Western cities are hugely multicultural, with every religion under the sun represented. Where I grew up in south London, you could choose from Buddhism, Hinduism, Secularism, Sikhism, Judaism, Jainism (you could even be a Crystal Palace FC fan:[3] we used to call that 'masochism').

Given that world of huge religious diversity, Christians are frowned upon for claiming that Jesus and Jesus alone is the only

---

3.   Crystal Palace Football Club is a professional soccer club based in South Norwood, London.

way to God. I know many Christians who are deeply uncomfortable about this and feel awkward about sharing their faith with people from other religions. (When I was at theological college in the 2000s, the college even organised a training day entitled, 'Is Evangelism a Sin?') We live in an age in which the chief virtue has become 'tolerance' — we must tolerate other people, other beliefs, not tell people that they're wrong. That's the way to build a compassionate, peaceful, civic society. The last thing we need is people going around trying to *convert* others.

Can evangelism work in a such a climate? In a nutshell: no. The moment you reduce the gospel to just another religious option on the smorgasbord of world views, you rob it of its power. But I don't believe we have to do that. Instead, I think it's possible to carve out space for effective evangelism and gently push back on the myth of tolerance.

I say 'myth' quite deliberately. I think the modern idea of tolerance is exactly that and a dangerous one. First, because 'tolerance' is deeply disrespectful. Think about this for a moment: what is it we generally *tolerate*? Things that are generally a bit unpleasant or annoying, usually because those doing them don't have the maturity to do otherwise. I tolerate my toddler when she draws with crayons on the wallpaper. I tolerate the cat when it widdles on the sofa. When I encounter an adult who thinks in a different way than I do, simply *tolerating* them would be deeply patronising. Rather I listen, I ask questions, I try to find out what they think and why.

And that leads to the second problem with tolerance: it's a licence to ignore those who are different from us. If we can write off whole communities with a patronising, 'Oh, that's just the Muslims...', then we have no motivation to actually engage with people. Conversely, if we recognise that we all have deep convictions and beliefs and those will often differ, now we need to learn to listen, to find ways to disagree without being disagreeable. Provided those conversations are a two-way street, wherein lies the problem?

For the last twenty years, I've had hundreds of evangelistic discussions with Muslim friends, many of which have been pretty animated. My Muslim friends are well aware I would love them to encounter Jesus and become Christians — and that has never been a problem. At the same time, I'm perfectly aware that my Muslim friends wish I would abandon Christianity and become a Muslim. And that's not a problem either — I respect their passion. The deepest friendships are not formed by pretending we all believe the same, or by tolerating people like naughty toddlers, but by recognising our differences and talking about them honestly.

Thus the first step to overcoming the fear of evangelism that prevents many of us from sharing Jesus with joy and conviction is to push back, gently and politely but firmly, on the creeping relativism, pluralism and myth of tolerance that has descended on our culture like a fog. Recognise where it has affected us, and the church too, causing many of us to buy into the idea that religion is a private matter.

Why do I believe in evangelism? I believe because the gospel is a public matter and if it's true, it changes *everything*.

FEAR OF GIVING AN ANSWER

The second fear that sometimes holds us back from sharing our faith with joy and exuberance is the numbing terror of *What Happens If They Ask A Question I Can't Answer?* One of the exercises I often like to use when I teach church groups on evangelism is to invite the audience to spend five minutes listing the toughest question about their faith they've heard from a friend or colleague when evangelising. Often only one or two hands go up — there's often a nervous silence. I then rephrase the question: 'If you've *never* shared your faith with a friend or colleague, what's the question that you're afraid of being asked? What's the question about Christianity that, if somebody asked you, would be so terrifying that it'd almost be better if the ground opened up and swallowed you whole, rather than you have to answer it?' Usually a forest of hands shoots up and question after question gets suggested: the problem of evil, God and science, violence in the Old Testament, Joel Olsteen's teeth — and dozens more.

Now there's a whole branch of Christian theology concerned with how one tackles questions like that — it's called 'apologetics' (not to be confused with 'apoplectics', which is what I sometimes experience when I read some of the modern popular atheist writings).[4]

The Bible talks about this in a number of places, for instance 1 Peter 3:15: 'but in your hearts, honour Christ the Lord as holy, always being prepared to make a defence [Greek: *apologia*] to anyone who asks you for a reason for the hope that is in you; yet do it with gentleness and respect'.

Notice Peter's point there. The Christian faith, our hope, is something for which we can give reasons. Christianity is not a nice idea, or a warm fuzzy feeling, or something we're asked to believe just because we believe, but something that if somebody asks us *why* we believe it, we should be able to give reasons.

That's fascinating, because in some ways it cuts against the grain of how we sometimes think about our faith as twenty-first century Christians. We live in a culture, as we've seen, in which the concept of 'truth' has eroded and it's been replaced with 'feelings'. Watch two people debate about any contentious ethical, moral or political issue and see how quickly people start shouting at each other, or protesting how the other side is 'offensive' (or if the debate is online, look for people typing in CAPITAL LETTERS). We've segued from 'I think therefore I am' to 'I feel, therefore I emote'.

And we're not immune from this in the church and it sometimes creeps into how we think about evangelism. Imagine that a non-Christian friend bounces up to me and asks, 'Andy, why are you a Christian?' And, so I switch seamlessly into Testimony Mode™: 'Well, thanks for asking! Some years ago, I met this guy at work — he had the cubicle next to mine — and we became friends. We

---

4.   For a popular response to the popular forms of atheism, see Andy Bannister, *The Atheist Who Didn't Exist (or: The Dreadful Consequences of Really Bad Arguments)* (Monarch Books, 2015).

used to play cricket together. Well, it turns out he was a Christian and one day he invited me to attend a course at his church, called Alpha. It sounded fun, so I went. The people were very friendly, the food was delicious, and in time I became a Christian'.

Is anything wrong with that story? Well, not in and of itself, but what if we rerun the narrative: 'Some years ago, I met this guy at work — he had the cubicle next to mine — and we became friends. We used to play cricket together. Well, it turns out he was a Buddhist and one day he invited me to attend a course at the local Zen Buddhist Centre. It sounded fun, so I went. The people were very friendly, the food was delicious, and in time I became a Buddhist'.

Here's the thing: if my answer to the question 'Why are you a Christian?' is the story of how I became one, then there is a problem, because that wasn't the question I was asked. The feelings-based culture that we live in often encourages us to give *How-Shaped Answers* to *Why-Shaped Questions,* but in so doing we miss something crucial. If the best we can offer to commend the Christian faith is a set of feelings or a personal story, then we have a problem, for we live in a culture where there are a myriad feelings on offer. Thousands of beliefs, ideologies and religions promise that you'll feel good, happy and fulfilled. (By contrast, the gospel actually promises you may feel worse: 'Take up your *cross* and follow me' is a pretty tough demand.)

There is only one good reason to believe in the Christian faith and that's if it's *true*. And evangelism only works if we believe that with every fibre of our being, and if we are willing to take the time to think through how to commend Christ to our friends, neighbours, and colleagues. I believe evangelism really does work — but we need to take seriously the biblical mandate to 'always be prepared'.

I first learnt this myself back in the 1990s at Speakers' Corner at Hyde Park in London. I'd been persuaded to go along one Sunday afternoon to try preaching on the street to Muslims ('How hard can it be?' my friend had insisted). I ascended a borrowed stepladder and was faced with a crowd of several hundred, well practised in the art of heckling and taking Christians to pieces. And I heard questions and objections to my faith that I'd never even considered before. As I got down from the ladder, my head spinning, one thing was abundantly clear to me: evangelism needed more than just a sense that Jesus was a good idea, or some of the half-remembered platitudes I'd picked up from being raised in a Christian home.

Over the next few months, I poured every spare moment into reading all that I could to answer the questions of my new Muslim friends, as I returned every Sunday afternoon to Speakers' Corner to climb my stepladder and face the crowds all over again. Through that baptism of fire, God gave me a love of Muslims, a love of public evangelism and a love of engaging with people's tough questions.

Now not everybody needs to climb a stepladder and preach on the street, but I think the lesson that I learnt back then is one that is applicable to all of us. We need to be willing to put the effort in, to 'always be prepared', as 1 Peter 3:15 puts it, if we're going to be equipped to answer people's questions and challenges, whether genuine or hostile.

But apologetics isn't just about answering people's questions; it's also about learning to *ask* really good questions.[5] In fact, this is the simplest form of evangelism and can often be incredibly effective: as somebody once remarked, try asking the other person questions until they finally ask you one. For example, whenever I meet somebody who says they're an atheist, I like to respond: '"Atheist" tells me what you *don't* believe. So what *do* you believe?' Find out what animates your friends, what your colleagues are passionate about, what they're *living* for — the more questions you ask, the greater the chance they'll be willing to ask you what *you* believe — and the more you'll understand your friend when you do get an opportunity to share Jesus, and thus can connect the gospel to their world.

This can work with hostile questions too. A year or so ago, I was speaking at the medical school attached to a large university near

---

5.   See Randy Newman, *Questioning Evangelism: Engaging People's Hearts the Way Jesus Did* (Kregel, 2004).

Toronto. After I spoke, a student came marching up to me. Without even so much as a 'Hello', he announced: 'I hate Christianity.' 'Really?' I replied, 'Why?' 'Because of the Bible', he snapped back. 'It's anti-gay, anti-science, anti-reason, anti-progress, anti-diversity and anti-women.'

Everything in me wanted to reply with similar energy and defend the gospel, but I decided I'd try a different tack. 'What's wrong with being anti-women?' I asked. The student looked at me as if I'd gone mad. 'Well … well … well it just *is*', he said. 'That's not an answer', I said. 'Come on, what's wrong with being anti-women?' We went to and fro for five minutes before he finally said: 'I know that it *is*, I can't tell you *why*'. That gave me the space to gently say: 'I agree that it's wrong to be anti-women. And I don't believe the Bible is — indeed, I believe that the Christian claim that men and women bear incredible value and dignity because they're made in God's image is the only possible ground for human rights'. I then pushed a little further: 'Tell me, are you a medical student?' 'Yes', he replied. 'Well,' I continued, 'then with the very greatest of respect, you need to find a real basis for medical ethics. Because one day when you're a fully qualified doctor, you'll be faced with ethical challenges — and if the only basis for your treating people with respect is 'it just is', then God help your patients'. He stared at me quietly and finally said: 'You've given me a lot to think about'.

Questions are very powerful: they can make people think, they can challenge without causing an argument and they can open up a conversation. 'Why do you think that?' is a very disarming question.

A few months ago, the organisation I worked for helped to organise a mission week at the University of Toronto. One of the most exciting stories for me that came out of the week was a first-year student who plucked up the courage to talk to one of her classmates about the Christian faith. She began by asking questions about what her friend believed. She listened well and finally her friend asked her what she believed. Intrigued, her friend then came to one of the lunchtime events during mission week and stayed behind to talk at length to the speaker. Later that day we heard that she had prayed to receive Christ. What began with a simple conversation, ended with a student giving her life to Christ. That's why I believe in evangelism: because the gospel powerfully resonates with people's lives, when we take the time to listen to their questions, to engage and to allow the Spirit to work through us and our conversations.

FEAR OF FAILURE

But there's one last fear that often holds us back from evangelism and that's the fear that evangelism doesn't actually work, that despite our best intentions, hopes and wishes, the gospel isn't actually effective, that the modern world is so hostile, so sceptical, so apathetic that evangelism isn't possible anymore.

But that simply isn't true.

First, let's disavow ourselves of the idea that the modern Western world is somehow unique. We forget that the first-century world in which the church began was deeply hostile to the Christian faith. Yet the church spread like wildfire. We forget, too, that in much of the world today, the culture is far, far more antagonistic to the gospel than in the contemporary West. Yet despite that, look at how the gospel has grown in China, or is growing in the Muslim world, or in some of the most difficult trouble spots of the world.[6]

Second, one of the things we love to tell at times are Christian horror stories. We love to sit around and bemoan how the church is shrinking, how the culture is going to hell in a handcart, how the media is increasingly secular and so forth. Maybe some of those things are true, but such stories neglect the work of what God is doing and how there are green shoots everywhere. One of my friends wrote a book looking at the amazing stories of where the church is growing in the UK and Europe — he called it *God's Unwelcome Recovery* — 'unwelcome' because many secular voices dislike it, but also 'unwelcome' because many Christians have bought into

---

6. See Lamin Sanneh, *Whose Religion is Christianity?: The Gospel Beyond the West* (Eerdmans, 2003).

the idea that the church is dying — maybe because sometimes it's tempting to hide behind such a myth.[7]

There are many reasons I believe in evangelism —
• because the gospel is true
• because it's powerful
• because it engages people's honest (and dishonest) questions
But primarily I believe in evangelism because it works — not in a naively pragmatic sense, but because time and time again, I've seen that when the gospel is preached in a way that engages people, God shows up. The question isn't whether evangelism is effective: the question is whether we still believe this. And if not, why not?

But tied up in all of this is one last question. What do we think the gospel *is*?

Perhaps you think that's an obvious question, but the more I've wrestled with some of the issues in this chapter, the more I've realised that at times we have a tendency to lose track of what the gospel is. Without realising it, we slip into Christianity *plus*: Christianity *plus* politics, Christianity *plus* moralism, Christianity *plus* our theological hobby horse. And when people reject the 'plus' — for example, identifying Christianity with a particular brand of politics and then rejecting the politics — we mutter that the gospel has failed, when what's actually been rejected is not Jesus but a caricature of the gospel.[8]

The gospel, at its heart, is incredibly simple: the news that there is a creator God, who loves us and wants to know us, a God from whom we're separated by our rebellion and self-centredness. But He is a God who chose not to abandon us, despite our rejection of Him, but stepped into history in the person of Jesus, lived the life that we should have lived and died the death that we should have died, in order to deal with our brokenness. And His defeat of evil and injustice was demonstrated by His resurrection — and if we

---

7. Sean Oliver-Dee, *God's Unwelcome Recovery: Why the New Establishment Wants to Proclaim the Death of Faith* (Monarch Books, 2015).

8. See Bruxy Cavey, *The End of Religion: Encountering the Subversive Spirituality of Jesus* (NavPress, 2007).

place our lives completely and wholeheartedly into His hands and say 'Your will be done', He will begin the process of restoring and remaking us, bringing us back into relationship with Him.

And that gospel is free. It demands *nothing*. Which is where the problems start, because most of us have considerably more than nothing and want to drag it into the equation. 'Hey, God, look at my efforts. Look at my hard work. Look at my right thinking. Look how nice I am.' Sometimes we contaminate the gospel with our politics, or our self-righteousness, or our moralism — and these things stink, as all dead things do. And nothing drives people away more than a rotting corpse. Evangelism hasn't failed, but some misrepresentations of the gospel have. Maybe we should cheer their passing.

A few weeks ago, I took part in a dialogue at a Canadian university with an atheist professor — at least, the last time we dialogued, he was an atheist; now he self-describes as an 'agnostic'. As we dialogued in front of the capacity crowd, he shared how he had been raised in a religious home, but how as a young man he'd rejected that rigid religiosity, especially the way that it refused to entertain any questions. But as we spoke that evening, he said, with tears in his eyes, 'I miss God. I *really* miss God. I wish I had the faith you had, Andy. I want to find my way back to that'.

I did my best to share with my friend that evening the story of what God has done in Christ — a Jesus who said 'those who seek will find'.

There are many reasons why I (still) believe in evangelism. But the primary one is because in Jesus God has made the first move — stepping out of His comfort zone in the incarnation that He might meet us. And now He calls us to do the same, empowered by the Spirit, bearing witness to others of the wisdom, the truth, the reality, the power, and, above all, the beauty of the gospel.

2

WHY I (STILL) BELIEVE IN THE BIBLE

Iver Martin

I'm going to 'come clean' on two counts.

First, I must have been brainwashed! I was brought up in a home that believed the Bible. My father was a Christian minister who taught the Bible every Sunday in church and my mother was a school teacher who was also a Christian. My upbringing was neither idyllic nor perfect: my parents argued sometimes and my father wrestled with his own unique personality. Yet, as I grew up, I saw a stability and a loving conviction in them and within the church which I have never encountered anywhere else.

I went to Sunday school and learned from an early age the timeless stories about Abraham, Moses, David, Daniel and Jesus. When I was twelve I went to a church camp where there was more Bible teaching. When I was fourteen I chose to profess my faith openly and come into church membership, and all through high school I was involved in Scripture Union. Many of my childhood and teenage friends also went to church and the girl I married shared the same Christian convictions and love for the Bible. In all my youth, despite its temptations and challenges, I never seriously questioned its truth. I still believe essentially what I believed when I was fourteen because I see no reason not to. Hence, in the eyes of many people I have blindly and unthinkingly followed my upbringing and must therefore be brainwashed — unless, that is, the Bible is true, in which case I've been right all along.

But my upbringing alone is not the explanation of why I am a Christian. It is not true that if you are brought up in a Christian home you'll necessarily 'turn out' to believe the same things as your parents. I know many people who had a similar upbringing to mine and have not embraced the Christian faith. I know others who started out as believers and then turned away from the Christian faith. Neither is it true to say that because I was brought up in a Christian environment I believed without thinking or asking important fundamental questions.

I can remember in my twenties wrestling with why I believed what I did. I began to read books that argued in defence of the Christian faith, particularly those by Francis Schaeffer. The more I read, the more convinced I became that the Christian faith provided answers that no other religion could offer. I still sometimes stop and ask myself why I am a Christian. I try to ask it honestly, and even attempt sometimes to imagine what I might be like if I was not a Christian.

There are three reasons why I am a Christian:

The first is a conviction that the existence of a supreme Being explains why we are here.

Second, the evidence behind the resurrection of Jesus Christ is so compelling that I can't escape from being persuaded that He, as opposed to every other religious leader, is the real thing.

Third, despite the many difficulties in understanding some of its teaching, the Bible is the only place where I can find a rational and reasonable explanation of who God is, what He is like, why humanity is a contrast between the noble and the horrific, and what God has done to rescue us. The Bible gives me the explanation as to why my species, the human race, is so impoverished, violent, corrupt and self-centred; but it insists that no matter how low a

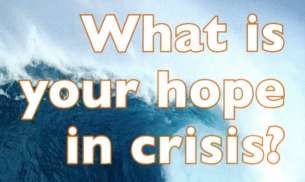

What is
your hope
in crisis?

When disaster strikes

In this world, death, unforeseen tragedies, and sicknesses strike everyone. With the coronavirus, we have all had to face the reality that we cannot predict or control many things. These painful and frightening events produce a sense of loneliness, confusion, and fear of a future that is uncertain. If we are honest, we have to admit that these recent worldwide events have forced us to acknowledge our limitations.

Through all that has happened, God has given every person on earth the opportunity to think about the most serious matter in life: to find and to know Him. God is challenging us to face our own mortality — *will you listen?*

We must face God

When you are in a crisis, your focus on life is sharpened. Suddenly the theory of 'survival of the fittest' sounds very hollow, and you see it for what it is: cruel and hopeless. When facing death, you suddenly know that life is something precious and that there is something after death. The Bible teaches that a loving and holy God made us, and that we are accountable to Him. He lovingly warns us of the fact that we must face His justice. As the Bible says, *'As it is appointed unto men once to die, but after this the judgement.'* (Hebrews 9:27)

Stop and think

Even if you hate to admit it, the wars, plagues, fires, floods and such things throughout history, are warnings from God's own hand, designed to awaken our consciences – His wake-up call to us, emphasising our lack of thought for our souls.

Our greatest concern in life should not be a virus or cancer or economic disaster, but to prepare ourselves for eternity.

Signs of mercy

The message God is sending is that you need His forgiveness and mercy. We all have broken His commands and have sinned against Him – against His holiness and justice. Sin is seen in all of our lives – in the lies, the pride, the self-centredness, the gossip, the hatred, the lustful looks, even time wasted. How, you may ask, can God forgive you of all these sins?

Jesus ~ our only hope in trouble

To show us His love and forgiveness, God sent His Son, the Lord Jesus Christ, into this world to pay the price of the sin-debt we owe to Him. Jesus willingly paid that penalty by suffering and dying on the Cross on our behalf, and was raised to life again.

To be saved from the final judgement and from the eternal consequences of sin, you must trust in Jesus Christ only, turn from your sins and surrender your life to Him. If you do, God promises to forgive you and give you eternal life. There is hope in the face of tragedy only in Jesus Christ. *"Here is a trustworthy saying... Christ Jesus came into the world to save sinners."* (1 Timothy 1:15).

"If we say that we have no sin, we deceive ourselves, and the truth is not in us. If we confess our sins, he is faithful and just to forgive us our sins, and to cleanse us from all unrighteousness." (1 John 1:8–9)

For your soul's sake, cry out to God. Seek to know who God is by reading especially one of the accounts of the life of the Jesus Christ (e.g. the Gospel of John).

If you would like a free Bible study pack to help you think about these things, please contact us. The Open-Air Mission is a Christian society (est. 1853) supported by hundreds of churches. We promise that nobody will call at your home and your data will be kept secure.

Name (Mr/Mrs/Miss) ....

Age (if under 16) ....

Address ....

....

.... Postcode ....

Send to: The Open-Air Mission,
PO Box 678, Abingdon, OX14 9NA
email@oamission.com   www.oamission.com

person sinks, that person is still a human being, made in the image of God. It is because of what the Bible teaches that I believe that God can transform even the worst of humanity, no matter how far they've fallen. God is the ultimate rescuer, and His story is found in the Bible.

The other matter on which I would 'come clean' is that I can't *fully* explain why I truly believe the Bible. Neither do I have the answers to some of the questions that people ask, such as, 'Where did Cain get his wife?' or 'Why does God allow suffering?'[1] I can't scientifically prove the truth of the Bible any more than I can prove the existence of God. Nobody can produce 'empirical evidence' which can demonstrate that the Bible is the message of God to the world. Even if there were a video of Moses writing the first five books, that would not prove that he was being inspired by God to do so.

The bottom line is that *the Bible proves itself*, as Jesus promised in John 7:17 — 'If anyone's will is to do God's will, he will know whether the teaching is from God' (see also John 5:32; John 16:14; 1 John 5:6). This why I always recommend that those who seriously want to find out about it should start by actually reading the Bible for themselves.

Throughout the rest of this chapter, rather than trying to refute every argument that people raise against the Bible in a detailed manner, let me try to put into a few words why I believe it and what it means to me as a Christian.

WHAT IS THE BIBLE?

But first, what is the Bible? The Bible is truly unique, different from any other book you will ever come across. It is startling, threatening, powerful and life-changing. Some of it is bizarre. There are catastrophic events, talking animals, fire from the sky; the ground opens up and swallows people, the sea splits in two,

---

1.　See: http://www.ligonier.org/learn/articles/explaining-anomalies.

the dead are raised to life again. There is murder, theft, deception, plotting, mystery and adultery, with no attempt to cover up the faults of even the best of people.

The message of the Bible is about God — who He is and what He is like. But it is also about me — who I am and what I am like. It tells me where I fit into this crazy, magnificent and lonely universe and, most importantly of all, it explains where I have gone wrong and how I can know God.

It is a collection of sixty-six separate books, written by various authors over a period of fifteen hundred years. Each book is connected to form a 'unity' around the person, death and resurrection of Jesus. It is divided into the Old and New Testaments: the Old Testament written before Jesus' incarnation and the New Testament written after it. Some of the books are historical narrative, some are song, some are prophecy and others poetry.

By the end of the second century A.D. the Bible had come to be recognised by the Christian church as the authoritative word or message of God. From then on it came to have a central place at the very heart of the Church, and to this day, Christians all over the world ground their faith in what the Bible teaches.

IS IT BELIEVABLE?

So why believe a book that was written so long ago, in such a different cultural context and in which there seem to be so many strange concepts?

First, although the Bible contains material which is not always easy to understand, it is nonetheless not unreasonable. There is plenty that is strange, yet nothing in the Bible is absurd. The Bible never says that black is white or that a circle is a square. Whilst unusual and even 'impossible' events occur, none of it completely defies logic. Even the most hardened secular critic has to admit that, despite his scepticism, it is conceivably possible that the Bible is true. None of it is illogical, as long as you're prepared to bring in the 'God factor'.

The miracles are often cited as events which beggar belief. For example, the parting of the Red Sea (Exod. 14), which created a pathway on which the Israelites could travel on dry land, is an event which is, to say the least, highly unlikely in any 'normal' sense — unless, that is, there is a God who controls nature and is prepared to temporarily suspend its laws on certain occasions to bring about what He wants. If you insist upon only believing what happens 'normally' and choose to disregard the miraculous, you are then saying that God either cannot or does not interrupt the norms of nature. But surely if God is Creator then He also possesses the authority to modify natural norms to bring about His own plan if He so chooses.

One of the Bible's most ridiculed passages is Numbers 22:28 where the donkey belonging to a man called Balaam speaks to him. Some scholars explain this away by saying that the story was never meant to be taken literally. It is rather, they say, a parable — a story with a meaning. But, once again, such an 'explanation' discounts the possibility of *God* stepping in and doing something impossible. Is it absolutely impossible for God to intervene, on a one-off basis, where in the normal natural course of events an animal would not be able to speak?

Every miracle is an impossibility — that's what makes it a miracle! So whether it is Jesus walking on water, a dead body rising from a grave, the Red Sea parting in two, or a donkey being given the power of reason and speech for just one minute, each one of these is a natural impossibility. What makes it possible is God's intervention, which is precisely the point of each event. I have never seen a miracle but I believe that they occasionally happened because God directly and supernaturally suspended the laws of nature to make Himself known and heard. Impossible? Yes and no.

Back in the 1980s when microelectronics was a fledgling industry, I worked in a semiconductor manufacturing factory. I was part of a team of engineers with whom I used to enjoy long debates over dinner, particularly during the nightshift, as long as things were going well on the production line. Often the conversation would turn to religion and on one occasion we debated what was impossible and possible.

I remember trying to convince my colleague that some things were just by nature impossible so I asked him, 'How possible is it for a man to survive unaided for two hours under water?' His response was that the possibility was 'finite but small'. At first I thought he was playing with words, but he was actually right. Scientifically, although the body cannot survive under water for a long time, yet, statistically, if you assert something as impossible the only way you can prove it is to take every permutation into the equation. In other words, if you were to *prove* that it is impossible to survive for two hours under water you would have to literally immerse every living person under water for two hours. Until then, you can only say that, biologically, it is highly unlikely for anyone to survive under water for two hours.

By the same token, while it is normally impossible for any man to stand on the surface of water, you can't say it is impossible without taking every possible permutation into account. In the case of Jesus, the one permutation which makes it possible is that He was God. If Jesus was truly God, then it is both possible and reasonable to believe that He possessed the authority and power to suspend the normal laws of gravity or water surface tension in order to walk to His friends in a boat in the middle of the sea of Galilee and to spectacularly display His divinity.

The same factor explains every miracle in the Bible. The Bible is not a science book. It does not try to explain how things happen but it tells what happened and in some cases explains why.

THE MESSAGE OF THE BIBLE

The second reason why I believe the Bible is its message. It explains firstly that the universe and everything contained within it did not just come into being randomly or arbitrarily but that God chose to bring everything into existence for a reason. In other words, you and I are here for a purpose which has been determined by a supreme Being. The first chapter in the Bible tells us that behind the universe there is a personal, living, all-powerful Creator who is perfectly good, identifies Himself as God and who made the universe because He wanted to.

Secondly, the account of creation tells us that humankind possesses a unique characteristic: the 'image' and 'likeness' of God. In contrast to every other created being, the first humans were able to communicate with God within a perfect relationship. They were also able to speak, think, investigate, ask, reason, create and manage, as well as enjoy a unique relational consciousness in which they were able to connect with and love one another.

The Bible then goes on to describe how, despite the perfection in which the original human beings lived, there came a specific point in time when a disruption took place between humans and God, which resulted in a catastrophic separation between the whole world and God. This is what Christians call the Fall. Genesis 3 tells us that Adam and Eve chose to disregard a simple command. In doing so they chose to distrust God's goodness and disbelieve His promise. God said one thing; they chose to go down a different road. They turned their backs on God.

While many voices in my head ask, 'Why did it have to be that way?', I'm left with the choice — did it happen or not? If it happened it explains that the world's brokenness, misery and corruption can be traced back to a single point in time, a space-time fall. From that moment all of the misery, hate, cruelty and fear which is such a feature of life came flooding into the human race. What's more, because we, as a human race, chose to go our own way, our relationship to God became one of distrust and hostility. That is why it is a myth to imagine that people everywhere are seeking after God. It is the opposite. Men and women generally want to hide from God rather than find Him.

It is the Bible that explains all of this, but there is more. Because the Bible is God's message it describes the world from God's perspective. Because God is perfect, holy and just and because we are accountable to Him, we stand under His righteous condemnation, which means that every human being deserves His ultimate punishment. It is important to stress this because the perception that many people have of God is that He resembles a giant Santa with whom everything one day will be all right. The Bible gives a very different picture.

But it goes on to tell of how God eventually did something unimaginable to rescue people from sin and condemnation. He literally came down to rescue us. He did not just *reach down* to rescue — but He *came* into this world by becoming human. He did not change into a human. He did not cease to be God in order to be human. He became human *as well as* being God. There came a moment in human history when amongst every other conception taking place, a baby was conceived in the womb of a young girl in Nazareth without a sexual union ever having taken place, in which God became a microscopic gestating foetus, in order to go through every stage of human development.

It is this which explains Jesus' extraordinary life and power. If you're only prepared to believe what obeys 'the observable laws of science', then, of course, the life of Jesus will be largely unintelligible. But if, like me, you come to believe that the man Jesus of Nazareth was actually God, you'll have no problem believing that He walked on water, changed water into wine, healed deaf and blind people, and even raised the dead. What I find most breathtaking is not that God can feed five thousand people or raise the dead, but that God became a human in the first place. It is perfectly logical to believe that if He was God, Jesus could feed five thousand people. What is utterly mind blowing is that Jesus was God whose nappies had to be changed!

The story of Jesus, which lies at the heart of the gospel message, is found in the four gospels, written by four authors: Matthew, Mark, Luke and John. Each of these, from his own individual and slightly differing perspective, traces the life of Jesus from birth right through to His horrific death, and then to His resurrection and ascension.

The story of Jesus fast-forwards from Bethlehem to the time when He had grown up. He appears suddenly as a man with the most winsome charisma, authoritative personality and inexplicable power. Each account follows Him from town to village, teaching, healing and drawing thousands of people in amazement as they watch and listen to Him. As I read the four astonishing accounts of the life and death of Jesus, I have to ask whether these accounts are plausible.

There is nothing in the gospel narratives to suggest that they are anything but a straightforward reporting of events as they happened, without any attempt to embellish or alter the facts. There are variations in these accounts but they do not contradict each other. Each of them represents the event as seen by a different eyewitness.

One example is the gospel written by Luke. Luke was not actually an eyewitness of Jesus but a Gentile doctor. He was also a historian whose concern it was to find out facts and document them. He did this by going around and meticulously gathering evidence from primary sources.

To put it bluntly, Luke bears all the hallmarks of a geek. There are some people who are geeks by nature. They're usually the ones who are 'different' in school because they love to study instead of playing football and avoiding homework.

But we'd better be thankful for geeks because without them the world would be a much worse place. When I feel unwell and consult my GP, I want him to be a geek! I want him to have studied medicine and to take his career seriously. If my doctor acted like a clown and told jokes instead of trying to diagnose my condition, I'd never want to see him again. When it comes to my health I want someone boring who knows what he or she is talking about.

When I read Luke I can't help imagining that he has spent years of his life studying and writing. And that's exactly what I want of him because he is telling me about the most important Person who ever walked the face of the earth and how that Person can reconcile me to God.

Presumably, having heard the rumours about this phenomenal Jesus, Luke sets out to establish the truth about Him in all its detail; so he naturally goes to interview the eyewitnesses. The project is a serious one; so naturally, like a good investigative journalist, he makes a point of interviewing the people who saw Jesus and takes copious notes of what people tell him. The result is a dossier compiled for someone called Theophilus (Luke 1:1–4) in which he honestly sets out the facts as related to him during his investigation.

What compels a man at the height of a successful career to drop everything and make a point of writing about a Galilean carpenter? He not only writes about Him as a historian from an objective perspective, but as a journalist who later travelled alongside Paul on his journeys, some of them dangerous. If Jesus was a fraud, why did Luke decide to commit the rest of his life to the message about Jesus, and what could he possibly have gained from knowingly writing a false account of Jesus' life?

Let me come back again to the plain facts. There is nothing about the gospel narratives that suggests anything other than an honest retelling of the Jesus story as recalled by those who witnessed Him.

In her book, *Not God's Type*, Dr. Holly Ordway, a professor of literature and one-time atheist, explains how she came to discover the remarkable uniqueness of the Bible by reading the gospels:

> I read through the Gospel narratives again, trying to take in what they said. I had to admit that — even apart from everything else I had learned — I recognized that they were fact, not story. I'd been steeped in folklore, fantasy, legend, and myth ever since I was a child, and I had studied these literary genres as an adult; I knew their cadences, their flavour, their rhythm. None of these stylistic fingerprints appeared in the New Testament books that I was reading.[2]

Paul, who wrote much of the New Testament, is another example of someone whose commitment to the gospel cannot be explained outside of a conviction about the truth of Jesus. Paul (or Saul, as

---

2.   Holly Ordway, *Not God's Type* (Chicago, Moody Publishers, 2010), 117.

he was formerly called) was a successful Jewish leader, highly respected by his peers and the people.

At the height of his influence the gamekeeper turned poacher! Saul, the ultra-zealous Pharisee, who saw it as his life's calling to protect the Jewish faith, was converted into Paul the preacher of Jesus! You can read about his 'Damascus Road' conversion in Acts 9.

He knew that by changing sides, he would lose friends and family, and that, by becoming an open follower of Jesus, his life would now be in danger. Indeed, it was only a matter of time before he would be killed. Why did this man, Saul, give up everything, including his own life, if he wasn't absolutely convinced that the gospel was true?

REVELATION

A third reason why I believe the Bible is that, by studying the Bible, I get to see in God what I don't understand — like the Trinity, for example, in which God is revealed as one God, and at the same time He is Father, Son and Holy Spirit. It may be impossible to explain how God is both one and three at the same time but if we put to one side the question how, it actually makes sense for God to be plural as well as singular. If God is a plurality in which relationship already exists, then when He creates beings to be in relationship with Him and one another, it all adds up. God is in Himself a relational being, hence what He creates in His image will naturally be relational.

I only know about the Trinity because the Bible reveals it. Granted, I must decide whether to believe that proposition. I may choose to disbelieve it, but for me, although there is always a voice in my head that asks, 'Why three and not four?', the Bible comes back with the same insistence — God is Father, Son and Holy Spirit. And I am left with the choice: do I believe it or not?

But then again, what gives me the right to understand everything about God? Does it not make sense that God is outside our sphere of time and space? Does it not make sense that God is incomprehensible — outside our ability to understand? If God were to fall neatly into our ability to comprehend, He would no longer be God. He would be just another created dimension. God is beyond our comprehension — He is Other!

If, in all of this, you're asking, 'Is all this believable?', you're not alone. Timothy Keller, in his *The Reason for God*, makes the point that, although most people know that there are many great stories and sayings in the Bible, their response is, 'You can't take it literally.'[3] He then goes on to challenge the various historical, literary and cultural objections raised by those who refuse to accept its teaching, concluding thus: 'Only if your God can say things that outrage you and make you struggle will you know that you have got hold of a real God and not a figment of your own imagination. So an authoritative Bible is not the enemy of a personal relationship with God. It is the precondition for it'.[4]

THE WORD OF GOD

Christians often describe the Bible as the 'Word of God', believing it to be infallible, inerrant and inspired by God. What does all of that mean?

First, we do not mean that God Himself physically wrote the Bible. It was primarily written by a variety of human authors, amongst whom were Moses, David and Solomon, who wrote parts of the Old Testament, and Matthew, John and Paul, who wrote much of the New Testament.

Neither did God *dictate* to the various authors what they should write. When we say that the Bible is 'inspired' we do not mean that the authors heard God's voice telling them what to write. Neither does the word 'inspired' mean that the authors were just enthused or excited about what they were writing.

Rather, when we say that the Bible is inspired, we mean that the authors wrote what God led them to write by His Holy Spirit. They

---

3.   Timothy Keller, *The Reason for God* (London: Hodder and Stoughton, 2008), 97.

4.   *Ibid*, 114.

were not in a trance. Nor were they always aware of exactly what was happening. They simply wrote in their own style and language, but what they produced was ultimately determined by God and eventually recognised by the church as God's authoritative Word.

If what's in the Bible is what God wants to be there, it means that what is in the Bible is what God wants us to hear. It means that the Bible perfectly tells the whole truth and can be trusted.

When Jesus lived on earth, He recognised the authority of the Bible of His day (the Old Testament), insisting that it was the voice of God (Matt. 22:31), that it would never disappear (Matt. 5:18) and that it 'could not be broken' (John 10:35). Moreover, Jesus foretold that an addition to the Old Testament would be written by His disciples under the power and guidance of the Holy Spirit (John 14:25–26; 16:13–14). This happened exactly as He promised. Today we have a completed Bible in which we can have full confidence, not least because Jesus endorsed the Old Testament and inaugurated the New.

THE INFLUENCE OF THE BIBLE

There are many books in my house. In the kitchen there are books that give instructions about how to make superb lasagne. But I have no relationship with these books. They are tools, like every other tool in the kitchen. Other books tell me where to walk in Scotland, where the planets are located in the night sky, and how to fix my central heating boiler. I am hugely thankful for all these but I have no meaningful love for them — why should I?

I have other books that contain poetry and the words of songs. I can be caught up in a good story or captivated by brilliant writing. Fictional stories are thrilling but that's where my relationship with them begins and ends. I have no relationship with any of my books, even the ones that move me to tears. I can be inspired and even changed by a good biography, but no book in my possession has affected me in the same way as the Bible. I feel empty if I go too long without reading it. And that is because I, along with Christians wherever you find them all over the world, believe that God speaks personally to us in its pages.

Of course, God could choose to communicate to humanity by other means. He could just speak with an audible voice. But if He wanted to give the same message to every generation and every culture, He would have to speak repeatedly in all of these diverse places and in every era. Instead God has chosen to communicate to the whole world by way of a timeless written document which has been translated into more languages and has reached more people in more cultures than any other book.

The Bible still flies off the shelves and today in many places in the world there is simply not enough supply to meet the demand. The Bible is different. It is alive and powerful — troubling, disturbing, effective, dynamic, magnificent. Its timeless message has impacted more lives and transformed more people than all of the world's most powerful influences.

I would suggest two things to anyone asking for an introduction to the Bible.

First: read it for yourself. A university degree is not necessary because in most places it is a reasonably simple book to read. Note down what you don't understand and persist in reading it.

Divided into two, the Old Testament, which spans several thousand years, tells the story of how God created the universe, how the first humans rebelled against God, how God continued to relate to the human race through the family of Abraham, and how He promised that one day He would send Someone who would bring redemption and forgiveness.

The New Testament begins with the birth of Jesus Christ. Thereafter, the four gospels tell the story of His life, death and resurrection before going on to tell of how the friends of Jesus went into various parts of the Roman Empire telling people about Jesus. The rest of the New Testament explains why Jesus died, what His resurrection means, how a person can come to faith in Jesus, what it means to be a Christian and what God promises to do in the future.

Second: keep an open mind. It never ceases to amaze me how many people approach the Christian faith with their minds already made up. Tim Keller cautions against the kind of prejudice in which people read their own preconceived understanding, shaped by their own cultural background, into what the Bible says: 'I counsel them instead to slow down and try out different perspectives on the issues that trouble them. That way they can continue to read, learn and profit from the Bible even as they continue to wrestle with some of its concepts'.[5]

So, whether it's the place of women, the anger of God, the seemingly innocent deaths in the Old Testament, human sexuality, or even the sacrifice of Christ, we should not read the Bible in the light of the expectations of our own modern Western culture. Instead, we should allow for the possibility of God's higher perspective to which ours must be subject.

Finally, if the Bible really is the living Word of God and if it's true that God speaks in its pages, then anyone picking it up should prepare for the unexpected.

For all the reasons discussed above I (still) believe in the Bible.

---

5.   *Ibid*, 109.

3

WHY I (STILL) BELIEVE IN A CREATOR

JOHN ELLIS

The Voyager 1 space probe launched in 1977 and passed out of our solar system on the 25th August 2012. Two decades earlier, on Valentine's day 1990, it turned, as it were, for one wistful look at home, and from a distance of 3.7 billion miles took and sent back a photograph of earth. In it the earth's size is less than a single pixel; the planet appears as a tiny dot against the vastness of space, almost lost in bands of sunlight scattered by the camera's optics. This arresting, unsettling, unimpressive pixel prompted Carl Sagan's lyrical meditation, *Pale Blue Dot*. It is a remarkable piece of writing.

> From this distant vantage point, the earth might not seem of any particular interest. But for us, it's different. Consider again that dot. That's here. That's home. That's us. On it everyone you love, everyone you know, everyone you ever heard of, every human being who ever was, lived out their lives. The aggregate of our joy and suffering, thousands of confident religions, ideologies, and economic doctrines, every hunter and forager, every hero and coward, every creator and destroyer of civilization, every king and peasant, every young couple in love, every mother and father,

hopeful child, inventor and explorer, every teacher of morals, every corrupt politician, every 'superstar,' every 'supreme leader,' every saint and sinner in the history of our species lived there – on a mote of dust suspended in a sunbeam.

The earth is a very small stage in a vast cosmic arena. Think of the rivers of blood spilled by all those generals and emperors so that in glory and triumph they could become the momentary masters of a fraction of a dot. Think of the endless cruelties visited by the inhabitants of one corner of this pixel on the scarcely distinguishable inhabitants of some other corner. How frequent their misunderstandings, how eager they are to kill one another, how fervent their hatreds. Our posturings, our imagined self-importance, the delusion that we have some privileged position in the universe, are challenged by this point of pale light. Our planet is a lonely speck in the great enveloping cosmic dark. In our obscurity – in all this vastness – there is no hint that help will come from elsewhere to save us from ourselves.

The earth is the only world known, so far, to harbour life. There is nowhere else, at least in the near future, to which our species could migrate. Visit, yes. Settle, not yet. Like it or not, for the moment, the Earth is where we make our stand. It has been said that astronomy is a humbling and character-building experience. There is perhaps no better demonstration of the folly of human conceits than this distant image of our tiny world. To me, it underscores our responsibility to deal more kindly with one another and to preserve and cherish the pale blue dot, the only home we've ever known.[1]

This description is a luminous, religious, agnostic piece — luminous in juxtaposing our smallness and our grandeur, religious in the sense that it offers a coherent world view, and agnostic in that it finds all confident religions, ideologies, and economic doctrines implicitly wanting. They have all failed to bring ultimate salvation to mankind. It is forlorn and wistful, and certain that no outside help will come.

---

1.   Carl Sagan, *Pale Blue Dot: A Vision of the Human Future in Space*, 1997 reprint, pp. xv–xvi.

BEING LOST AND BEING WRONG

One of the early adverts for a GPS navigation system quipped that whilst the Global Positioning Satellite system may have cost the US government $12 billion to put into orbit, the cost to you of harnessing this technological marvel was (then) only a comparatively paltry $399. Indeed, it has been said recently that as a result of such technologies, we are losing the 'art' of getting lost. What does it mean to be lost?

At minimum it means to be unsure of your direction of travel — how to get where you want to be. But to be truly lost means more than this. It means to be unsure of where you are. Any journey is impossible without knowing where you are to start with. Hence the over-told joke of the man asking directions greeted with the reply, 'If I wanted to get *there,* I wouldn't start from here!'

The problem of knowing where you are cannot be remedied without some form of bearing from outside. Some form of existential truth has to be gained, deduced or given concerning one's surroundings, sufficient for identifying one's point in space. Even triangulating one's bearing from compliant stars or satellites requires external reference points as a means of giving 'place' to the present.

To speak of the experience of lostness in life is almost a cliché. Dante starts his *Divine Comedy* with the famous words, 'In midway of the journey of our life I found myself within a darkling wood, because the rightful pathway had been lost'.[2] And it matters little whether one would prefer to be in Las Vegas or on a warm beach in the Seychelles; if you are lost in the woods, simply wishing you were elsewhere is unhelpful. The key thing is honesty, surely — realism. And yet with regard to this lostness, we are often self-deceiving. We are often very willing in the dark woods to screw our eyes shut and think of that beach. It seems we are only too willing to be teleported by the local in the joke to start from somewhere other than here, anywhere other than here.

---

2.   Dante: *The Divine Comedy Inferno Canto* I:1-60 The Dark Wood and the Hill [Tr Rossetti 1865].

But if we are to know our place in the universe, we must resist the impulse to self-deception, no matter how tempting.

OF DESCARTES AND SATELLITES

Since the Enlightenment and the famous encapsulation of it by Descartes in 1637 — 'I think therefore I am' — the dominant world view takes it as self evident that by reason and rationality we are able to discern all things, and thus locate ourselves and recover from our lostness on that *Pale Blue Dot*.

Prior to the Enlightenment it was reasonable to arrive at truth by one of four means: by revelation (*God says*), tradition (*the elders say*), experience (*I have experienced it*) or reason (*I think*). Now it is generally assumed we are largely reduced to two: reason and experience. But beware the chronological snobbery of despising the simple souls who arrived at their world views on the basis of revelation or tradition.

Consider the nature of any rational demonstration: it begins with premises and proceeds through logical deduction to conclusion. If the premises are true and the logic is valid, the conclusion is correct. Even if the logic is perfectly sound, however, the conclusion is folly if the premises are untrue. Consider the following syllogism: *All Martians are infallible; I am a Martian; therefore I am infallible.* The logic is correct, the terms unambiguous, and yet the conclusion utterly nonsensical because the premises are not true (at least one of them is not; I have never met a Martian and for all I know they are indeed utterly trustworthy!). This argument is impeccable and one hundred per cent valid as an argument, yet utterly meaningless as a truth claim.

The very nature of argument means that deductive logic flows forward based on the prior steps. Of itself it does not contribute anything new to the content of the conclusion. The conclusion is only true if the premises are true. This means that for knowledge of the truth we need something outside the argument to constitute the true premise(s). And argument cannot establish the truth of the premises since this would simply be a circular argument.

Now admittedly the conclusion of an argument cannot be true if the laws of logic are disobeyed. But the conclusion, shocking to most modern minds, is that in the end all the knowledge we have must go back to, and rest on, something that is not argument — neither deductive logic nor a rational demonstration that such-and-such premises entail such-and-such conclusions — but a true premise. Logic alone cannot be the origin of a truth claim. For that we need something else.

To say that some things are beyond reason is not the same as saying that such things are illogical or go against reason. But to find our place on the *Pale Blue Dot* we will need more than logic alone. The GPS receiver in the hand is useless if all the satellites fall to Earth. These external reference points constitute the truth claims upon which the triangulation works. These are the premises of argument.

OF ORIGINS AND BATTERIES

A more simple and likely way of getting lost or remaining lost is of course that the humble battery in the receiver fails. If we are to understand our place in the universe or on our planet or in our time, we have to answer three questions that all world views and narratives must answer: how did we get here, what went wrong, and how will it be put right? No realistic human being in the twenty-first century has a problem with posing the central question, namely that something has indeed gone wrong. Carl Sagan agrees implicitly with the second ('there is no hint that help will come from elsewhere *to save us from ourselves*') and goes some way to explaining the third: either we are trapped within that pessimistic reality or we must save ourselves.

It is, of course, rationally possible to dispense with the central question and reply that nothing is *wrong*; all we observe is that *Homo Sapiens Sapiens* is played out.[3] Global warming may do for

---

3. See, for example: Richard Dawkins, *River out of Eden: A Darwinian View of Life* (Science Masters Series BasicBooks, 1995), 133.

us what a meteor did for the dinosaurs, and all the achievements, and indeed all our 'imagined self-importance, the delusion that we have some privileged position in the universe...'[4] will be shown up for what they are. Some other species will take over, or none, and we are none the better and none the worse for that. It's just one of those things. But, indeed, though this is logically tenable, it is a conclusion that is impossible to live by. And even within the 381 words of Carl Sagan's prose, both views are expressed. Something is wrong ... our sense that something is wrong is an illusion. But to observe the dilemma or to experience the ambivalence requires consciousness. It is the battery in the receiver.

Paul Davies, physicist, cosmologist and astrobiologist, who is consistently keen to point out that he is no believer in God, nevertheless admits, 'The physical species *homo* may count for nothing, but the existence of mind in some organism on some planet in the universe is surely a fact of fundamental significance. Through conscious beings the universe has generated self-awareness. This can be no trivial detail, no minor by-product of mindless, purposeless forces; we are truly meant to be here'.[5]

But how on earth do we have the *hubris* to assume that anything is wrong? Annie Dillard's lyrical reflections of her year at Tinker Creek in the Blue Ridge mountains of Virginia won the 1975 Pulitzer Prize for general non-fiction. In it she watches the death of a robin. She muses concerning the indifference of nature to the robin's 'slow and gruelling' death, and her own sense that something tragic has happened. The robin dies and '... nature is no less pleased; the sun comes up, the creek rolls on, the survivors still sing. I cannot feel that way about your death, nor you about mine, nor either of us about the robin's ... We value the individual supremely, and nature values him not a whit'.[6]

She has a point. And she goes on to consider, viewing this divergence of reactions as it were from a high and abstract

---

4.   Carl Sagan, *Op Cit.*

5.   Paul Davies, *The Mind of God — Science and the search for Ultimate Meaning* (Penguin Books, 1992), 232.

6.   Annie Dillard, *Pilgrim at Tinker Creek* (HarperPerennial, 1998), 178-9.

perspective, that these two views cannot be reconciled. She asks who is right? And it is worth quoting in full:

> Either this world, my mother, is a monster, or I myself am a freak. Consider the former: the world is a monster. Any three-year-old can see how unsatisfactory and clumsy is this whole business of reproducing and dying by the billions .... But wait, you say, there is no right and wrong in nature; right and wrong is a human concept. Precisely: we are the moral creatures, then, in an amoral world. The universe that suckled us is a monster that does not care if we live or die .... This view that a monstrous world running on chance and death, careening blindly from nowhere to nowhere, somehow produced wonderful us. I came from the world, I crawled out of the sea of amino acids, and now I must whirl around and shake my fist at that sea and cry 'Shame!'[7]

So, like a bad chess player who places his hand on one piece and takes it off to move another, I have touched the issue of consciousness and, before even trying to advance that piece on the board, moved my hand to the question of ethics or morals. But really the two are not terribly far apart. The point is, how did these two pieces come to be on the chessboard at all?

HOMO SAPIENS SAPIENS

In his preliminary argument concerning the inadequacy of physico-chemical reductionism to explain consciousness, the agnostic philosopher Thomas Nagel describes the prevailing world view and its regnant authority within science. He also lays bare his incredulity regarding the presumed cultural authority of this most basic form of the narrative of our origins:

> Physico-chemical reductionism in biology is the orthodox view, and any resistance to it is regarded as not only scientifically but politically incorrect. But for a long time I have found the materialist account of how we and our fellow organisms came to exist hard

---

7.   *Ibid.*

to believe, including the standard version of how the evolutionary process works. The more details we learn about the chemical basis of life and the intricacy of the genetic code, the more unbelievable the standard historical account becomes.[8]

Here is the crux of the problem. If we are lost, not just in a foreign town, but in the narrative of our own lives, on the *Pale Blue Dot*, how can we trust our mind to triangulate our position if we believe that mind is just the accidental collocation of atoms? After all, evolution goes faster the faster death goes, and yet we have a sense of misapprehension regarding this whole business of 'reproducing and dying by the billions' as the derivative authority for *Homo Sapiens Sapiens*. There comes a troublesome and legitimate concern about the reliability of the only tool for the job, the human mind.

IS THERE ANYBODY OUT THERE?

How are we going to find truth? And let us get something out of the way at the start. Truth is where you find it. It is often said that the Christian faith is a crutch for the weak. Even if it were true, however, that Christians constituted all and only the weakest of men, that would not have any bearing on whether the claims of Christianity are true or false. Troublingly of course to such a critique, it is hugely relevant that Jesus did not come to the power brokers and elite of first-century Palestine only to be relegated afterward to a creed of the weak and powerless. He came precisely to those whose very vulnerability is considered the argument against Jesus' claims. It is akin to arguing that a new cancer drug cannot be efficacious, as its producers claim, because it only heals the sick.

In the terminology of Socratic logic, to conclude that Christianity is false because some of its adherents believe for inadequate reasons, and may find it a comfort in weakness, danger or fear of death, is to commit the genetic fallacy — namely to assume that

---

8.   Thomas Nagel, *Mind and Cosmos: Why the Materialist Neo-Darwinian Conception of Nature Is Almost Certainly False* (Oxford University Press, 2012), 5.

a belief is rendered false by showing how it came to be held (its genetic origins). Of course that holds true for atheism too. *Touché*!

But here, I would humbly suggest, we have a divergence of credibility. The Christian world view holds that the minds we possess came from the creation of the relational, trinitarian, rational God who said, 'Let us make man in our image' (Gen. 1:26). And in the parallel creation account in John 1, Jesus is referred to as The Word, that is, the *Logos,* who is with God from the beginning and is God.

For the consistent atheist, committed to philosophical naturalism or physico-chemical reductionism, the mind is just atoms and neurotransmitters, and the position of determinism is hard to argue against. In other words, the naturalist in pursuit of truth has to make a cognitive choice (though goodness knows with what!). As David Berlinski has written, 'The most unwelcome conclusion of evolutionary psychology is also the most obvious: if evolutionary psychology is true, some form of genetic determinism must be true as well. Genetic determinism is simply the thesis that the human mind is the expression of its human genes'.[9]

If you instinctively reject genetic determinism, very good. But you have to realise the fissure you open in doing so. In the old 'nature versus nurture' debate, as Berlinski succinctly puts it, if you want to hold that the environment doesn't determine how we think and act (we are free to respond to stimuli including abstract epistemological and ontological arguments), then we are not controlled by our genes. And if we are not controlled by our genes, then we are not controlled by evolution (which selects those genes). You can't have it both ways. So if you wish to read on (thank you; I do not take that for granted!) and consider the issue of truth claims for and against the existence of God, then *you* are hovering with your hand over both pieces on the chess board, and you may have to ask for a special dispensation to move them both forward at once.

---

9. David Berlinski, *The Devil's Delusion* (Basic Books, Perseus, Random House Second ed., 2008), 177.

THE SUPERNATURAL NATURALIST AND THE NATURAL THEOLOGIAN

As an ophthalmologist I work with people who have good sight and wish to protect it and people with sight loss who wish to arrest it or reverse it. We have made advances in therapy and in our understanding of the physiology of sight and the embryology of the developing mammalian eye. It is something of a truism to refer to the wonder and beauty of some of these discoveries, of which more in a moment. But where I and much of our profession almost always fail, is in the care of those who have gone beyond the reach of therapy and surgeries — the care of the sight impaired, and the significantly sight impaired (blind). This may be bound up with the psychology of the 'fix it' attitude of my profession, and implied failure is therefore met with denial or suppression. Fortunately we are surrounded by skilled, compassionate and experienced colleagues in the Royal National Institute of Blind People and other agencies who do a much better job where it is most needed.

Legal blindness is defined in most countries and by the World Health Organisation as a standard of sight considerably better than absolute 'blackness', as many of us imagine it. But one situation where this is indeed the case is when both eyes are removed in infancy for bilateral, life-threatening tumours (retinoblastoma).

One such 'patient' was Martin Milligan who had both eyes surgically removed because of cancer early in his life, before any formed memories, and at the stage where the infant brain is plastic and developing rapidly. So he has essentially never known sight. Wonderfully, for our present purposes, he became an academic philosopher. In a series of published letters between Milligan and Brian Magee (a sighted philosopher) they discuss the epistemological implications of this 'handicap' (categorically *never* Milligan's word), namely absolute blindness. Indeed that is the correct place to start, and the most startling thing to understand correctly. Milligan does not perceive himself to want for anything in terms of sensory experience of the world and there is never even the remotest hint of self-pity in any of his writing.

This reflection is a crucial one for Milligan since — along with other similar sighted vocabulary, even including colour — he feels he can understand fully without experience everything the sighted can. He is aware of no gap in his cognitive knowledge of the world. But he goes beyond this, and is aware of no gap in his sensory experience of the world, no feeling of lacking anything and no compromise in his ability to apprehend reality — all of reality. He forms, he believes, an utterly cogent, coherent reality without sight.

It is no use saying that he is mistaken; that is too patronising. Neither is he alone in this. Tom Jernigan, past president of the American National Federation of the Blind, stated that blindness is not a handicap but just a difference. Nevertheless, the sighted Magee does wrestle with his own incredulity at hearing this, and even his correspondent's apparent satisfaction with his lot.

But this leads very naturally to Magee suggesting a self-evident, though hypothetical, corollary. It would have been possible for the whole world to have been born blind. Had this been the case, we would doubtless be content having never known anything else, but we would be walking and living in the middle of a whole spectrum of reality that we could not know. Indeed, like the flawed but oft repeated 'elephant analogy' of world religions (all that touch have a part, true but partial, and none the whole of the truth), this situation could only be realised from the perspective of one outside that scenario — in the case of the blind, the first person born with eyes open; in the case of the elephant, the only sighted person who sees the centuries of groping priests, gurus and holy men from a position apart. In the case of the elephant analogy the metaphor thus becomes self-defeating and it is surprising that it is still used and loved.

Our senses are contingent. They are what they are, but they might have been otherwise. And there is presumably a whole potential, perhaps even an infinite potential portfolio of senses that we might have had but lack. And their possession might alter our view of reality as much as sight conferred on an all-blind world would.

We then come quite naturally to the thought that if we cannot know what we do not perceive, no finite creature can understand its own nature. As has already been said, authoritative self-awareness in the manner described by Descartes cannot rest on argument alone; it requires true premises. And true premises must be derived from observation (simple or the most elevated scientific experiment), revelation, or tradition before they can be tested in logic. And, dealing with those we observe, these observations are limited by our contingent senses. And Milligan's point is that we are almost certainly all in the same boat with regard to total reality: 'it is nearly all passing us by without our having any means of knowing what we are missing'.[10]

Putting this another way, from the materialist's perspective, when someone says that the world, this world, is all that there is or all that there can be, what they must mean is that our senses are utterly sufficient to apprehend reality, and that reality is utterly bound in scope to match those perceptive senses. I hope I am not misrepresenting the materialist perspective. But a brief acquaintance with history — even just the last hundred years — shows that even the relatively uneducated are now familiar with concepts that were not even conceivable to the best of minds in 1917.

What cannot be known cannot be known, and what cannot be put into words cannot be put into words. But that there will be discoveries, none are more likely to enthusiastically embrace than the materialists who are very often the strongest advocates of the version of history that views the arc of human scientific discovery as moving ever onward and upward. No matter that some have called out that such progress is slowing, and that we often mistake technological progress for scientific.[11] The fact remains, even if in diminished measure.

The issue is in the substrate for the premises upon which we build our arguments to describe truth. If we are too enlightened to allow for revelation (God telling us how reality really stands) or the tradition of the elders, then we are cast solely on observation. And observation is always incomplete. Revelation as an epistemological

---

10.   Brian Magee and Martin Milligan, *Sight Unseen* (Oxford University Press, 1995), 37.

11.   James le Fanu, *Science's Dead End* (Prospect magazine; July 2010:Issue 173).

authority for the Christian is complete, because God's spoken word is now complete (John 20:30–31; Rev. 22:18–19) and because Jesus has completed that revelation in Himself (Heb. 1:1–2).

There only remains this, as expressed by Brian Magee and Martin Milligan:

> That which exists unapprehended by us is as real as what we apprehend ... The notion that there must be something quasi-magical about whatever might exist beyond the limits of possible human experience is misplaced, and so we stand in need of some sort of demystification of the unknown. All that there can possibly be is more of reality, and that is all. If there is a God then he is part, or all, of reality; and if he is permanent then his very permanence makes him, in the most literal meaning of the word, everyday.[12]

Classical Christian belief holds (unlike Greek, Gnostic or Buddhist philosophy) that God is the author of all matter and that matter (atoms) is therefore beautiful, though marred and fallen. God was pleased with what He made (Gen. 1:31) and made all that was made (John 1:3). When Jesus appeared after His resurrection, frightening His disciples into fearing they saw a ghost, He asked for, and was given, fish to eat (Luke 24:42). The detail of the biographer here is such that we are told how it was cooked (broiled, not sushi!).

Thus as a Christian I am fully committed to matter and atoms and a rational mind, and a basis for ethical decision-making, but the materialist must be a mystic, believing in morals without reason and reason without origins. Since God exists He is part of that reality (not inseparable from it as a Monist or Pantheist would claim, nor are we gods as New Age religions claim). And His very permanence does indeed make Him 'everyday'.

SCEPTICAL ABOUT SCEPTICISM

So far, though, most of this has only been grounds for unbelief in materialism — or, from the Christian perspective, unbelief in unbelief. After all, the claim of Christianity is that 'God is there

---

12.   Brian Magee and Martin Milligan, *Sight Unseen* (Oxford University Press, 1995), 218.

and He is not silent'[13] and that indeed He has spoken, in direct contradiction to Carl Sagan's claim that there is no hint that help will come from 'elsewhere'.

But before leaving unbelief, what of the *God of the gaps* argument? To briefly summarise, God was invoked by more primitive people in earlier times as an explanation for all that we could not understand. When something could not bridge the gap between two points, 'God did it' was the easy filler to smooth the way for lazy brains. And as science grew, the gaps inevitably diminished and this God was squeezed out of His hiding place in these fissures of ignorance.

The problem is not that this view misrepresents God, but that it misrepresents science — or rather misrepresents the nature of discovery and epistemology. As it is doubtless quite simple to show, as science has grown, the gaps have not shrunk but widened. We have elegant experiments to show that light is both particle and wave, but these models cannot be reconciled. We cannot reconcile general relativity and quantum physics. As discoveries increase so do candidate hypotheses for further investigation. God (if He ever resided in the gaps) seems to have increased His jurisdiction, not diminished it. He is more glorious as a result of science, not less so.

When Darwin first published *The Origin of Species* in 1859, the interior of the cell was considered simple protoplasm. No one then could have envisaged the internal protein factory, the primary amino acid chains nor their secondary, tertiary and quaternary structures as proteins, their gating, switching, conformational changes, induction, transport, relationship to other structures and molecules and the effects of errors in their coding.

Indeed, a recent paper on the evolution of vision makes a startling admission in this regard. Beginning with Darwin's famous quote from *The Origin of Species* that the formation of the mammalian eye 'with all its inimitable contrivances' is a staggering challenge to the credibility of the theory he proposes, it is added that Darwin

---

13. *He Is There and He Is Not Silent* is the title of a book by Francis Schaeffer (Tyndale House Publishers, 1972).

drew support from the fact that 'numerous gradations from a simple and imperfect eye to one complex and perfect can be shown to exist'. This is true in the sense that numerous more simple forms of light-sensitive organisms do exist. But when the author looks at the actual complexity of a protein capturing a photon, beginning the cascade that registers light, he has to look as far back as single cells so primitive that they have no nuclear membrane (prokaryotes). These cells exist in fossil records as far back as 3.5 billion years ago, only 1 billion years after the formation of the earth's crust. Of the highly complex folded protein rhodopsin, he admits: 'The problem here is that even as far back as the prokaryotes the complex seven transmembrane domain arrangement of opsin molecules seems to prevail without simpler photoreceptors existing concurrently. Darwin's original puzzle over ocular evolution seems still to be with us at a molecular level'.[14] The Darwinian conundrum is sub-cellular.

In *The Origin of Species*, Darwin quickly and rightly moves on from his concern with the eye to admit that the real problem is the question of 'how life itself first originated'.[15] As Darwin remarked in a letter, 'The first origin of life on this earth, as well as the continued life of each individual, is at present quite beyond the scope of science'.[16] At the time of writing the conundrum remains unsolved.

MOVING THE CHESS PIECES

Richard Dawkins, Richard Lewontin and Francis Crick all say the same thing — that one must look apparent design in biology or biochemistry straight in the face and see the obvious suggestion of design and deliberately resist that inference as the refuge of the intellectually destitute and remember that all this came about by

---

14. Williams D. L., *Light and the evolution of vision* (Cambridge; Feb 2016 Eye; 30), 177.

15. *Ibid*, 173.

16. Darwin Charles (1868) *The variation of animals and plants under domestication* Quoted in: Juli Peretó et al. *Charles Darwin and the origin of life* (Life Evol Biosph (2009) 39:395–406).

chance. This you must conclude with the mind that was formed by that same chance, and was not fashioned as a tool fit for this deduction. And you must hold that your cogent view of reality rests secure on true premises, even though these cannot logically be complete, since observation and scientific enquiry are not yet complete, and you cannot travel forward in time by a century to see what will then be 'prosaic' fact. You must have faith that there will indeed be discoveries and that none of these will unseat your existing theory, indeed they will be guaranteed only to further confirm it.

Returning to the three key epistemological questions (how did we get here, what went wrong and how will it be set right?), the arguments so far advanced deal predominantly with the first question: how did we get here? And it may be that that is a route to faith for some. It was not for me.

In my case that central question torments me. What has gone wrong with the human race on the *Pale Blue Dot* is only what has gone wrong with me, writ large. I am at war with everyone — with God, with my fellow *Homo Sapiens Sapiens* and with myself. I hate this warfare but I cannot seem to relinquish my weapons. The difference between me and the 'generals and emperors ... [and their] rivers of blood spilled... so that in glory and triumph they could become the momentary masters of a fraction of a dot'[17] is only one of opportunity and degree.

I am selfishness and ugliness and guilt and shame — a mess of wasted opportunities, squandered blessings and lost opportunities. I have taken to myself too much credit for petty successes and squirmed out from under too much deserving opprobrium. I shift blame and judge others most harshly for the very sins I most frequently commit. I have occasionally flirted with the notion of taking refuge in the non-judgmentalism of modern liberalism, but repeatedly find it fails. For a brief moment it feels wonderful, but it is unsatisfying if it turns out to be the whole show, the entire world view. As an end in itself it is inadequate, because as well as this guilt, I feel a vacancy.

---

17.   Carl Sagan, *Op Cit.*

Victor Frankl, a survivor of Auschwitz, concluded that life is not primarily a quest for pleasure, as Freud believed, or power, as Adler taught, but a quest for meaning. I find that to be true. We are worshippers (to use the Bible's word) and in this regard I find its analysis fits with my self-understanding — I need a bigger cause than myself to live for. We need something transcendent, or we lose ourselves in the 'unbearable lightness of being'.

God has put in us an instinct to desire weight and ballast. We all need to know we are here for a reason, that our time on earth has meaning. But I don't come up to the mark, and I know it, and I don't get to set the mark or standard. As I place my hand on the chess piece of right and wrong, I find I have no right to move it forward.

A critic of Christianity may say at this point that my need is precisely what you would expect and does not constitute a truth claim, that Christianity is in the end only moralistic, therapeutic deism. We like that kind of thing (clean living) because it makes us feel good. And we believe in God (though He is a tame and rather distant deity).

This does not bear even the slightest resemblance to real Christianity. In any case it is an inconvenient truth that many of the best minds, 'converted' to Jesus Christ, do not fit the stereotype of the weak in need of a crutch. Rosaria Butterfield wrote of her change of world view: 'This word — conversion — is simply too tame and too refined to capture the train wreck I experienced in coming face-to-face with the living God'.[18] And C. S. Lewis wrote, 'Amiable agnostics will talk cheerfully about "man's search for God". To me, as I was then, they might as well have talked about the mouse's search for the cat.'[19]

Real Christianity is not a creed or a path to enlightenment or a lifestyle or a way to feel better about yourself. Christianity is a Person; it is Christ. And that is a truth claim which stands to be accepted or rejected independent of my, or anyone's, need for it to be true.

---

18   Rosaria Butterfield, *The Secret Thoughts of an Unlikely Convert* (Crown & Covenant Publications 2012), Loc82 Kindle edition.

19.   C. S. Lewis, *Surprised by Joy - The Complete CS Lewis Signature Classics* (HarperCollins Publishers London), Loc11833 Kindle Edition.

For me the search for truth begins and ends with Jesus Christ. I cannot do justice to the beauty, the sufficiency for every pain and joy shared, the brightness of Truth personified, the piercing light, the wildness and the wakeful fear, that is Jesus Christ. I know Him a little; I owe Him everything. In answering, 'Why I (still) believe', I could make no other defence than to say my reason is the Person of Jesus Christ. He is ballast in a weightless world, reason in a mad world, beauty in an ugly world and light in a blind world.

Sagan was right in one sense to group all those 'thousands of confident religions, ideologies, and economic doctrines' together. All of them applaud and respect power, and none more so than the 'religion' of philosophic naturalism. After all, evolution's doctrine of the survival of the fittest is the very distillate of the worship of power. But Jesus Christ stands alone and apart and reveals a God we would never have imagined and could never have created. In a world that worships power, He came in weakness and vulnerability to win us back, through dying a common criminal's death in an occupied state, after an unjust trial. After all, 'Power can fence us in, but only sacrificial love can find us out. Power can win when we are ranged against it, but it cannot win us'.[20]

Jesus is proof that Carl Sagan is wrong; He stands in a category by Himself and demands a response, but does so with all the winsome appeal of One who knows that 'man is born to trouble as the sparks fly upward' (Job 5:7) from 'inside' that experience.

There is nothing magical or hidden here; this is spiritual need meeting material reality. He encouraged His first followers to touch Him — 'Then he said to Thomas, "Put your finger here, and see my hands; and put out your hand, and place it in my side. Do not disbelieve, but believe"' (John 20:27) — and they marvelled that they did ('That which was from the beginning, which we ... have touched with our hands' — 1 John 1:1). He came to bring us home, kicking and screaming if need be, to move us to the last question: how will it be put right? How will all things be put right?

---

20.   Os Guinness, *Fool's Talk* (IVP books, 2015), 73.

All things are right when He is in the centre and all things are wrong when anything else is. He told His first followers why He came: '...the Son of Man [Jesus' term for Himself] came not to be served but to serve, and to give his life as a ransom for many' (Mark 10:45). Who would have guessed that when God came, He would come in such humility, to suffer and die the cruellest of deaths to bring us home? If this Jesus is at the centre, all things are in order, and we lay down our weapons willingly and find we are no longer lost in our own story. He has brought us home.

All of the above is why I (still) believe.

4

WHY I (STILL) BELIEVE IN A GOOD GOD[1]

VINCE VITALE

To be honest, I thought Christianity was for people who didn't think hard enough. That was my assumption as I began my undergraduate studies in philosophy at Princeton University. But I met some Christians who convinced me that, given how much was at stake, I should at least give God a chance.

And so I began reading through the Bible for the first time. I would cross things out and add what I was sure were improvements in the margins, but before long my attitude towards Christianity began to change. As I continued reading the Bible, I started to believe that Jesus had lived the most beautiful life ever lived. I also came to think that the Christian faith was intellectually satisfying, and I learned that there were incredibly smart people exploring the philosophical questions about God with relentless rigour, and still coming to the conclusion that God exists.

Nevertheless, I had objections, and the topic of this chapter was one of the biggest ones: how can there be a good God if the world is so full of evil and suffering?

---

1. Portions of this chapter are taken from *Why Suffering?: Finding Meaning and Comfort When life Doesn't Make Sense* (New York: Hachette, 2014), which is co-authored by Ravi Zacharias and Vince Vitale.

In just the last forty-eight hours, one friend got in touch to say that his Aunt had died from cancer; another friend wrote from the Middle East to say, 'We are only metres away from where a bomb exploded. The entire neighbourhood is shut down and there has been news that there may be other explosions following this one.' Then I received an email from another dear friend: 'This very hour is the six-year anniversary of my suicide attempt. I feel vulnerable, alone and forsaken. Please could you pray for me?' And then this morning I woke up to hear of terrorist bombings in Brussels that have killed more than thirty people.

Suffering is never far from any one of us, but why would that be the case if God exists? God is supposed to be all-powerful; if so, then He has the power to stop suffering. God is supposed to be all-loving; if so, then He would desire to stop suffering. And yet our world is filled with all sorts of horrors.

If you or I stood by and watched serious suffering when we could stop it, others would rightly call us evil! How then can we call God loving? This is what is often referred to as *the problem of evil* or *the problem of suffering*.

There are no easy answers here. In one of the first conversations I had on this topic, my aunt, Regina, expressed to me how difficult it is to see her son Charles struggle with a serious mental illness. Being more concerned at the time with the question than the questioner, I started spouting some of my abstract, philosophical ideas about why God might allow suffering. After listening very graciously, Aunt Regina turned to me and said, 'But, Vince, that doesn't speak to me *as a mother*'.

I should have remembered that when Jesus arrived at His friend Lazarus's tomb, He chose not to defend His perceived tardiness but instead to shed tears with Lazarus's sisters, Mary and Martha (John 11). One of the most important things to me about my Christian faith is that I have a God who does not just provide reasons and explanations, but who weeps alongside us when we suffer.

Still, there is a lot that can be said and has been said about why a world created by God might include suffering, and sometimes considering these reasons can help us to believe in God despite suffering, to trust God amid suffering, and to hope with confidence for a time beyond suffering.

So what I want to do here is offer nine responses to the question 'Why suffering?' I strongly resist any one-size-fits-all answer to this question, but I think all of the responses I will present have something to be said for them, and I think that is significant. In a courtroom, one witness who testifies to the defendant's innocence might not be very persuasive. But if you had nine witnesses, who *all* testified to the defendant's innocence, each having seen things from a different perspective, that would be very compelling evidence.

Therefore I want to present a variety of perspectives on which God can be seen as loving and good despite the existence of evil and suffering. Each of the approaches can be thought of as a witness to the goodness of God. You might not be convinced by any one of them on its own, but the fact that there are so many responses, so many witnesses, so many apparent sightings of divine goodness is strong reason to conclude that God is, in fact, good.

A RESPONSE OF FREEDOM

To find a first Christian response to the challenge of suffering, we can turn to the first pages of the Bible.

What we find there is a story of people who are in intimate relationship with God. But then they hear this voice in their ears, 'Did God actually say, "You shall not eat of any tree in the garden?"' (Gen. 3:1). And they begin to doubt God. They begin to doubt that He knows what's best for them; they begin to doubt that He is *for* them; ultimately they begin to doubt what He has actually said — His word.

And then they sin; they do what they know deep down they should not do — not a big sin, just eating a piece of fruit that they were told not to eat. No big deal, right? But it starts them down a path. First we're told that they felt shame. They were convinced that God wouldn't want anything to do with them any more, and so they hid themselves from God. Then they began accusing each other. Adam pointed at Eve and said, 'She did it!' (in essence pointing his finger at God as well by referring to Eve as 'The woman whom *you* gave to be with me' [Gen. 3:12, emphasis added]), and Eve pointed at the serpent and said, 'He did it!'

From temptation to doubt to disobedience to shame to hiding to finger-pointing to suffering. Is there really a question about whether this story speaks the truth about the human heart? When I read it, I have to admit that it resounds with the truth about me.

And so the Bible starts with a story of people who were created *free*. Why? Because God didn't want to force people into relationship with Him. He could have! He's powerful enough to just force us to do whatever He wants us to do.

But what do we call a relationship where a more powerful person forces a less powerful person into submission? We call that abuse. We call that slavery. And that is not the way you treat someone you love.

God hates suffering; it is not what He wants. But He is absolutely committed to not treating us like slaves. The Christian God is not a tyrant. A tyrant just wants obedience; he doesn't care how he gets it. The Christian God is a father, and a loving father wants His children to freely trust Him.

According to the Bible, the explanation for so much of the suffering we see and experience is the misuse of free will. Maybe that sounds like an exaggeration to you. It once did to me, but not anymore. There was a boy named Euan with whom I used to fight as a teenager. I was unkind to him. The very same free will that God gave me to help him up, I used to push him down.

A few years ago I heard that Euan had killed himself. The Bible says, 'the wages of sin is death' (Rom. 6:23). Would Euan have killed himself if I had been kind to him, offered my hand to him? I don't know.

Sometimes when I try to explain sin to people they want to tell me that I'm exaggerating, that really I'm pretty good. It's not like I've *killed* anyone! Actually, that's a much harder statement for me to affirm than you might expect. And what if God shone a light not just on Euan but on the rippling effects of all of my unkindness over the years?

I am convinced that our tendency is to vastly underestimate the consequences of our free choices.[2] Therefore, if we are going to sincerely ask the question 'Why suffering?' we need to look not only at God but also at ourselves. We need to be honest enough to answer as G. K. Chesterton once did in a newspaper response to the question, 'What's wrong with the world?':

'Dear Sirs,

I am.

Sincerely yours,

G. K. Chesterton'.[3]

---

2. You might ask, 'Even if human free will helps to account for a lot of evil and suffering, is it relevant to so-called *natural evils* such as earthquakes and tornadoes?' The Christian philosopher Peter van Inwagen notes that earthquakes and tornadoes are not intrinsically evil; indeed, they can be awe-inspiring and beautiful. They are only evil when people are in the wrong place at the wrong time. Van Inwagen suggests that at some point in the earth's history, God raised beings to a state of rationality and moral awareness and then brought them into intimate relationship with Himself. In that state of untainted union with God, van Inwagen wonders whether these first human persons would have had a sort of sixth sense that always allowed them not to be in the wrong place at the wrong time. The loss of this sense when these persons fell into estrangement from God, van Inwagen theorises, would be just as natural a consequence as the loss of human language is for a feral child. (Interestingly, it has been documented that when some animals sense Rayleigh Waves [vibrational waves] ahead of a coming tsunami, they identify them as a sign of danger and move inland. Humans also have sensors in their joints allowing them to detect Rayleigh Waves, but, when this occurs, humans fail to process these waves as a warning of danger.) Humanity is not living in the loving, nurturing relationship with God it was most intended for, and therefore human beings are not functioning properly in their environment. For van Inwagen's discussion of these points, see his article 'The Magnitude Duration and Distribution of Evil: A Theodicy' (*Philosophical Topics* 16.2, 1988) and his book *The Problem of Evil* (Oxford University Press, 2006).

3. The American Chesterton Society is inclined to think this anecdote is true; however, documentary evidence of it has not been found. In any case, it is a poignant example of recognising the need to look within the human heart to make sense of the world around us.

A RESPONSE FROM MORALITY

The second response I want to touch on is a response from morality. The world's most famous atheist, Richard Dawkins, once gave this summary of atheism: 'There is, at bottom, no design, no purpose, no evil and no good, nothing but blind, pitiless indifference.'[4]

And so when someone challenges me — a Christian — with the problem of evil, we actually have a point of *agreement*, because they are agreeing with me that this quote from Dawkins is wrong; they are agreeing with me that, when we look around our world, there are some things that are not the way they are supposed to be; there are some things that we have to be able to point at and say, 'That is genuinely, objectively evil'.

It would be genuinely, objectively evil even if we didn't think it was. Even if someone thinks it is okay to bomb an airport, they are wrong. Even if someone thinks it is okay to commit genocide, they are wrong. And even if Hitler had won World War II and the whole world had come to think that it was okay to commit genocide, they would still be wrong.

There is a moral law that transcends human opinion. But if there is this overarching moral law, then (as Ravi Zacharias has pressed) doesn't there need to be a moral law-*giver*?

If I drive 100 miles per hour, I have broken British law. Why? Because a legitimate governmental authority has given a speed limit law.

If I cheat on my wife, I have not broken British law, but I have broken a moral law. Who is the authority that gave *that* law? Who could possibly be in the legitimate position to make a moral law that governs the entire world across all cultures and all times?

Atheism thinks evil shows that there is no God. I think it shows the exact opposite! Moral evil requires a moral law, and a moral law requires a moral lawgiver. Only God is in position to provide a stable, transcendent, moral standard that allows us to call good 'good' and to call evil 'evil'. Ironically, the person who objects

---

4.   Richard Dawkins, *A River Out of Eden* (New York: Perseus, 1995), 133.

to God because of evil can only make his objection by already assuming the God that he was intending to disprove.

A RESPONSE OF HUMILITY

One of the assumptions smuggled into the thought that suffering disproves the existence of God is this: if God has good reasons for allowing suffering, *we* should expect to know what those reasons are.

But why think that? When parents decide to move their family from one city to another, this genuinely can be very difficult on a young child. In the moment, the child might be certain that all happiness is behind him, that his parents hate him and that for all practical purposes his life is over.

And, yet, even such outrage on the part of a child does not mean that the child's parents are wrong to make the move, and it does not mean that they don't love their child. In fact, it's very likely that it was precisely the good of their children that weighed heavily in the parents' decision.

You can see the analogy: if parents' reasons are sometimes beyond what a child can fully grasp, why then should I be surprised when some of God's reasons are beyond what I can fully grasp?

Or consider when I take my pet dog, Buster, to the vet. Buster doesn't understand why I need to allow him to suffer the pain of a needle or undergo a painful surgery. And when I sit Buster down on the couch and try to explain to him that this surgery is important so that he won't get a terrible disease, I don't get very far! That's not because of a lack of ability on my part; it's not that I'm not communicating well enough. Buster simply isn't the sort of being that can understand why I do some of the things I do.

My understanding is higher than Buster's understanding. The understanding of parents is often higher than that of their children. Why then should we be surprised when God's ways are higher than our ways?

Over the last thirty years, there has developed a large and growing philosophical literature asking this question. In its current philosophical guise, this approach goes by the name *sceptical theism*. But it's not a new approach; the Bible affirms it in several places, for instance in the Book of Isaiah:

> For my thoughts are not your thoughts,
>   neither are your ways my ways,
>   declares the LORD.
> For as the heavens are higher than the earth,
>   so are my ways higher than your ways
>   and my thoughts than your thoughts
>   (Isa. 55:8–9; compare Rom. 11:33–34).

Or, as God inquired of Job,

> Where were you when I laid the foundation of the earth?
>   Tell me, if you have understanding.
> Who determined its measurements — surely you know!
>   (Job 38:4–5)

I'll give you one chance to guess the number of universes I've created. Am I really in any position to lecture God about how He should have created the universe?

If God is as great as Christians claim He is, then sometimes not fully grasping the fullness of His reasons is exactly what we should expect. And if it's exactly what we should expect to find if God *does* exist, then our finding it can't be strong evidence that God does *not* exist.

A RESPONSE OF GRACE

It's typical to think of the problem of suffering like this: we picture ourselves in this world of suffering; then we picture ourselves in a very different world with no suffering or at least far less suffering. And then we wonder, 'Shouldn't God have created *us* in the other world—the world with far less suffering?'

That's a reasonable thought. But we forget to ask, 'Would it still be *you* and *me* — and the people we love — who would have come to exist in that very different world?'

This is the question that motivated my Ph.D. research, and the technical name for the theory that emerged is *Non-Identity Theodicy*.[5] I can explain it with a true story.

There was a pivotal moment early on in my parents' dating relationship. They were on their second date. They were standing on the Brooklyn Bridge, overlooking the picturesque New York City skyline, and my dad noticed a ring on my mom's finger. So he asked about it, and she said, 'Oh, that's just some ring one of my old boyfriends gave me. I just wear it 'cause I think it looks nice'.

'Oh, yeah, it is nice,' my dad said, 'let me see it.' So mom took it off and handed it to him, and my dad *hurled* it off the bridge and watched it sink to the bottom of the East River! 'You're with me now,' he declared; 'you won't be needing that anymore'.

And my mom loved it!

But what if she hadn't? What if she had concluded my dad was nuts and ran off with her old boyfriend instead? What would that have meant *for me*? (If you can believe it, fifty years later my dad still interrogates my mom about who that old boyfriend was, and my mom still flatly refuses to say!)

I might be tempted to think that, if Mom had wound up with her old boyfriend, I could have been better off. I might have been taller. I might have been better looking. Maybe the other guy was royalty. That would have been cool! I could've lived in a castle! But, actually, that's not right. There's a problem with wishing my mom wound up with the other guy, and the problem is this: 'I' never would have existed.

Maybe some *other* child would have existed. And maybe *he* would have been taller and better looking and lived in a castle. But *part* of what makes me who I am — the individual that I am — is

---

5. A *theodicy* is an (at least partial) explanation of why God allows suffering. *Non-Identity Theodicy* explores the idea that without suffering the people who would have existed would have been different from — i.e., would have been *not identical* to — the people who actually exist. *Non-Identity Theodicy* takes cues from excellent work published by the philosopher Robert Adams in the 1970s. See Robert Merrihew Adams, 'Must God Create the Best?', *The Philosophical Review* 81 (1972) and Robert Merrihew Adams, 'Existence, Self-Interest, and the Problem of Evil', (originally published in 1979, but revised), in Robert Merrihew Adams, *The Virtue of Faith and Other Essays in Philosophical Theology* (Oxford: Oxford University Press, 1987).

my beginning: the parents I have, the sperm and egg I came from, the combination of genes that's true of me.

Asking 'Why didn't God create *us* in a world with far less suffering?' is similar to saying 'I wish my mom had married the other guy.' I'm sure my mom and her old boyfriend would have had some very nice kids, but 'I' would not have been one of them.

We often wish we could take suffering out of our world while keeping everything else the same. But it doesn't work that way. If something as small as the throwing of a ring into the East River can change who comes to exist, imagine how radically who comes to exist would be changed if God miraculously removed all vulnerability to suffering. Imagine if He took away free will every time we thought to hurt someone, or if He radically changed our natural environment — if weather systems and plate tectonics didn't behave as they do, if we were never susceptible to disease, if the laws of thermodynamics had undergone a redesign. What would be the results?

One likely result is that none of *us* would have lived. Sometimes we understandably wish that the world had been very different. But, in doing so, we unwittingly wish ourselves — and those we love — right out of existence.[6]

And I don't think God likes that idea!

In fact, I think one of the things that God values most about this world — even though He hates the suffering in it — is that it is a world that allowed for *you*. I believe God desired you. Not because you are better, or smarter, or funnier, or better looking than the other creatures God could have created,[7] but simply out of *grace* — unmerited love, the love of a parent standing over a newborn child.

The question, 'Why do you love your child?' doesn't even make sense to the parent. *What do you mean why do I love her? She's my child. I made her. She's in my image. She has my nose.*

---

6. None of this implies that we cannot one day live in an eternal state where there will be no evil or suffering. It is a person's *origin* that establishes his identity. Once he comes to exist, however, his *future* can take many different forms, despite personal identity being maintained.

7. I am reminded here of the Psalmist's words: 'what are mere mortals that you should think about them, human beings that you should care for them?' (Ps. 8:4 NLT).

What does God think of you?

I wonder what the instinctive answer of your heart was when you read that question. The Christian message is that God loves you, even as you are, as much on your best day as on your very worst day, with a love that you cannot lose, with a love that is not to be earned but simply to be returned. And one of the things God values about this world is that it is a world that allowed for you to come to exist.

My family has had quite a bit of disability in it. Some people would say that because of the suffering caused by their disabilities, it would have been better if my cousin Charles had never existed, and if my Uncle John had never existed. There would have been less suffering overall; the world would be better off.

I adamantly disagree. It's because I knew Charles and John intimately that their suffering was so frustrating. But it's also because I knew Charles and John intimately that I can understand why God loves them so deeply, and why God would value a world that allowed for them to have life and to be offered eternal life.

The problem of suffering is therefore reframed in the form of a question: could God have wronged us by creating us in this world and offering us eternal life, rather than creating a different world in which we never would have lived?

There is a strong analogy here between divine creation and human procreation.

We know that intentional human procreation will result in serious suffering, because even the most fortunate of human lives includes serious suffering. Even more than that, we know that one day any child we bring into existence will suffer death.

Why, then, do we think that having a child is morally okay, and even can be loving and courageous? Because the child who comes to exist would not have existed otherwise. In human procreation we risk great suffering, but in doing so we give to someone the gift of life. What I have been suggesting is that, similarly, in creating and sustaining this world rather than some very different world, God gave each of us the gift of life and the offer of eternal life with Him.

Here is the result of this reasoning: if you think it would be evil to create people into a world that you know will produce serious suffering in their lives, you will not only need to call God evil, you will also need to call evil anyone who decides to have a child. What follows is that if there is good reason to think that human procreation can be an act of love, there is also good reason to think that God's creation could be an act of love.

A RESPONSE OF LIFE TO THE FULL

For a fifth response, think of what is, in your opinion, one of the greatest lives ever lived. Consider it in detail. Think of the person's character and how it was formed. Think of the person's relationships. Think of his or her great triumphs, their sacrifices, their steadfastness for what is good and true.

Now, try in your imagination to subtract from that person's life all possibility of suffering. Subtract the suffering that shaped the culture and family they were born into, the suffering that formed their character, the suffering they fought against, the suffering that they carried others through.

What happened? All of a sudden that life doesn't look anything like the great life that you were initially so inclined to celebrate.

Without the possibility of significant suffering, practically every great true story in history would be false. No one would ever have made a significant sacrifice for anyone else. No great moments of forgiveness and reconciliation. No opportunities to stand for justice against injustice. No compassion (because nothing to be compassionate about), no courage (because no dangerous situations requiring courage), no heroes, no such thing as laying down one's life for another (John 15:13).

Is it so obvious that God would create this world rather than our own? Criticism without alternative is empty. If not our world, what world should God have made? I find that the longer I reflect on how much good would have been lost in losing the *possibility* of the bad, the harder it is to give a compelling response to that question.

A RESPONSE FOR ETERNITY

Moreover, God does not need to choose between the goods of this world and the goods of heaven. He can choose both — some for a time, and then others for all time.

It is easy to forget that, if God exists, our current perspective is not the full perspective. The Bible says that the eternal life that God offers to every person will be one where 'He [God Himself!] will wipe every tear from their eyes', where there will be 'no more death or mourning or crying or pain' (Rev. 21:4, NIV).

Imagine aliens who managed to tap into a video feed from earth, but all they could see was the hospital delivery room when I was being born. They watched as the doctors forcefully told my mom to do things that made her scream in pain, and then, when she could take no more, the doctors got out a knife and cut right into my mom's stomach. They took me out — blood everywhere — and even though my mom was reaching out for me and screaming for me, the doctors immediately rushed me away from her. What would the aliens think of the doctors?

If all the aliens saw were the first few moments of life, they might be convinced the doctors were evil. Only from a fuller perspective would they be able to see that the doctors actually cared for my mother extremely well, and in fact saved my life.

On the Christian understanding of reality, what we currently see is only the first few moments of life — literally just the birthing process of human history! We will always come up short if we attempt to find the full explanation for suffering in this life alone. This life is only the smallest fraction of our lives; we are going to live forever, and the vast, vast majority of our lives can be spent without death or mourning or crying or pain. Although so difficult to imagine now, the eternal life we are intended to wake up to will be so vivid, so robust, so real that we will know the utter relief of opening our eyes to find that the bad dream of all of our suffering is finally over.

At the beginning of the Book of Job, Job loses everything — his wealth, his livestock, his family. At the end of the book, God gives back to Job a double portion of everything that had been lost (Job 42:10): twice as many animals, twice as much wealth.

But Job only gets back the *same* number of children. Why is that? Perhaps because Job still had his original ten children. They have not been lost. Job is not with them for a time, but perhaps he will be reunited with them for all time. In the life to come, God can give back to us so much of what has been lost. He can fulfil so many of the dreams that have been shattered.

A few months ago, one of my students, Ariel, found out that her brain is prone to bleeding, and that she would probably die within a few years.

Shortly after she received that diagnosis, Ariel shared with me that she found herself looking in the mirror, observing the limited mobility on her right side, and she can remember asking herself, 'Is this the healthiest I am ever going to be?' 'Is this the strongest I am ever going to be?' 'Is this the prettiest I am ever going to be?'

And then Ariel told me of the deep peacefulness that came over her as she remembered the answer to those questions — 'No. Absolutely not'. She spoke about the joy of knowing that one day her body will be able to do far more than it ever has before. I know Ariel loves to snowboard, so I asked her if she thought there would be snowboarding in eternity, and I wish you could have seen how unhesitatingly and how confidently she responded, 'Absolutely! And soccer too!' And I wish you could have seen the radiant smile on her face as she said it.

When deep suffering comes, it tries to get us to believe that there is nothing more to life than the worst. But one of the privileges of being a Christian is being invited into a bigger story, to see life from a wider perspective, and to know — in the deep sense that brings true peace — that suffering is not your end.

A RESPONSE AT THE CROSS

For the next response let me tell you my favourite story from my childhood.

I was about six years old. I was playing football on my neighbour's front lawn with a bunch of older kids, and I was getting knocked around pretty good. I came running home crying to my mom, who was out on the front porch, yelling to her, 'I'm not tough enough! I'm not tough enough!'

So guess what she did. My mom did what any loving mother of a six-year-old son would do. She bent down into quite an athletic stance, hung her nose out in the air, looked at me lovingly, and said, 'Punch me in the nose! Punch me in the nose! Come on! You are tough enough! Punch me in the nose!'

At first I just looked at her like she was crazy, and indeed she was, but she persisted: 'Punch me in the nose!' Well, she asked for it. I don't know what sort of psychological state I must have been in, but finally I reared back and gave my mom a straight right hand, and, to my astonishment, blood began pouring out of her nose and down her face.

Then came one of the most gorgeous images I have ever seen. *Through the blood* came the most dazzling, radiant, joyful smile, and my mom said, 'Now get back out there!'

You might not know what to make of that story. Understandably so! What a bizarre thing for my mom to do. What an unthinkable, messy, bloody thing to do. But what an extravagant display of love.

My mom chose to bring me into this world, knowing there would be suffering. And when the suffering came, and my eyes filled with tears, she bent down, and stepped into my suffering with me, even though that meant suffering at the hands of her own child.

That is one picture of Jesus on the Cross, where God did something unthinkable and messy and bloody — where God bent down, and stepped into our suffering, even though it meant suffering at the hands of those He created.

Why? Because that's what a loving parent does. Christians believe in a God who, like my mom, was willing to come and suffer alongside us. The night before Jesus died, as He wrestled with what He knew the next day would bring, He said to His friends, 'My soul is overwhelmed with sorrow to the point of death' (Matt. 26:38, NIV).

There is no depth of agony and helplessness we can experience in this life that the Christian God does not understand.

The atheist philosopher Friedrich Nietzsche actually may have said it best: 'The gods justified human life by living it themselves — the only satisfactory theodicy ever invented.'[8]

Though Nietzsche was writing of the ancient Greeks and remarkably doesn't make the connection to Christianity, the connection is clear. When we look to the Cross, we find in Jesus a God who loves us enough to suffer with us, and therefore a God we can trust.

A RESPONSE OF RELATIONSHIP

Surprisingly, the objection from suffering — raised invariably in the West — is less frequently raised in the parts of the world where people appear to be suffering most. Somehow those who have suffered most, rather than consistently denying God, often have the greatest confidence in the goodness of God.

I've often wondered about this. Perhaps this is in part because there are certain things about God's goodness that can be known only by inviting God into our suffering and experiencing Him in the midst of it. In philosophy, this type of experiential knowledge is referred to as *non-propositional knowledge*, which is to say that it can't be fully conveyed by words, by writing it down in a book to be read.

Quite a lot of our knowledge is like this. My wife, Jo, and I recently spent time in Florence, and we had the privilege of viewing Michelangelo's *David*. To be honest, it didn't feel like much of a privilege as we stood in line in the rain for two hours waiting to get in. Nor did it feel like a privilege when Jo and I 'discussed' our difference of opinion about whether it was worth continuing to get drenched to see something that we had already seen countless times in photographs and on television. In the end, we did a *marriage*

---

8.   Friedrich Nietzsche, *The Birth of Tragedy and the Genealogy of Morals*, trans. Francis Golffing (Garden City, NY: Doubleday, 1956), 30.

compromise. Jo wanted to stay, and I wanted to leave, and so we compromised and we stayed.

And when we saw the *David* — in person, up close — we were both utterly grateful that we did. Only then did we *know* what all the fuss was about. We knew something by experiencing that piece of artwork firsthand that had not been conveyed to us — that *could not* be conveyed to us — by postcards or documentaries.

Much of our knowledge is knowledge gained by experience, and this is even more frequently the case when we start talking about knowledge relevant to relationships. I know my wife's face. But no matter how many pages you gave me, and no matter how much detail I included, I could never express to you the fullness of that knowledge in writing. That knowledge I can only share with you by introducing you to her.

And I could say the same of simply knowing Jo — knowing who she is. I could tell you about Jo all day long, but still I would not come close to expressing to you the fullness of my knowledge of who she is. That depth of knowledge can be acquired only through the interactions of intimate relationship.

Perhaps this is also true of knowledge of God's goodness and knowledge of His response to suffering. Maybe much of that knowledge, as well, cannot be known by philosophical argumentation, but only by inviting God into our suffering — by voicing our frustration to Him during it, by praying to Him through it, by experiencing it together in real relationship.

To me, one of the most depressing images in the Bible is that when Jesus' suffering was at its worst, all of His friends 'deserted him and fled' (Mark 14:50, NIV). Suffering's greatest cruelty is its isolation.

But the experience of suffering is radically different when someone who loves you is right there with you every step of the way. As a Christian, you never have to go looking for someone who understands your suffering; you never have to go looking for someone who cares. That Someone is always with you, even dwelling within you.

The meaning in suffering and in God's response to suffering is largely to be found not in theorising, but in living day to day beside the God who suffers with us and for us. The Christian response to suffering is primarily not a response of ideas, but a response of a Person and a response of relationship. It is the response of knowing not just about God, but God Himself — 'I had heard of you by the hearing of the ear, but now my eye sees you' (Job 42:5).

A RESPONSE THAT MAKES A DIFFERENCE

We've taken a brief look at a few of the perspectives from which God can be seen as good and loving despite the suffering of this world. Perhaps you are not fully persuaded by each perspective — by each witness — but the fact that there are so many witnesses, all pointing to the goodness of God, is strong reason to believe they are seeing accurately; the love of God does shine into even the darkest corners of this world.

It's worth mentioning one final problem of suffering. This is the problem of how we're going to deal with suffering, and that's a problem for every one of us, regardless of what we do or do not believe about God. When suffering comes, when death comes, who will bear it with us? And who will see us through it?

The answers to these questions were never more obvious to me than about three years ago when I sat at the hospital bedside of Joe, the father of one of my best friends. He was dying of cancer.

It was on Joe's front lawn that I started crying on that unforgettable day when I punched my mom in the nose. Now it was Joe who was feeling not tough enough. The doctors had given him only a few weeks left to live, and he told me that, although he had always been confident that God exists in some way, he was finding himself increasingly scared about what comes next.

As we spoke, what became clear to me was that Joe's understanding of the central message of Christianity was that you should try to do more good than bad in your life, and then just hope that in the end your good deeds will outweigh your bad deeds. If they do, something wonderful awaits. But, if they don't, you're in trouble.

I was never so incredibly thankful to be sitting before someone as a Christian. Every other way of seeing the world would have had nothing to say. As an atheist, I would have had to say there is no hope at all beyond the grave. If I adhered to almost any other religion, I would have had to tell Joe that he was basically right — it was about whether he had done enough to earn God's approval — and therefore had every reason to fear what was next.

Only as a Christian could I explain to Joe that while God *does* want us to do good, that is *not* what makes us right with God. What makes us right with God has nothing to do with anything we do or ever could do, but rather with what Jesus has already done — once, and in full, and for all.

I explained that if we trust in Jesus Christ, we no longer need to fear judgment, because Jesus has already taken the judgment for everything we have ever done or will ever do wrong. I explained that when Jesus died on the Cross, that was God taking on to Himself all of the darkness in our lives — the suffering, the guilt, the shame, the failure — so that we could be free of it. That was God saying He knows it's too much for us to bear, and so He bore it Himself. That's how much He loves us.

When I asked Joe if this made sense, he replied, '69 years and I never thought of that. I thought Christianity was one thing, but it was something else entirely. This turns everything upside down'. There was an extended pause, and then Joe said, 'You know, Vince, you spend your whole life trying to make up for your mess-ups, but this finally explains how we can deal with guilt'.

I asked Joe if he wanted to pray with me to put his trust in Christ and he said that he did. With great conviction he thrust out his arm to me. We clasped hands, and we wept, and we prayed, and as we finished praying he exclaimed a loud 'AMEN!'

Joe asked me if my wife knew this great truth about Christ as well. I said that she did, and he responded, 'It must be a happy life'. And then, after a thoughtful pause, 'Now I'm actually looking forward to what's next'.

Some think the problem of suffering should push us away from God. For me, it's precisely because I feel the problem of suffering so severely that I am led to trust the only God who has proved that He can do something about it.

That's why I (still) believe in a good God.

5

WHY I (STILL) BELIEVE IN JESUS

Maher Samuel

The English philosopher John Stuart Mill once wrote, 'Mankind can hardly be too often reminded that there was once a man named Socrates. That is correct, but it is even more important to remind mankind that a man named Jesus Christ once stood in their midst'.[1] No one can deny the influence of Jesus Christ on human history in general, and on the history of Western civilization in particular. Yale historian Jaroslav Pelikan wrote, 'Regardless of what anyone may personally think or believe about Him, Jesus of Nazareth has been the dominant figure in the history of Western Culture for almost 20 centuries. If it were possible, with some sort of super magnet, to pull up out of history everything that bears at least a trace of His name, how much would be left?'[2]

Consequently, for every truth seeker, it is worth making the effort to be acquainted with this pivotal character in history. It is not reasonable to show interest in this unique character without reading the oldest and most comprehensive writings about Him,

---

1.   J. S. Mill, Essay on Liberty, 1859; in Sinclair, Upton, ed. *The Cry for Justice: An Anthology of the Literature of Social Protest* (John C. Winston Co., 1915).

2.   J. Pelikan, *Jesus through the centuries: His Place in the History of culture* (Yale University Press, 1985), 1.

namely the four gospels. When the seeker reads about Jesus in these documents, many things will draw his/her attention — such as: His moral supremacy, His obvious rationality which never contradicted his deep spirituality and His unveiling of human nature like no one else. What is more, one must also note His distinguished and comprehensive revelation of reality — He did not stop at the accurate revelation of visible reality with all its religious, political, moral and social dimensions, but He also revealed both the unseen and the ultimate reality. In this chapter I will focus on two points, clearly revealed throughout the gospels, namely the uniqueness of His person and the uniqueness of His mission.

THE UNIQUENESS OF JESUS' PERSON

Jesus made very strange and unique claims about Himself, claims that mean He cannot be regarded as merely a guru, religious leader or prophet. First, I'll look at four of them and then provide four arguments that make the rejection of these claims very difficult.

a) His relationship with God

Jesus spoke about having a unique relationship with God that excludes Him from being merely a prophet or religious leader. He asserted that he who has known Him has known God, and whoever has seen Him has seen God, and that no one knows Him except the Father; neither does anyone know the Father, except the Son. He spoke of Himself as the Son of God, not in the sense of sonship known to the Jews at that time. They understood that the angels are sons of God, and so was Adam, as they were directly created by God. However, Jesus called Himself the *only* Son of God. He had a kind of sonship that no one shared with Him. He was bold enough to tell God Himself, 'All I have is yours and all you have is mine' (John 17:10, NIV). He said that the Father is in Him, that He is in the Father and that He and the Father are one (John 8:19; 14:7, 9; Matt. 11:27; John 3:16; 10:29–33; 5:20; 10:30, 38).

b) His relationship to time.

He spoke about His eternal coexistence with God; that also lifts Him above being a mere human being. He spoke about a love between Him and God that existed before the foundation of the world and about glory that He shared with God before the world existed. He told the Jews, 'before Abraham was, I am' (John 8:58). We should understand this claim exactly as the Jews themselves did, for they picked up stones to stone Him. They immediately recognised that He was claiming to Himself the same nature of being as the Lord Jehovah who revealed His nature to Moses as the uncreated eternal being — 'I am who I am' (John 16:28; 17:5,11; 8:58–59; Exod. 3:14).

c) His relationship with the Scriptures

All the activities and teachings of Jesus were in a Jewish environment that strongly venerated the Scriptures and believed them to be prophetic and infallible. In this context, Jesus came and He venerated the authority of Scripture no less than they, whether in His personal life, in His teachings or in His debates with those who opposed Him. The strange and amazing thing is that He continuously asserted and repeated that He Himself was the focal point of the Scriptures and their main theme (John 5:39; Luke 24:27)! Isn't this an exaggerated claim? How can an ordinary person, or even a great prophet, be the theme of all the Scriptures? Take John the Baptist: Jesus testified that he was greater than a prophet, though the Old Testament only refers to him twice (Mal. 3:1; Isa. 40:3). So one can see that the claim to be the centre of all Scripture cannot be made by one who thinks himself to be a mere prophet. Some studies show that there are more than three hundred prophecies about Christ in the Old Testament.

d) His relationship with mankind

He taught His disciples that true leadership and greatness lie in becoming a servant to all. He Himself had not come to be served but to serve. He didn't serve only those needy ones who came to Him, but went about searching for them. There are dozens of stories that confirm this, the last of which was that He bent over in the upper room like a servant to wash His disciples' feet (Matt. 20:26–28; Mark 10:45; John 4:4–26; Luke 19:1–10; John 13:1–17). However, while He taught this and acted it out, He claimed that He had another relationship with humans — one that appears superficially to be contradictory to the concept of serving. He claimed, for example, that He had authority to forgive people's sins, to give them life and also that He will judge them in the Last Day! Could this be a mere human (Mark 2:10; Luke 7:48; John 10:10; 5:22)?

GREAT CHALLENGES

These very powerful claims suggest an insanely egocentric personality. It is possible to reject or ignore these claims, but there are four challenges that make this rejection much more complicated than it may initially seem.

a) Miracles

His claims were accompanied by supernatural signs and wonders that were admitted by many, even His enemies (John 11:47-8). For many reasons they were unlikely to be fabricated by His followers. Some of the reasons are cultural; for example, how could Matthew and Mark, as Jews, write about a bleeding woman touching Jesus, or about Him touching a leper or touching the dead, or going to heal the daughter of a Canaanite woman, testifying that her faith was great (Mark 5:21–43; 1:41; 7:25–30; Matt. 9:18–26; 8:3; 9:25; 15:22–29)? For Jews these stories are unthinkable and offensive.

Some of the reasons are theological, for His miracles were very much linked to His teaching which was not understood by His disciples then! Feeding the huge crowds with the five loaves is followed by long and deep teaching about Himself as the bread of life, teaching which His disciples did not understand. The miracle of opening the eyes of a man born blind was immediately after teaching about Himself as the light of the world. The miracle of raising Lazarus from death was immediately after revealing Himself as the shepherd who will give His sheep eternal life, which provoked the Jews to kill Him. The healings on Sabbath days were to confirm that the Sabbath was made for man and not man for the Sabbath (John 6:1–13; 25–40; 8:12; 9:1–12; 10:1–33; 11:28–44; Mark 2:27).

Other reasons are psychological — many of the miracles which the disciples recorded show their failure and weakness, which makes recording them unlikely in a culture of shame and honour.

b) Morality

These claims were accompanied by His very high moral standard which is difficult to ignore and which undermines the possibility of His lying in these claims about Himself and His mission.

He dealt with people as ends, not means. Tax collectors and sinners came close to Christ to listen to Him, sit with Him and enjoy a relationship with Him (Luke 15). The question that presents itself is: what was it in Jesus' personality that attracted them in that way? I believe it is nothing other than His treatment of them as ends and not means. What about the sinful woman to whom He gave great value despite the scorn of the religious community toward her, the scorn exemplified in the behaviour of Simon (Luke 7)? What about His forgiveness to His murderers in an unrivalled sort of unconditional love even at the expense of self (Luke 23)?

c) Intellectuality

His claims were accompanied by intellectual abilities that dispel any suspicion of mental disorder. Dallas Willard said that Jesus is the greatest thinker of the human race and the most intelligent person who ever lived on earth.[3] Notice His respect for rationality and its indispensability to entering the kingdom (Mark 12:34).

---

3. Dallas Willard, *Jesus the Logician* (Christian Scholars Review, Summer 1999), 610.

Consistency with the laws of logic was obvious in His debates and arguments. For example, in an *a fortiori* argument your debater objects to the validity of B and at the same time accepts the validity of A. If you are able to prove that the evidence for the validity of B is stronger than that of A, he is obliged to accept the validity of B. In many instances, Jesus applied this with his debaters (John 4:21–24; Matt. 12:9–14; John 10:31–41). He also used hypothetical syllogisms in which you come to a necessary logical conclusion from certain propositions or hypotheses. He also utilised 'avoiding the two horns of a dilemma'; when debaters tried to corner Him, where normally He would have to choose between two problematic solutions, He was consistently able to find a third solution (Matt. 7:11; 22:15–22, 23–33).

d) Resurrection

He crowned these claims by rising from the dead — which can be persuasively argued using the minimal facts approach. Reading the four gospels, there are at least five great hindrances to the rejection of His resurrection.

The death of Christ. Christ died on the Cross. This is documented outside the New Testament — in the Talmud, Tacitus and Josephus. Proposing that He lost consciousness for a length of time and later recovered shows ignorance of the monstrosity of crucifixion and what He went through.

The burial. The writers of the gospels specified the names of the two people who buried Him. They were not anonymous or weak; they were accessible to the public, making it quite easy to verify the claims of the gospel writers (John 19:38–41; the gospels were written within 20–25 years after the events).

The empty tomb. The disciples filled Jerusalem with the news of Jesus' resurrection and they started in the very temple before the chief priests. How easy would it have been to prove them wrong if the dead body of Jesus could be found (Acts 2, 3, 4 and 5)?

The testimony of the eyewitnesses. It is an agreed method of knowledge. The names of those who saw Him were mentioned and they were not hallucinating. He appeared to one, then two, then seven, then twelve, then five hundred who were still around when Paul wrote about the resurrection of Christ and they could be referred to. They also were not embarrassed to mention the fact that the first eyewitnesses were women, although this strongly conflicted with Jewish culture and tradition (John 20:11–18, 24–29; Luke 24:13–35; John 21:1–14; 1 Cor. 15:6).

The drastic change in the disciples. Until the moment of Jesus' arrest, the disciples were just a small group, weak, wavering, doubting the truth about Christ. But suddenly everything changed and they became bold men and women in their testimony and defence of the veracity of their faith and their certainty about Christ's resurrection (John 20:19; Acts 2, 3 and 4). There is no explanation for this abrupt and strong transformation except that something supernatural had happened that could bring it about.

THE UNIQUENESS OF JESUS' MISSION

I still believe in Jesus not only because of who He is, but also because of what His mission was, which I'll summarize in three points. First, as the true light He came to expose the falsehood of religion and its destructive effects on humanity. Second, as the incarnate God-Man, He came to correct the distorted image of God in our minds on one hand and to present the original and ideal human on the other. Third, as the promised Messiah/Lamb of God, He came to provide holistic perfect salvation from the human predicament through His death and resurrection.

a) Exposing religion

Jesus was not a conventional religious leader and He didn't come to establish a new religion. The reader of the gospels can easily recognise that they emphasise His unfriendly dialogues and His strong conflicts with religious leaders, conflicts that eventually led to His murder (Matt. 23:1–5, 31–33; 15:14; Mark 7:5–7). Jesus claimed that He is the light of the world, the light by which we see light (John 8:12). Accordingly, He exposed the true nature of religion and its destructive effects on human rationality and morality.[4] By religion I do not refer to the *sensus divinitatis*, an intrinsic awareness of divinity in the heart of every human as described by Calvin.[5] Nor do I refer to different academic definitions of religion which as a matter of fact can't settle on one general definition.[6] I mean rather the malicious blend of mind-set, attitudes and practices that Jesus exposed and condemned. This blend, I assume, is simply a reaction of a corrupted heart toward the *sensus divinitatis* itself. It is customarily made to appease human fears deriving from the pains of life and uncertainty about the afterlife by appealing to the Supreme Being who plots reality to one's benefit. It seeks to soothe the conscience and relieve guilt by atoning for sins through religiosity, in order to feed man's pride and evil desire to feel superior to others. This is the religion which Jesus exposed, and, interestingly enough, what Jesus exposed two thousand years ago is the same religion that I see around me here today in the Middle East, whether it takes a Jewish, Christian or Islamic appearance.

In the following lines, I shall mention briefly some of what Jesus has exposed.

Religion is a system that reduces morality to a set of do's and don'ts. This was always an issue of dispute between Jesus and the Pharisees

---

4. Violence, discrimination, pornography, bribery, sexual harassment are very common in the Middle East where religion is very important in the daily life of its people. For example, a 2009 Gallup poll on the importance of religion in daily life in different countries showed Egypt as one of the most religious countries in the world — ninety-seven per cent. In the same year other polls showed Egypt as the highest country in visiting pornography sites on the internet and in sexual harassment on its streets!

5. 'There is within the human mind, and indeed by natural instinct, an awareness of divinity', John Calvin, *Institutes of the Christian Religion* (Philadelphia: Westminster, 1960), 1.4.3.

6. Charles Kimball described the problem of defining religion in his book, *When Religion Becomes Evil*: 'The word religion evokes a wide variety of images, ideas, practices, beliefs, and experiences — some positive and some negative. Putting these disparate elements into a coherent frame of reference is no small task'. (pp. 15–16). Michael Peterson has written, 'Arriving at a precise definition is notoriously difficult, because all of the proposed definitions seem subject to counter example' (*Reason & Religious belief; an Introduction to the Philosophy of Religion* [Oxford University Press fifth edition], 6).

in all His conflicts with them — He heals on a Sabbath, He sits with tax collectors, His disciples eat without washing their hands, etc. (Mark 3:1–6; Matt. 9:10; 15:2). Such a view causes the moral act to be mechanical and lifeless, rather than being an aesthetic and creative one that naturally originates from a moral soul that is created in the image of God and living in fellowship with Him. Moreover, it turns the moral act into a purpose in itself to achieve self-satisfaction, deepening the selfishness and egocentricity of religious people.

Religion is a system that consumes the religious with holy objects/traditions and ignores the holy One to whom they point. There is no doubt that a true relationship with God necessitates different holy practices. However, these are an outward expression of an inner reality that is strengthened by them. It is impossible for these practices, no matter how numerous, to create that inner reality. They eventually nullify the word of God and the relationship with Him (Mark 7).

Religion is a system that considers doing good to be a legal way of atoning for the bad. As time goes by, the religious person thinks he/she will accumulate good deeds that will enable him/her to do bad deeds if the account balance allows it (Matt. 23:23–24)!

Religion is a system that deeply satisfies chauvinism and the sense of superiority. It is a deep-seated desire in the heart of human beings that results from many factors — spiritual, psychological and social. It ultimately leads to the contempt of others who are different in belief or religion, declaring them to be disbelievers. Then it becomes easy to subhumanise them. When this stage is reached there is no problem in casting them out or even killing them without feeling guilty. This is what Christ exposed in the parable of the Pharisee and the tax collector. It is also what Christ exposed when He revealed to His disciples what was in their hearts toward the Canaanite woman whom they saw as no more than a dog. But Jesus revealed what was in her heart — humility and faith (Luke 18:9–14; Matt. 15:21–28).

Religion is a system that hinders the critical and creative mind. If the religious person expresses difficult questions and doubts related to religion, it inevitably leads to him being looked upon as a traitor unfaithful to his beliefs. On the other hand, religion does not tolerate any kind of reformation or renovation; on the contrary, the more the religious person goes backward and holds on to what is old, the more he is appreciated and valued among his religious assembly. Jesus charged the Pharisees with foolishness and blindness for not using their critical minds with the traditions handed down to them. Moreover, He encouraged using their critical/creative mind in dealing with Scripture itself (Matt. 23:16,17,19)!

Religion is a system that kills the joy in people. It turns them into angry, fearful, hardhearted people as pictured by the elder brother in the parable of the prodigal son. The religious people that Christ exposed were exactly that: the head of the council was angry and bitter, even when a woman bent for eighteen years could stand up straight, Simeon was bitter and angry with Jesus simply because He allowed a sinful woman to touch Him, and so on (Luke 15:11–32; 13:10–17; 7:39).

b) God's image and human form

Jesus' mission as the God-Man was to correct the distorted image of God in the human mind, and to regain the original ideal form of humanity which was completely perverted through sin. As a psychiatrist, I can see that many of our fears and pains result from a distorted conception of God in our minds which is instilled in us by the culture in which we grew up. It is obvious from the Lord's Prayer that the request on which all other requests are made is to separate God's name/image — 'Hallowed be Thy name' (Matt. 6:9) — from any cultural stain imposed on it. Through His words and actions, Jesus attempted to cleanse the conception of God in people's minds from many cultural stains that were then common and which I see today. I'll refer to three areas in which Jesus challenges culture.

God is the true Father. Fatherhood in the Middle East meant authority and control, not protection and provision. Films and novels, until a few decades ago, illustrated such an image: the father comes home from work, the kids go and hide, he sits to eat alone, then the rest of the family sit to eat after he has finished. In contrast, Jesus, after confirming to His disciples that whoever has seen Him has seen the Father, proceeded to provide an entirely different image. On the shore of the Sea of Galilee, the seven disciples were in a very critical situation — spiritually, they doubted His resurrection; emotionally, they were in deep frustration after their failure as disciples and even as fishermen; physically, they were shivering because of bad weather and hunger. Jesus came to them at dawn, made a fire, and prepared bread and fish. He cherished them, warmed them and fed them without a single word of blame (John 14:9; Luke 24:36–53).

God is the servant leader. Shocking the disciples, Jesus, after claiming to be God incarnate, bent down and washed their feet. By contrast, even to this day, leadership in the Middle East means dictatorship. The leader is the one who is greater than the rest, understands better than anyone, the only one who has the right to think, plan and command. Jesus was familiar with this picture and He condemned it and taught that the greatest is the one who serves, not the one who controls (John 13:1–16; Mark 10:42–45).

God is the unique King. Kings in general, and in the Middle East in particular, rise to their authority through manipulation and power. Jesus in His trial before Pilate affirmed that He is King, but His kingship is entirely different. It is founded on the power of the truth and not that of deceit or that of the sword (John 18:36).

It was part of Jesus' mission to re-depict the *imago Dei* which has been corrupted by sin. I'm fascinated by the tremendous beauty of the *imago Dei* as shown in Him and seen in at least three ways:

Wilful submission to God. Jesus shows all the wisdom and power which enable Him to decide and act independently but in reality He never took one step independently from the Father. He considered submission to God's will as His business, His food, His pleasure and the foundation of all His relationships (John 6:38; 4:34; 15:10).

Deep empathy with human beings. Jesus' complete freedom from egocentricity enabled Him to understand the feelings and needs of others. With the leper He touched him before healing him, because the man had been bereft of touch for a long time. With the old feverish woman He held her hand, as a simple touch was not enough for her. With children He hugged them, because touch was not enough for them (Matt. 8:3,15; Mark 10:16).

Meaningful and fruitful. He didn't enjoy a luxurious life, or even a typical poor man's life. He lived homeless and died crucified at the age of thirty-three. However, there is no other life that fed and still feeds millions with truth, goodness and beauty as His does. He talked about His joy and glory in accomplishing His mission on the night before His crucifixion (Luke 9:58; 15:11).

c) Holistic salvation & unexpected means

Jesus spelt out His mission in this sentence: 'I came that they may have life and have it abundantly' (John 10:10). From His name which means 'Saviour', and from the rest of His teachings, we can infer that this promised full life is a holistic salvation from the human predicament. This salvation is existential, moral, judicial and physical. Superficial evangelism watered down Jesus' salvation into something like a ticket for heaven, while in fact it is a great gospel (good news) in which the triune God restores humanity to be God's living image that represents Him and carries His presence, working with Him now in the evil world, and reigning with Him eternally in the new heavens and new earth. This was beyond the expectation of His Jewish disciples who understood salvation solely in physical and political terms. Moreover, He shocked them by revealing that the means of accomplishing this great salvation is nothing other than His death and resurrection.

In what follows I shall explain briefly the different aspects of His salvation, and the plausibility of His death and resurrection as its means.

Existential Salvation. The main aspect of Jesus' salvation is the existential aspect. Sin means independency and separation from God resulting in the loss of meaning and purpose in life. Reconciliation with God means regaining the ability to live meaningfully and to accomplish one's purpose. Of all the forty-six parables of Christ, probably none is as famous as the prodigal son (Luke 15:1–32). I see it as worthy of this fame because it might be the most effective in summarising the existential human impasse and the beauty of the reconciliation which Jesus came to achieve. Notice that man here is lost and dead in his rebellion. But amazingly, he was the 'greatly missed son'! Philosophers describe the wretched state of man as 'alienation' but provide no solution. Jesus in this parable states that alienation ends in the arms of the father, under the shower of his kisses, and through the restoration of the glory of sonship. The lost identity is finally found when he hears his father say, 'This, my son...'

The Egyptian philosopher and Nobel prize-winning novelist Naguib Mahfouz, in his novel, *The search*,[7] illustrates human alienation in a way similar to that of the prodigal son as alienation from the father. The story dramatically begins with a son standing at the bedside of his dying prostitute mother. In her last words she desperately advises her son to search for his father, after she reveals to him that his father is in fact alive and that she had lied to him all along (notice, the search began after the death of his mother, a prostitute symbolising material pleasure, and with the revelation that God is not dead, as asserted by Nietzsche).[8] She says, 'That's why you should not slacken in the search for your father'. The son thinks a little and then asks, 'Is it worth the trouble?' She replies, 'Without any doubt, son; in his parentage you will find respect and honour. He will deliver you from the humiliation of needing anyone... You will enjoy peace at the end of it all'. Sadly the son in Mahfouz's story never finds the father, but dies wishing he did. By contrast, the prodigal son's agonising journey ends in the arms of his loving father.

---

7.   N. Mahfouz, *The search* (Doubleday, 1991).

8.   F. Nietzsche, *The Gay Science* (1882), section 108.

Judicial Salvation. Indeed we are all victims but we are all offenders also. This is a fact that no one can deny except the exceedingly arrogant. Breaking moral laws has destructive consequences. If there is not a just authority that can judge and condemn the offender, the meaning of justice no longer exists. Because of our sins, we are all in the position of the offender who must face God the Judge. From here arises the need for a judicial settlement with God, if we seek reconciliation with Him. Therefore, from the beginning Jesus declared the absolute necessity of His death on the Cross to accomplish our reconciliation (Luke 9:22). For me, the Cross is an ocean that cannot be crossed, although I am fully convinced of its necessity and its effect. I will shed light briefly on this when I come to discuss its plausibility.

Moral Salvation. The salvation of Christ is existential in essence, founded on justice and practically actualised and fortified by morality. This is what John expressed when he said that Jesus came with blood and water (1 John 5:6). The blood lays the judicial foundation for salvation, and water in the Bible symbolises moral sanctification, the moral transformation that the Holy Spirit achieves in the souls of those who accept Jesus as their Saviour. This is what Jesus meant when He spoke to Nicodemus about being born from above (John 3:3). It is difficult to know how birth from above happens, but we should easily see its effects. It is a process of new creation that the Holy Spirit carries out in people. Paul explains it by saying it is the washing of rebirth and renewal by the Holy Spirit. It is clear in the rest of the Bible that the washing happens once, while the renewal continues throughout one's life (Titus 3:5).

Physical salvation. Although the salvation of Christ is, as Peter expressed, the salvation of our souls (1 Pet. 1:9), that does not mean that Christ ignored either the physical suffering that human beings endure or that which the whole creation experiences. Christ's salvation includes the restoration of everything to its original condition as God created it. Thus it includes the redemption of the body, the emancipation of creation, the reconciliation of heaven and earth, and the inauguration of the new heavens and the new earth in which righteousness dwells. But all of this will take place in accordance with a divine agenda. Jesus promised a coming world with a glorious physical condition that will be established in His second coming.

The mission of Christ is accomplished in an unexpected way which He continuously talked about — His death and resurrection! This is what the early church believed, so it worded its first creed, recorded in Paul's first letter to the Corinthians: 'Christ died for our sins in accordance with the Scriptures, that he was buried and that he was raised on the third day in accordance with the Scriptures and that he appeared to Cephas, then to the twelve' (1 Cor. 15:3–5). This creed clearly confirms that the salvation Christ offers is founded on the death of Christ and His resurrection.

The plausibility of Jesus' death as our salvation. Many today wonder how one man's violent death long ago can affect us today? It is a disapproval that has its merits if we say that Christian salvation occurs when someone believes in the death and resurrection of Christ. But the matter is totally different if we say that salvation is achieved through *union* with Christ who died and rose. The matter here is not just belief in a doctrine or a concept, and not even belief in a historical event, but rather faith in a Person. If we take into consideration that faith is a relationship and a union, then the person united with Christ shares in the death of Christ with all its results and in the resurrection of Christ with all its power. The necessity of the death of Christ for the achievement of salvation is not an opinion that Christians came up with, but it is what Christ Himself confirmed many times (Luke 9:22; Matt. 16:21; Luke 24:46). We may have difficulty grasping this but we cannot cancel out what He taught and remain His followers.

Whenever we speak of forgiveness, we are speaking of a price to be paid. Suppose a friend of mine borrows my car, drives it carelessly, destroys it, and then comes to me in regret and apologises, saying that he does not have the money to repair it. What should I do if I do not want to put him in prison, other than pay for the repairs myself? Whenever something goes wrong and there is a desire for repair, someone must pay, either the offender or the offended.

I remember one of my patients, a non-Christian, who was brought to the hospital in a coma because of a suicide attempt. After recovery, I started the psychotherapy sessions. He surprised me in the first session by saying, 'Save your efforts; I will commit suicide again'. He said that he was such a horrible person who had committed all sorts of evil and that he did not deserve to live. I started telling him indirectly and conservatively about the love of God and His forgiveness to those who repented. A few days later I noticed he had stopped coming to the sessions. I went to his room to check on him. He wasn't in the greatest of moods. We talked a bit and he said: 'You're just like the rest of the religious leaders who manipulate us into thinking that God is merciful and that He forgives sins. How could I commit all that I've committed and receive forgiveness just because I asked for it? Who pays the price for what I've done?' I told him, 'I have truly deceived you but not because I told you that God is willing to forgive you, but because I hid the most important news — there is Someone who paid the price'. I returned home that day certain that a reasonable person cannot accept forgiveness that has not been paid for.

The plausibility of the resurrection of Christ in achieving salvation. Dorothy L. Sayers once said that if there is a Creator and He has His reasons for allowing all this evil and suffering to happen in this world, then the least He could do is to come into this world and experience the suffering that His creation endures for Himself.[9] The Cross of Christ declares that He has done precisely that. The Creator experienced all kinds of suffering that His creation endures.

Building on Sayers' idea, one can argue that if God were gracious enough to experience all kinds of human suffering, wouldn't He be expected not to fall defeated in the face of evil? Assuming that death

---

9.   Dorothy Sayers, *Creed or Chaos?* (Harcourt Brace, 1949), 4.

is the greatest evil of all, shouldn't God be expected not merely to endure it, but also to overcome it? It is precisely here that the Christian doctrine of resurrection falls into place. It is where hope is at last found, where God Himself defeats the greatest stronghold of evil, death.

Moreover, through the resurrection we can rationally accept the claims of Jesus in regard to our salvation. His claims are no longer philosophical suggestions, but the credible claims of a Man who defeated death itself.

CONCLUSION

When I first read the gospels with precision and honesty, I could not help but acknowledge the immense number of conflicts that existed between Jesus on the one hand, and religious leaders on the other. I quickly came to the conclusion that He was no ordinary religious leader, nor did He come to establish a new religion.

It was then that I began to realise the uniqueness of both His person and His mission. I wholeheartedly and eagerly hoped that this awe-inspiring Man was no charlatan. I embarked on a journey of encountering the evidence. It was in His morals, His intellect, His miracles, and most significantly of all, His resurrection that I found a solid rational foundation for putting my faith in Him.

And today, after more than thirty years, through my relationship with Him as my Saviour and my experience of all that He promised, I can affirm that Jesus Christ is the Son of God and that He is well and truly capable of granting a fulfilled life to those who believe in Him.

For all the above mentioned reasons, I (still) believe in Jesus.

6

WHY I (STILL) BELIEVE IN THE HOLY SPIRIT

JOHN BLANCHARD

I have believed in the Holy Spirit for well over half a century, and still do, for two reasons, one subjective and one objective. The subjective reason is that He is constantly at work in my life; the objective reason is the evidence I find in the Bible.

In the Preface of *I believe in the Holy Spirit* (first published in 1975), Michael Green calls a certain approach to his subject 'the most exciting and disturbing movement of our times'.[1] Decades later, these adjectives still apply, as the subject excites many people and disturbs many others. For some, it finds its way into almost every discussion about church life and the lives of individual believers, focusing on subjects such as baptism in the Spirit, the gifts of the Spirit, the fullness of the Spirit, the anointing of the Spirit, being filled with the Spirit and the fruit of the Spirit, to say nothing of speaking in tongues, prophecy and a wide variety of experiences attributed to the Holy Spirit. On the other hand, the subject of the Holy Spirit disturbs many people, with the sad result that it leads to deep divisions in the church, a rupturing of personal relationships, misunderstanding and heartache — and, saddest of all, attitudes and actions that are unbecoming to Christians.

---

1.   Michael Green, *I believe in the Holy Spirit* (London: Hodder & Stoughton, 1975).

Examining all of these would take several books rather than a single chapter. In this chapter, I want to be simple and scriptural: simple, so that it is accessible to as many readers as possible, and scriptural, so as to be a faithful reflection of what the Bible says on the subject. I will quote a number of other sources, but my touchstone will be, 'What does the Scripture say?' (Rom. 4:3)

THE THIRD PERSON

First things first: who (or what) is the Holy Spirit? America's 'Battle Hymn of the Republic' includes the words, 'John Brown's body lies a-mouldering in the grave, but his soul goes marching on'.[2] John Brown was a passionate abolitionist who died before slavery was officially outlawed, but his successors claimed to sense his ongoing presence.

There are sceptics who think of the Holy Spirit in similar terms — and cite words by Jesus to back up their idea. As Jesus was approaching the end of His earthly life He told His disciples that after His death, 'I will ask the Father, and he will give you another Helper, to be with you forever' (John 14:16). Moments later He added, 'I am going away, and I will come to you' (John 14:28). As Jesus came back to earth physically for only forty days after His death (between His resurrection and His return to heaven), His promise is taken to mean that after His body was no longer with them they would be able to feel His presence as they reflected on the years He had spent with them, and the things they had heard Him say and seen Him do. In this way they would enter into a different form of relationship with Him — a kind of 'John Brown experience' — just as those who mourn the loss of loved ones today sometimes say, 'I know they are still here, I can feel their presence'.

If this is the kind of thing Jesus meant, then the Holy Spirit was nothing more than an emotional blanket those early Christians wrapped around themselves to give them comfort, confidence and courage as they faced the future without the real presence of Someone they had loved dearly.

---

2   Hymn by Julia Ward Howe, November 1861 (published in The Atlantic Monthly, February 1862)

It would also mean that twenty-first century believers should think of the Holy Spirit only in similar terms. Yet when promising His followers 'another Helper' and saying that in this way 'I will be with you', Jesus made it crystal clear that this other Helper would not merely be a post-mortem influence but a distinct living Person. This comes powerfully across in this statement:

> When the Spirit of truth comes, *he* will guide you into all the truth, for *he* will not speak on his own authority, but whatever *he* hears *he* will speak, and *he* will declare to you the things that are to come. *He* will glorify me, for *he* will take what is mine and declare it to you (John 16:13-14, emphasis added).

The word 'Spirit' (it would not have been capitalised in the original Greek) is neuter, so left to itself *could* merely mean some kind of influence, but it is impossible to miss the fact that seven times in these two sentences the Holy Spirit is referred to as 'He', a masculine pronoun, making it clear that the Holy Spirit is a *Person*. Yet the Bible goes far beyond that and makes it equally clear that the Holy Spirit is a *divine* Person, one of three in a Godhead the Bible identifies as the Father, the Son and the Holy Spirit.

THE TRINITY

When referring to the Godhead we commonly use the term 'Trinity' (from the Latin *trinitas*, which means 'threeness'). The word 'Trinity' is not found anywhere in the Bible, and we have no adequate word in English to express the nature of the different existences within the Godhead, but 'Trinity' summarises the Bible's teaching that God is three Persons yet one God. The word 'person' is the nearest we can get, though we must not use it to imply that within the Godhead there are three distinct beings each possessing a different nature.

It is also important to maintain the individuality of each of the Persons concerned. God is not made up of three parts; He is essentially one. Simply put, the Father is not the Son or the Holy Spirit; the Son is not the Father or the Holy Spirit; and the Holy Spirit is not the Father or the Son. Each of these three Persons is not only fully divine, but coequally so with the other two. God exists in the Persons of Father, Son and Holy Spirit; 'The whole undivided essence of God belongs equally to each of the three persons'.[3] If we struggle to understand this (and we do), we need to accept that a mystery is not the same as a misrepresentation. At the height of his ministry, the apostle Paul spoke for us all when he confessed, 'For now we see in a mirror dimly...' (1 Cor. 13:12).

Time and again the Bible links the Holy Spirit with creation. In writing about God bringing all created reality into existence, one of the Psalmists adds, 'When you send forth your Spirit, they are created, and you renew the face of the ground' (Ps. 104:30). This takes us further than Genesis 1:2. It tells us that the Holy Spirit keeps the created world living and moving along. In prophesying a time of great blessing, Isaiah said it would come when 'the Spirit is poured upon us from on high, and the wilderness becomes a fruitful field' (Isa. 32:15). As someone has put it, 'The power by which creation is energized is not so much like the power of a wound-up spring, as like the effect of an overwhelmingly powerful personality'.[4] Elihu, whose speeches often emphasised God's sovereignty, focused the Holy Spirit's creative power on humankind as he told his friend Job, 'The Spirit of God has made me, and the breath of the Almighty gives me life' (Job 33:4).

THE LIVING WORD

Earlier in the chapter I referred to the Bible as 'the living and abiding word of God' — but to do this is immediately to bring the Holy Spirit into the picture. Old Testament writers confirmed this. David introduced his last words by saying, 'The Spirit of the LORD speaks by me; his word is on my tongue' (2 Sam. 23:2).

---

3.   R. C. Sproul, *The Mystery of the Holy Spirit* (Fearn: Christian Focus Publications, 1991), 85.

4.   John Peck, *I want to know what the Bible says about the Holy Spirit* (Eastbourne: Kingsway Publications, 1979), 13.

The prophet Ezekiel's opening message included the claim that 'the Spirit entered into me and set me on my feet, and I heard him speaking' (Ezek. 2:2). The prophet Micah explained his ministry by saying, 'I am filled with power, with the Spirit of the LORD' (Micah 3:8). The prophet Zechariah reminded the Jews of his day of the calamities that had come upon their forefathers because they had not listened to 'the words that the LORD of hosts had sent by his Spirit through the former prophets' (Zech. 7:12).

This truth is repeatedly confirmed in the New Testament. Speaking to over a hundred believers soon after Jesus had ascended to heaven, Peter reminded them that even Jesus' betrayal by Judas Iscariot was a fulfilment of prophecy 'which the Holy Spirit spoke beforehand by the mouth of David' (Acts 1:16). Later, after he and John had been arrested and threatened by the religious hierarchy, he told friends that this, too, had been prophesied in the Old Testament 'by the Holy Spirit' (Acts 4:25). When Paul was under house arrest in Rome, he told those who refused to believe the gospel that the Holy Spirit predicted this 'to your fathers through Isaiah the prophet' (Acts 28:25). The writer of Hebrews quoted from Psalm 95 and cited it as something 'the Holy Spirit says' (Heb. 3:7). Later in the same letter he quoted from Jeremiah 31 and said the words concerned were a message by which 'the Holy Spirit...bears witness to us' (Heb. 10:15). In the first of his letters Peter said that when Old Testament prophets wrote about the death and resurrection of Jesus these were matters 'the Spirit of Christ in them was indicating' (1 Pet. 1:11).

Paul summed all of this up when he wrote, 'All Scripture is breathed out by God' (2 Tim. 3:16), and so did Peter when he said that 'no prophecy was ever produced by the will of man, but men spoke from God as they were carried along by the Holy Spirit' (2 Pet. 1:21). Yet the New Testament goes even further, claiming that its own words had the same origin. Peter linked Paul's writing with 'the other Scriptures' (2 Pet. 3:16), and the word 'Scriptures' means much more than any kind of writing. It translates the Greek word *graphe,* a technical term used over fifty times in the New

Testament, and referring *in every case* exclusively to God's Old Testament words. The point could hardly be clearer, and in the Bible's last book the apostle John urges his readers seven times to hear 'what the Spirit says to the churches' (Rev. 2:7, 11, 17, 29; 3:6, 13, 22).

None of this means that the Holy Spirit dictated the Bible's words, and that men did their best to remember what He had said. Instead, as Brian Edwards explains,

> They recorded accurately all that God wanted them to say and exactly how he wanted them to say it, in their own character, style and language. The inspiration of Scripture is a harmony of the active mind of the writer and the sovereign direction of the Holy Spirit to produce God's inerrant and infallible word for the human race.[5]

We can now go an important step further and say not only that the Holy Spirit caused the entire Bible to be written, but that He alone is able to convince us that it is true, explain its meaning and apply it effectively to our lives. John Calvin taught that the authority of the Scriptures is not truly recognised 'unless they are believed to have come from heaven as directly as if God had been heard giving utterance to them'.[6] This faith can be given only by the Holy Spirit.

Wayne Grudem writes,

> It is one thing to affirm that the Bible *claims* to be the words of God. It is another thing to be convinced that those claims are true. Our ultimate conviction that the words of the Bible are God's words comes only when the Holy Spirit speaks *in* and *through* the words of the Bible to our hearts and gives us an inner assurance that these are the words of our Creator speaking to us.[7]

---

5.   *Nothing but the Truth* (Darlington: Evangelical Press, 2006), 39.

6.   *Institutes of the Christian Religion,* trans. Henry Beveridge (London, James Clarke & Co., Ltd., 1962), Vol. 68.

7.   *Systematic Theology* (Nottingham: Inter-Varsity Press, 1994), 77.

To give just one New Testament illustration of how this works out, the writer of Hebrews explains the intricate details of Old Testament temple worship then says that this is something 'the Holy Spirit indicates' (Heb. 9:8).

The practical application of this is seriously searching. In writing about the depths of biblical truths Paul wrote that these are things 'God has revealed to us through the Spirit' (1 Cor. 2:10), then added a solemn warning: 'The natural man does not accept the things of the Spirit of God, for they are folly to him, and he is not able to understand them because they are spiritually discerned' (1 Cor. 2:14). Jesus said much the same thing when He told unbelieving hearers, 'Whoever is of God hears the words of God. The reason why you do not hear them is that you are not of God' (John 8:47). This perfectly explains why unconverted people often reject the Bible as being utterly irrelevant to their lives, or openly mock it as being no more than pious piffle or a collection of random sayings that have no authority. The reason they treat the Bible like this is not because they can prove their case, but because they are spiritually incapable of grasping its truth. In the words of the English biblical scholar George Findlay, 'The unspiritual are out of court as religious critics; they are deaf men judging music'.[8]

THE VITAL PRESENCE

This points us towards the calamitous truth that without the Holy Spirit nobody can ever become a Christian. Writing about those who made empty claims about their spirituality, but whose lives betrayed their real nature, Jude pinpointed the problem: they were 'devoid of the Spirit' (Jude 19). Paul was equally blunt when he wrote to Roman believers: 'Those who are in the flesh cannot please God. You, however, are not in the flesh but in the Spirit, if in fact the Spirit of God dwells in you. Anyone who does not have the Spirit of Christ does not belong to him' (Rom. 8:8–9).

---

8.   *St Paul's First Letter to the Corinthians* (Erdmans), 59.

Paul calls the Holy Spirit 'the Spirit of God' and 'the Spirit of Christ', and speaks of the believer being in the Spirit and having the Spirit dwelling in him. These are two ways of describing the same experience, but they both point to the one fearful fact that without the Holy Spirit's indwelling presence a person 'cannot please God'. No amount of religion, respectability, sincerity, zeal or 'spirituality' will do, as these are self-generated substitutes for God Himself.

At an annual carnival held in Basel, Switzerland, at the beginning of Lent, many who defile it with debauchery wear masks to hide their identity. The local Salvation Army uses this custom to warn people of their spiritual danger by placing billboards and posters around the city with the German words '*Gott seieht hinter deine maske!*' ('God sees behind your masks'). God sees behind all our religious, moral and spiritual masks and condemns all of our pretensions.

Nobody knew this better than Paul, who relied heavily on his own self-righteous efforts until he realised that in terms of making him right with God they should be written off as 'rubbish' (Phil. 3:8) — the translation of a Greek word commonly used of dung. The prophet Isaiah was equally blunt when he wrote, 'We have all become like one who is unclean, and all our righteous deeds are like a polluted garment' (Isa. 64:6); the last two words would describe a cloth stained with menstrual fluid. There is a big gap between acknowledging sin and accepting that it can never be balanced or outweighed by our religion or good works, and an even bigger gap between doing that, abandoning all trust in them, and flinging oneself on Jesus as Saviour.

Paul underlined this by writing, 'no one can say "Jesus is Lord" except in the Holy Spirit' (1 Cor. 12:3). Even the most ungodly person can mouth the words 'Jesus is Lord', but as Leon Morris points out, 'Paul is not denying this. He is saying that the words can be uttered with full meaning only under the influence of the Holy Spirit. The Lordship of Christ is not a human discovery. It is a discovery that is made and can be made only when the Spirit is at work in the heart'.[9]

---

9. Tyndale New Testament Commentaries: 1 Corinthians (Leicester: Inter-Varsity Press, 1985), 165.

Jesus told His disciples that when the Holy Spirit came He would 'convict the world concerning sin and righteousness and judgment', and went on to say that the fundamental, universal sin of which people need to be convicted is 'that they do not believe in me' (John 16:8-9). This is what Matthew Henry called 'the great reigning sin... which is at the bottom of all sin'.[10] People may feel guilty about particular sins without being aware of their corruption and depravity, or of their need to trust in the Lord Jesus Christ as their Saviour.

George Whitefield insisted, 'The light of natural conscience never did, never will, and never can, convince of unbelief'[11] — and 'without faith it is impossible to please [God]' (Heb. 11:6). Only the Holy Spirit can remedy the situation. This means that only the Holy Spirit can make anyone a Christian, and Jesus underlined this when explaining the necessity of the new birth to the religious leader Nicodemus. He began by telling him, 'unless one is born again he cannot see the kingdom of God', then added that this meant being 'born of the Spirit' (John 3:3, 6, 7). The Holy Spirit is the One who brings those 'dead in... trespasses and sins' (Eph. 2:1) to spiritual life; as Paul later confirmed, 'the Spirit is life' (Rom. 8:10). Only the Holy Spirit can bring about the miracle of the new birth and lead a person to genuine repentance and saving faith.

This brings us to a question that has troubled countless Christians — but need not be asked: *has every Christian received the Holy Spirit?* The reason it ought never to be asked is that the New Testament is saturated with the answer.

Negatively, there is not a single case after Pentecost in which Christians are commanded to receive the Holy Spirit. They are commanded to 'walk by the Spirit' (Gal. 5:16, 25), to 'maintain the unity of the Spirit' (Eph. 4:3), to '[pray] in the Holy Spirit' (Jude 20) and to be 'filled with the Spirit' (Eph. 5:18), but *never to receive Him.*

---

10. Matthew Henry's Commentary, ed. Leslie F. Church (London: Marshall, Morgan &Scott, 1960), 397.

11. *Seventy-five Sermons on Important Subjects*, Vol II (The Pennsylvania State University Library), 158.

Positively put, the New Testament teems with the clearest possible assertions that Christians have already received Him. We can see this even if we confine ourselves to Paul's letters. He told Roman believers, 'you have received the Spirit of adoption as sons' (Rom. 8:15). He asked those at Corinth, 'Do you not know that … God's Spirit dwells in you?' (1 Cor. 3:16) He reminded those at Ephesus that 'we both have access in one Spirit to the Father' (Eph. 2:18). He told those at Philippi that as believers we 'worship by the Spirit of God' (Phil. 3:3). Finally, he commended those at Colosse for their 'love in the Spirit' (Col. 1:8). A Christian may not always be conscious of the Spirit's *presence*, but he would never *be* a Christian in His *absence*!

THE FRUIT OF THE SPIRIT

When the editor of this book invited me to contribute to it and suggested certain areas that I could cover, he was afraid that he was pointing at a whole book rather than one chapter. I now know what he meant! — and can look here at only one aspect of the Holy Spirit's work in the life of the Christian. This is what the Bible calls 'the fruit of the Spirit', and its teaching has its most focused expression in these words: 'But the fruit of the Spirit is love, joy, peace, patience, kindness, goodness, faithfulness, gentleness, self-control' (Gal. 5:22-23).

Some Bible scholars have suggested that these virtues can be seen as three groups of three, but it is more important to notice that 'fruit' is singular, not plural. The Greeks had four words for 'love': *eros* meant physical love; *storge,* the kind of love seen within family relationships; *philia*, tender affection; and *agape*, the word used here. Hardly ever used in classical Greek, it meant love in its highest imaginable form, what someone has called 'the queen of all Christian graces'.

'Love is …' is the name of a comic strip created by the New Zealand cartoonist Kim Casali in the 1940s and now, long after her death, syndicated worldwide. The cartoons can be touching,

humorous and cute, but none matches *agape*. In down-to-earth terms *agape* love means that whatever another person says, does or believes, however much you disagree with their view, their attitudes or their lifestyle, and however they act towards you, you will act towards them in a way deliberately calculated to bring about their greatest blessing and their highest good.

The supreme example of this is seen in the death of Jesus in the place of those who are God's enemies by nature. His followers are called to 'Love your enemies' (Matt. 5:44) and to 'overcome evil with good' (Rom. 12:21). Only the Holy Spirit can enable a Christian to do this!

'Joy' is far deeper than happiness, which so often is a reaction to favourable happenings. True joy is based on the believer's unchangeable relationship with God. It was while Paul was in prison that he wrote, 'Rejoice *in the Lord* always' (Phil. 4:4, emphasis added).

Czechoslovakian pastors once told me that during their persecution by Soviet Communists, 'In prison, we learned not to ask, "Why?", but just to say, "Praise the Lord!"' When James urged his readers, 'Count it all joy, my brothers, when you meet trials of various kinds', he added a reason for doing so, which was that these trials were being used by God to help in making them 'perfect and complete' (James 1: 2, 4). Paul's testimony is telling: with all the pressures of his ministry, anxious care for struggling young churches, and in particular his heartache over problems in the church at Corinth, he can still tell the believers there, 'In all our affliction, I am overflowing with joy' (2 Cor. 7:4), which elsewhere he defined as 'the joy of the Holy Spirit' (1 Thess. 1:6).

'Peace' is painfully elusive in a world racked with conflict, strife and discord at international, national, social and personal levels, but, in every situation Christians face, the Holy Spirit is able to bring peace. This peace has been defined as 'tranquillity of mind based on the consciousness of a right relation to God'.[12] It is something

---

12.   Kenneth W. Wuest, *Wuest's Word Studies: Galatians* (Grand Rapids,Wm. B. Eerdmans Publishing Company, 1944), 160.

the world can neither give nor take away; it is 'the peace of God, which surpasses all understanding' (Phil. 4:7).

'Patience' follows naturally from deep, inner, God-given peace, and perfectly translates the Greek *makrothumia*. In Greek, *makros* means 'long' and *thumo* means 'temper'; the fruit of the Spirit enables the Christian to be 'long-tempered' instead of short-tempered. Jesus displayed 'perfect patience' (1 Tim. 1:16) in facing provocation and persecution; the Holy Spirit leads His followers to do the same.

'Kindness' refers to disposition rather than to action. The Greek *chrestotes* is related to a word that would have been used of mature wine that was not harsh or bitter. 'Kindness' is a texture of character, a sweetness of spirit, a mildness of manner.

'Goodness' is kindness in action, aiming at everything that is 'good and right and true' (Eph. 5:9). Paul was delighted to find believers in Rome 'full of goodness' (Rom. 15:14).

'Faithfulness' hardly needs any explanation. A Christian should be reliable and trustworthy, true to his word and promises. The Bible says of God that 'all his work is done in faithfulness' (Ps. 33:4) and also that even when the going gets tough His people can 'entrust their souls to a faithful Creator' (1 Pet. 4:19). The Holy Spirit enables them to do so.

'Gentleness' renders *prautes,* which has been called 'the untranslatable word', because no single English word captures its full meaning. It often appears in our English Bibles as 'meekness', but must never be thought of as meaning weakness. Moses was 'very meek, more than all people who were on the face of the earth' (Num. 12:3), but was a man of great courage and determination, who could blaze with righteous anger and was chosen by God to lock horns with Pharaoh and lead the Israelites out of their Egyptian captivity. Supremely, Jesus was 'gentle [*praos*] and lowly in heart' (Matt. 11:29). When Paul pinpointed serious failures among Corinthians he assured them that he did so 'by the meekness and gentleness of Christ' (2 Cor. 10:1). Meekness is strength under control. It deals rightly with wrong, but knows nothing of malice, unrighteous anger or revenge.

'Self-control' is exactly what it says on the tin. The original Greek word incorporates *kratos* (strength). Self-control means 'the controlling power of the will',[13] a costly, never-ending discipline that only the Holy Spirit can produce in us.

BAPTISM AND FULLNESS

This chapter has had to be brief, and I am aware that two of the most controversial Holy Spirit themes are missing. The first is *the baptism of the Holy Spirit*, which some say is a 'second blessing' Christians need so as to be lifted into a deeper spiritual experience that will make their Christian work powerfully effective. This is not the place to examine in detail any of the complicated claims that are made, but we can take a straightforward look at one key biblical statement: 'For just as the body is one and has many members, and all the members of the body, though many, are one body, so it is with Christ. For in one Spirit we were all baptized into one body — Jews or Greeks, slaves or free — and all were made to drink of one Spirit' (1 Cor. 12:12–13).

Three crucial things open up the meaning of this passage. The first is the repeated use of 'all', which rules out the claim that what is spoken of is for only some believers, those chosen by God to excel in either gifts or effectiveness. The second is the tense of the repeated 'were', which is aorist indicative passive. Simply put, the passage describes what had happened in the past, once for all, to all of the people concerned. The third is the effect of the event, which was to place them 'into one body', which can only mean the Christian church; the Lord Jesus Christ is 'the head of the church, his body' (Eph. 5:23).

Pulling this together surely makes it clear that the passage is speaking about believers' conversion, and not about some eclectic post-conversion experience they should be seeking. As Donald Grey Barnhouse rightly put it, 'No one may ask a believer whether

---

13. W. E. Vine, *Expository Dictionary of New Testament Words* (Edinburgh: Oliphants Limited, 1940), 114.

he has been baptized with the Spirit. The very fact that a man is in the body of Christ demonstrates that he has been baptized with the Spirit, for there is no other way of entering the body'.[14] To say that people can be Christians but not baptised in the Spirit is to play fast and loose with this passage of Scripture.

The second controversial theme is *the fullness of the Holy Spirit*. Although there is a welter of teaching on this subject, we can again concentrate on just one passage, this time a very short one: 'And do not get drunk with wine, for that is debauchery, but be filled with the Spirit' (Eph. 5:18).

Paul is writing 'To the saints who are in Ephesus' (Eph. 1:1), all of whom had 'heard the word of truth, the gospel of your salvation, and believed in [Christ]' (Eph. 1:13). But the command to be filled is addressed today to *all* who share these believers' saving faith. As with the passage about Spirit baptism there is space here for only a few crucial points.

The first is that this is a positive command. It is not a theological proposition or a suggestion that Paul's readers might like to consider as an interesting option. God is not asking for our approval, but for our obedience.

The second is that it is a permanent command. The verb 'be filled' is in a present tense (in direct contrast to the aorist tense we noted when considering Spirit baptism). A biblical illustration will confirm the difference. To remedy a shortage of wine at a wedding Jesus told his disciples, 'Fill the jars with water' (John 2:7). This too was a command about filling, but in this case 'fill' is an aorist (once for all) tense, not a present (continuous) tense. They were to fill the jars once, not to keep on filling them. The command to be filled with the Spirit is completely different, and Christians looking and longing for a once-for-all, dramatic experience that will mean they are filled with the Spirit from then on are on a wild goose chase.

The third is that it is a passive command. The wording is not, 'Fill yourself with the Spirit', but 'Be filled with the Spirit'

---

14.   Cited by Leon Morris, Spirit of the Living God (IVP), 91f.

(literally, 'Be being filled with the Spirit'). Fullness of the Spirit is not something Christians can bring about; it is God's work, not theirs. We sometimes speak of a person who achieves great things in life as being 'self-made', but nobody filled with the Holy Spirit is self-filled. Such an experience is never something about which the person concerned can boast as an achievement; it is always and only a gracious work of God in their life.

The fourth is that it is a pictorial command — in the sense that being set alongside the negative command 'And do not get drunk with wine' helps us to grasp its meaning. Alcohol is a food (but not a nutrient) and as the level of its consumption increases it gradually takes over the drinker's central nervous system, so that their thoughts, words and actions are radically affected, leading eventually to 'debauchery'. Simply put, the person concerned is no longer in control, but under the dissipating influence of ethyl alcohol. The picture Paul is painting is one of comparison and contrast. The comparison is that to be filled with the Holy Spirit is to have one's thoughts, words and actions directly, deeply and decisively influenced by His nature and power. The contrast is that being filled with the Spirit does not mean spiritual intoxication. Its outcome is not frenzy but fruit, and the fruit of the Spirit is not excitement, but character. The Spirit's ministry is to bring the sinner to the Saviour and then to make the sinner like the Saviour. Christians are being transformed 'from one degree of glory to another' and this transformation is 'from the Lord who is the Spirit' (2 Cor. 3:18). It is the work of the Holy Spirit to make us increasingly reflect the character of Christ.

The fifth is that it is a pressing command, in that being filled with the Spirit is not God's responsibility but ours. We must decide whether or not we are determined to be filled with the Spirit, and we must constantly seek not to grieve the Holy Spirit, but to long for Him to make us more and more Christlike. Jesus promised that those who 'hunger and thirst for righteousness' (Matt. 5:6) will be filled — and 'hunger and thirst' are in the present tense! We should seek to 'cleanse ourselves from every defilement of body and spirit, bringing holiness to completion in the fear of God' (2 Cor. 7:1). We should want to have done with self-promotion, self-satisfaction, self-justification and self-assertion. We should constantly strive not only to be good, but to be godly. We should echo the prayer of Robert Murray McCheyne: 'Lord, make me as holy as a pardoned sinner can be made'.[15]

In October 1954 the Holy Spirit moved gospel truth from my head to my heart. Ever since, He has been guiding, instructing, strengthening, rebuking, correcting, enabling and blessing me, and giving me a sure and certain hope of the eternal glories of the 'new heavens and a new earth' (2 Pet. 3:13).

I (still) believe in the Holy Spirit!

---

15. Quoted by Andrew Bonar in *Memoir & Remains of the Rev Robert Murray McCheyne* (Oliphant, Anderson & Ferrier 1892 edition), 159.

7

WHY I (STILL) BELIEVE IN THE CHURCH

Joe Barnard

Imagine the church to be a woman dragged before an unruly crowd of protest. Accusations fly from blurry faces like rotten tomatoes and worm-eaten apples. A public prosecutor quiets the swelling complaint in order to name the allegations against the accused. He enumerates the failures of the church in the following order.

First, the church is a moral failure. Voltaire first noted that the church, contrary to her avowed intent, does not actually improve the morality of her adherents. The accusation is made that the opposite is true: the institution set up to improve the inward manners of the heart ('be ye perfect') in fact corrupts them. For anyone astonished by this claim, the evidence set forth is the conduct of the clergy. If headlines are true, measured by lust for sex and drive for power, some church leaders are the fraternal twins of secular politicians.

Second, the church is a social failure. This is set forth in two ways. On the one hand, there is the sad joke of church unity. Perhaps Paul did — the critic sighs — in a moment of fatal optimism believe that the gospel would squash the powers of rivalry, partisanship, bigotry and spite in order to give birth to an angelic society, in which neither gender, race, income, nor status mattered but Christ was all-in-all. But consider the facts. Church history is not a romantic comedy in which blacks and whites exchange a kiss of peace, men and women embrace, and Catholics and Protestants happily waltz. Church history is a Darwinian drama in which imperialism, repression, rivalry and violence enable the strongest to survive.

On the other hand, to see another dimension of the social failure of the church, one can rehearse the angry criticism of Nietzsche, who took the charge of Voltaire (that the church is a corrupting influence) and inflated it to say that the flourishing of the church is the enfeeblement of the species. According to Nietzsche the sinister power of the church is to re-label virtues as vices and vices as virtues. How, Nietzsche would ask, did self-promotion, assertiveness, ambition, desire for fame and pride — traits considered heroic in the past as they are celebrated in pop culture and success literature today — become evil? The responsibility falls squarely on the shoulders of the church. Accepting the teaching of a rejected Messiah, she propagated the belief that humility, meekness and self-sacrifice were virtues while self-confidence, pride and the desire for self-fulfilment were soul-rubbish to be swept away.

Third is the political failure of the church. In spite of the origins of Christianity, a heart-warming tale in which a king rejects power in order to achieve victory through goodness, trust, truth and love, the church has shown less reserve when offered the sceptre and the rod. With a surgeon's honesty, the historian Paul Johnson describes how, in the effort to suppress division, clarify doctrine and numerically grow, the early church became 'in many striking ways a mirror-image of the (Roman) empire itself'. Thus the church mutated from a 'suffering and victimized body, begging for toleration, into a coercive one, demanding monopoly'.[1] Although the image of an armed and politicised church is a faint memory, the shadow of the Inquisition and the self-harm of religious warfare still blacken the reputation of the church today.

The fourth accusation is the spiritual irrelevance of the church. The day of tent-revivals are done. Speaking about contemporary spiritual appetites, Francis Spufford quips, 'Most people don't have

---

1.   Paul Johnson, *A History of Christianity* (London: Penguin, 1976), 76.

a God-shaped space in their minds, waiting to be filled... Most people's lives provide them with a full range of loves and hates and joys and despairs, and a moral framework by which to understand them, and a place for awe and transcendence, without any need for religion'.[2]

The empirical data of diminishing church attendance seems to corroborate the claim. If relevance is measured by the degree something is missed when absent, the relevance of the church in the twenty-first century appears to be slightly above the level of printed Encyclopaedias. The general consensus is that life has moved on and better things are available.

Fifth is the religious irrelevance of the church. Religion can be thought about in different ways. One way is to think about religion as the set of beliefs, practices, values and habits — the world view and lifestyle — that glues a society together. The benefit of this description is that it enables one to categorise secularism alongside Christianity, Islam, Hinduism and Buddhism as a world religion. Now once a person is able to think of secularism in terms of world view and identity, she begins to see that secularism is more than a competitor of the church. Secularism is the spiritual replacement of Christendom. There is no competition between secularism and the church because the battle has been decided and the church has lost. This means that in the twenty-first century people do not opt in or out of a secular world view. Secularism is the pervasive, though often hidden, influence that shapes the identity of people regardless of whether or not they are members of the church.[3]

So there is the church standing in the dock, facing the scorn and resentment of Western society. What should be done with her? Is she a dangerous prostitute, luring children from truth and reality, needing to be detained, or is she a demented auntie who can be left alone to die among the elderly? Up until now there is no consensus.

However, perhaps a different perspective is available.

---

2. Francis Spufford, *Unapologetic: Why Despite Everything, Christianity Can Still Make Surprising Emotional Sense* (London: Faber and Faber, 2012), 5.

3. See Charles Taylor, *A Secular Age* (Cambridge: Harvard University Press, 2007), 1–25.

THE CASE FOR THE CHURCH

The allegations are daunting, the distrust is acute, and the confidence of believers is dwindling. With honesty and candour the Mount Everest of questions must be faced: why would any levelheaded person *still* believe in the church in the twenty-first century?

No reply to this question will be deemed acceptable by all. The church cannot be viewed, understood or valued simply from an empirical point of view. Instead, one must step beyond the fence of history in order to see the church from the height of God. Only from this vantage can one appreciate the irreplaceability of the church and perceive that, in spite of her blemishes and failures, the church is a gift to the world, worthy of love and celebration. Below, seven reasons are given to celebrate the church in a secular age.

THE REALITY OF THE CHURCH

The first reason to believe in the church is that the church is *real*. The church is, in other words, what the Bible says. She is, first and foremost, the assembly of God's people, the gathering of God's children from every tribe, nation, tongue and people. One must be clear that the performance of the church does not validate or invalidate this truth. The privilege and calling of the church is determined by the call and purpose of God.

Furthermore, the church is the temple, or residence, of God. This is one of the great themes of biblical history and one of the great revelations of the gospel. The Bible begins with God planting a garden so that He can dwell among human beings. Tragically, sin disrupts this fellowship and humanity ends up alienated from God. Much later God gives Israel a sacrificial system and a temple so that He can once again reside with people. But the story repeats itself and humanity ends up no closer to God. Now one of the startling teachings of Jesus was that God did not desire to dwell in a temple made of wood or stone but in the hearts of His people. Picking up on this, the apostles taught the early Christians that the people of God, the church, are the temple of God.

This point needs explaining. The eminent New Testament scholar Tom Wright helpfully describes the significance of the temple for Jews and Christians. He says, 'The Temple was not simply a convenient place to meet for worship. It was not even just the "single sanctuary", the one and only place where sacrifice was to be offered in worship to the one God. It was the place above all where the twin halves of the good creation intersected. When you went up to the temple, it was not *as though* you were "in heaven". You were actually there'.[4]

His point is that the temple was the unique place where heaven and earth overlapped and intersected. With this background, the church glistens like a diamond in a piece of graphite. The people of God, as the temple of God, have unique access to the Creator. He is not only attentive to their prayers and pleased with their worship, but present among them — uniquely — on earth as in heaven.

Once the reality of God's presence is seen, one must consider the reality of the peace and blessing available through the church because of God's presence. This blessing is captured in the Hebrew concept of *shalom*, which encompasses psychological, material, social and spiritual well-being. To be a member of the church is to be a member of God's family and to enjoy the privileges that come with having God as Father, Christ as brother, and the Holy Spirit as a renewing source of life and community. These privileges are not the natural right of humanity, nor are they available outside of the reality of the church. To use the dictum of the early Christian teachers, to have God as Father is to have the church as mother.[5]

THE MISSION OF GOD

The second reason to believe in the church is that the mission of God has not changed. The God of the Bible is the God who

4. N. T. Wright, *Paul and the Faithfulness of God, Part I* (London: SPCK, 2013), 96–7.

5. The history of the use of this phrase is given in Henri de Lubac, *Christ and the Common Destiny of Man* (San Francisco: Ignatius, 1988), 48–81.

acts with intention and purpose. From Genesis to Revelation we read of *Operation Creation Rescue*, a divine plan to supplant the brokenness of our natural and social worlds with the fullness of heavenly peace and blessing. This mission is a joint enterprise whereby God partners with human beings — beginning with Abraham, advancing to Israel, culminating in Jesus and flowing into the church — in order to overcome the forces of sin, death and evil.

This back story is essential because it puts the church in perspective.[6] The church is not one of a set of religious societies that can be substituted and replaced like parts of an engine. On the contrary, the church is the delegation of God, His earthly covenant partner who has been commissioned, trained and empowered to advance a heavenly mission in the world. Thus to believe in the church is to believe in God and, more specifically, in His righteousness, that is, His commitment and ability to finish the project that He began more than three thousand years ago with a promise to Abraham.

Much confusion resulting from the blemishes of the church would be avoided if people paid attention to the nature of the people that God gathers into His church for this mission. The church is not a selection of the wise, upright, dutiful and virtuous among our species, a kind of religious dream team. The opposite is true. In the Old Testament God is embarrassingly honest with the Israelites telling them that they were not elected as His servants due to their numbers, strength or moral superiority. They were chosen because they were little and weak, like children, and thus more apt to reveal His power and mercy. The same recruitment process is evident in the disciples of Jesus and later in the quirky assemblage of rich and poor, slave and free, Jew and Gentile that made up the early church. In no case does the Bible give reason to believe that the church is composed of better people than the world. Materially we are the same; what sets the church apart is the grace of God.

---

6. For the megaplot of the Old Testament, see Christopher J. H. Wright, *The Mission of God: Unlocking the Bible's Grand Narrative* (Downers Grove: Intervarsity Press, 2006).

Likewise, critics would be less shocked by the behaviour of the church if they were more attuned to the history of the Bible. Unlike the contemporary myth of progress, the Bible resists any *zeitgeist* of optimism that would imagine the road into the future to be straight, smoothly paved, free of potholes and easy to navigate. Whether one considers the lives of individuals in the Bible like Moses, David and Peter or whether one looks at the history of Israel under the Old Covenant, the pattern that emerges is one of a faltering people who struggle to grasp the mission, who fail spectacularly more often than they succeed and who frequently profane the very name they are commissioned to glorify. This is not to justify the sins of the church, but simply to say that, if one looks at the church through the spectacles of the Bible, one does not expect to see a spotless virgin but a fickle teenager in the pains of adolescence.

THE WISDOM, POWER, AND COMMUNITY OF THE GOSPEL

A third reason to believe in the church is that she alone is entrusted with the gospel. To appreciate the gospel one must say something about sin. Christians admit the full array of human needs: social, economic, material, psychological, political and spiritual. Likewise, Christians are glad to make use of all of the means available to help people. Yet the scalpel of God's Word uncovers one problem more universal and fundamental than any other, the misdirected desire and alienation that theologians call *sin*.

Sin is not something that governments, technicians, and scientists understand or can remedy, but like a poisonous chemical in the waterlines, sin ruins life and is ultimately fatal. At a personal level, sin is the pride and selfishness that splinters relationships, the greed, disinterest and malice that cause one person to hurt another. At a social level, sin is the catalyst behind bigotry, injustice, scapegoating and war. At an ecological level, sin is why human beings gleefully destroy their habitat in order to enjoy a few decades of ease, comfort and fun. In short, sin is why the world is a mess.

Now the gospel is the message that God knows about the problem, cares, and — here is the shocking headline — has acted decisively to fix the problem through the death and resurrection of Jesus. This news cannot be discovered through philosophy or science but is the gift of revelation.[7] Therefore, the church has a unique and grave responsibility in the world that cannot be fulfilled by any secular institution. She alone is the messenger appointed by God to proclaim the good news that a cure is available for the superbug of sin.

But the gospel is more than good news. It is *power*. This may be confusing for modern people who think of words as empty containers of information. God's words are different. They are creative, reviving and transformative, and this is especially true of the gospel.

For this reason Paul describes the gospel as the saving power of God. This means that the church not only has knowledge about a cure, but a message saturated with divine power that effects change where change is most needed — in the disordered hearts of sin-producing people. Therefore, the church is able through the grace of God to change lives more profoundly than any set of doctors or therapists. She alone is the midwife of God's redemptive work through the sharing of His Word.

But the gospel is more. It is the charter for a brand new society, a colony of heaven on earth. This new society is radically different from all others insofar as its community has nothing to do with ethnicity, family networks, wealth, status, beauty, fame, common interest or natural gifting. It is based entirely on a relationship with God through the person of Jesus Christ. This spiritual bond enables the church to attain to a degree of equality that surpasses any other community.

The equality of the church is based on three facts and one implication. The three facts are: (1) every human being is made in the image of God; (2) every human being is a sinner before God;

---

7. For the gospel as good news, see Tom Wright, *Simply Good News: Why the gospel Is News and What Makes It Good* (London: SPCK, 2015).

and (3) the only righteousness, or standing, or status that matters is a gift of love that comes through the righteousness, or standing, or status of Jesus Christ. These facts lead to one world-tilting, ego-subverting implication: the roots of inequality have no social importance in the church. However far the church falls short of her charter, the founding deed is clear. In Christ our differences are irrelevant; what matters is what we share in Him.[8]

THE UNRIVALLED BEAUTY OF THE CHURCH'S ETHICAL TEACHING

Ignore for a moment the hypocrisy of Christians and whatever treachery the church has committed in the past (more on that below). Beneath these misdeeds, tucked away in the original sermons of Jesus and the circulated letters of His disciples, is the most beautiful statement of what it means to be human in the history of the world. This teaching is the ethical inheritance of the church.

To begin, this teaching says that human beings are relational creatures whose satisfaction comes, not through the ego, but by sharing the self, first, through love of God and then through love of neighbour. The circle of neighbour, as Jesus unforgettably teaches in the parable of the Good Samaritan, is universal. No person is excluded from the duty of Christian love. Christians are commanded by Jesus to greet the unjust, to love their enemies and to forgive the guilty. Therefore, philanthropy, distilled to its highest degree of purity, is a mark of the authentic church.[9]

Second, the teaching of Christ is categorically opposed to any form of moral pretence or hypocrisy. Goodness and sinfulness are determined not simply by what a person does or does not do, but by the motives of the heart and, more deeply still, by the underlying loves that nourish and direct all thought and action. Thus, without blinking an eye to human depravity, Christians strive for total

---

8. Dietrich Bonhoeffer explores the equality within the church more fully. See Dietrich Bonhoeffer, *Life Together* (London: SCM, 1954), 10–15.

9. On Jesus as the inspiration behind philanthropy, see Paul Johnson, *Jesus: A Biography from a Believer* (New York: Penguin, 2010), 91.

perfection, the holiness that begins with a rightly ordered heart but takes flesh and becomes real through words, deeds and gracious relationships. In this way, the ethical ideal of the church achieves perfect balance. On the one hand, any good deed that does not issue from a good heart is culpable. On the other, any good heart that does not result in good deeds is insincere and, in truth, not good at all.

Third, a basic condition of the Christian life is community. The virtues celebrated by the church, and the vices spurned by her, are character traits that only grow in the soil of relationships. Likewise, these virtues uniformly promote and enrich the peace and unity of the community, which is intended to be so vitally connected that it reflects the synergy of a human body. This image of communal life scuttles the criticism of Nietzsche. The *agape* love of the church glows in comparison to any narcissistic set of values, whether they be the self-promoting heroism of the ancient world, recapitulated in the monstrous dictators of the twentieth century, or the self-promoting celebrity of the modern world.[10]

Fourth, the moral beauty of the Cross cannot be ignored. Charles Taylor describes how every moral identity is built on a moral source, which is the ultimate good that not only clarifies the aim of life but empowers moral living.[11] For Plato, the moral source was the Good itself; for John Stuart Mill, it was the principle of greatest happiness; for Kant, it was the idea of the rational agent; but for the church, the moral source is the *agape* love revealed in the sacrificial death of Jesus Christ. Critics must be challenged: is there anything more inspiring, holy and beautiful than God hanging on a Cross so that the debt of sin might be paid and so that His unremitting love can be proclaimed throughout the world?[12] This

---

10. David Brooks provides an insightful critique of the religion of the Big Me in *The Road to Character* (London: Penguin, 2015), chapter 1.

11. For a careful exposition of the importance of moral sources, see Charles Taylor, *Sources of the Self: the Making of Modern Identity* (Cambridge: Harvard University Press, 1989), 91–107.

12. Jonathan Edwards argues that the gospel could not be any more aesthetically pleasing. See Jonathan Edwards, *Religious Affections* (Edinburgh: Banner of Truth, 2001).

act of prodigal love is the wellspring of Christianity, the event to which the church returns day and night for inspiration, insight and power. No other moral source is so personal, humane, generous and, for those imprisoned in the self, disturbing.[13]

Finally, in spite of many ignorant preachers, there is no dualism in the Christian life. Christians do not believe that the material world is unimportant, much less evil, and Christians are never told in the Bible to give up this world (in the sense of creation) for a different one. The opposite is true. The Bible teaches plainly that humanity was created to be the caretaker of the natural world, that creation has suffered horrifically due to human selfishness and pride, and that the rescue mission of God is not just about redeeming humanity but saving creation from the consequences of human sin. Therefore, no Christian can abdicate the duty to love and care for the environment and to work for a just society. This is our human vocation.

THE SPIRITUAL RELEVANCE OF THE CHURCH

Relevance can be measured by the degree to which something is missed. Relevance can also be measured by the degree to which something is needed. Whether or not there is an appetite for the church in contemporary society is a moot point. The deeper question is whether society can function if the church disappears. One can explore this question from two directions, that of society and that of the self.

On the one hand, the distinguished sociologist Anthony Giddens argues that modern society both raises and suppresses fundamental questions regarding human existence. Among these are questions about the meaning of life, how to cope with finitude, or death, why human beings are different from the rest of the natural world and the prickly topic of personal identity. In spite of the treasury of scientific knowledge, modern society does not provide people with

---

13. The warmth of Christian love stands out in particular against the coldness of modern altruism as Larissa MacFarquhar reveals in *Strangers Drowning: Voyages to the Brink of Moral Extremity* (London: Penguin, 2015).

the resources needed to answer such basic questions. The result is brooding, unidentified anxiety.[14]

On the other hand, focusing on the self, the philosopher Robert Roberts describes how within a Christian psychology human beings have spiritual needs that cannot be ignored. He lists these as follows: a need for something so trustworthy that it can provide absolute security; a need to be loved by someone who knows us perfectly and whose love is dependable; and a need for an ultimate orientation that goes beyond all finite goals and purposes. To ignore these needs is to deprive the soul.[15]

Putting the stresses of society together with the needs of the self, one begins to see that the church has never been more relevant than now. To summarise the argument of Francis Spufford in the bestselling book, *Unapologetic*, Christianity makes better emotional sense of the real world than any other religion or philosophy. Christianity explains the crack in the world, our need for love, the big picture, who we are, and the route home. In addition, Christianity provides an absolute source of security and love in the person of an Almighty Father. No other form of spirituality is as comprehensive, coherent and satisfying as the Christian life. Perhaps this is why contemporary atheists, even while rejecting church doctrine, are attempting to emulate church wisdom and practice?[16]

THE IMPERFECT BUT TRIUMPHANT HISTORY OF THE CHURCH

The church is imperfect. No one would deny this. The church has committed grievous offences. No one would ignore this. But the history of the church is not the humiliating exposé that most people assume.

---

14. Anthony Giddens, *Modernity and Self-Identity: Self and Society in the Late Modern Age* (Cambridge: Polity Press, 1991), 35–70.

15. Robert C. Roberts, *Spiritual Emotions: A Psychology of Christian Virtues* (Grand Rapids: Eerdmans, 2007), chapter 3.

16. Alain de Botton pleads for a non-dogmatic recovery of basic elements of church wisdom and practice in *Religion for Atheists* (London: Penguin, 2012).

There is not space here for the shortest abbreviation of church history. For this reason, the tactic taken will be to utilise the work of Rodney Stark, a renowned sociologist of religion, in order to suggest that honesty demands a reconsideration of the church's reputation. The goal will not be to provide a definitive argument in favour of the church, but simply to blast the insouciance that leads people to condemn the church without regarding facts.

First, consider the crusades. Any educated person, upon hearing the name, spontaneously imagines sword-carrying Christians needlessly invading the Middle East in order to gain land, power and money. This story has been rehearsed time and again. Yet, in *The Triumph of Christianity,* Stark reaches a different conclusion. Summing up careful research, he says, 'The Crusades were not unprovoked. They were not the first round of European colonialism. They were not conducted for land, loot or converts. The crusaders were not barbarians who victimized the cultivated Muslims. The Crusades are not a blot on the history of Christianity. No apology is needed'.[17]

Now this judgment cannot be defended here. The takeaway is merely the suggestion that the reputation of the church as a corrupt institution responsible for as much evil as good (eg. the Crusades) is a prejudice that ought to be reviewed.

Here is a second example: the cold war between religion and science that, for most people, is symbolised by the trial of Galileo by the church. The tale spread through high schools and universities is that, from the birth of modernity, the church attempted to control and suppress scientific research because she saw that the discoveries of scientists would contradict the doctrines of theologians. On this topic Stark again calls for a paradigm-shift. He says, 'The original warfare between religion and science never happened; Christianity not only did not impede the rise of science; it was essential to its having taken place'.[18]

---

17. Rodney Stark, *The Triumph of Christianity* (New York: Harper Collins, 2011), 234.

18. *Ibid*, 294. Diogenes Allen gives a complementary history of the relationship of faith and science in *Christian Belief in a Postmodern World: the Full Wealth of Conviction* (Louisville, John Knox Press, 1989), chapter 1.

The argument of Stark reinforces the plea of George Wiegel that Europe should stop apologising about — and deliberately erasing — her Christian heritage. People deserve to know that, without the church, there would be no Europe, no West and no modern world.[19]

Regardless of whether one will accept a reassessment of past sins, history itself affords copious examples of the positive good that the church has done for the world. From philanthropy to gender equality, from salvaging Western civilisation to abolishing the slave trade, from supplying philosophic principles that underlie human rights to building hospitals, schools and universities, from giving hope and meaning to peasant life, to inspiring monumental works of art and music, the Western world would be unrecognisable apart from the influence of the church.

Finally, moving from the past to the present, one must celebrate the contemporary life of the church. Here the work of Philip Jenkins is ground-breaking. On the one hand, things are not as they appear in Europe. The church is growing even as traditional denominations lose clout and membership. On the other, a new Christendom is surfacing in the Global South that is becoming a lifeline of mission and support, feeding back into Europe what Europe once fed into the world.[20] Therefore, anyone attempting to write the epitaph of the Western church is acting presumptuously. The church dies only to be resurrected with renewed life, vision and energy.

THE FAILURE OF THE MODERN WORLD

The seventh reason to believe in the church is that the modern world has failed. The secular promise to deliver humankind from darkness to light has not happened. This is evident, first of all, by the naivety of the modern world. This term, naivety, is often used to describe

---

19. See George Weigel, *The Cube and the Cathedral: Europe, America, and Politics without God* (Leominster, Gracewing, 2005).

20. For an assessment of religion in Europe, see Philip Jenkins, *God's Continent: Christianity, Islam, and Europe's Religious Crisis* (Oxford: Oxford University Press, 2009). For the growth of the church in the global south, see Philip Jenkins, *The Next Christendom: The Coming of Global Christianity* (Oxford: Oxford University Press, 2011).

the credulity of pre-modern people who did not question religious beliefs. But modern people are no less naive than their pre-modern grandparents. In the psyche of our culture, scripted into a thousand advertisements, is a narrative of progress and a trust in science that is untested, unproven and manifestly religious. Recognising this, the sociologist and theologian Jacques Ellul says that the modern world is built on two myths, one of history and another of science.[21]

Furthermore, the modern world is idolatrous. Idolatry is the worship of creation instead of the Creator, investing meaning and power in things that cannot satisfy or fulfil the demands placed on them. One of the great themes of the Bible is that idolatry is addictive and dehumanising and that a fundamental aim of the mission of God is to free humanity from the bondage of idols. Now the modern world is no less idolatrous than the ancient world. The sticks and stones of Canaanite religion have been exposed to be frauds, but only to be replaced by the more sophisticated, but no less dehumanising, idols of money, sex and power. Thus there is as much need to identify and denounce idolatry in the twenty-first century as there was in the days of Elijah, Isaiah and the apostle Paul.

Finally, there is a totalitarian spirit in modern society. Hannah Arendt famously described totalitarianism as a power structure in the shape of an onion. Layer upon layer reinforced a fundamental lie. Now the totalitarianism of modern society is not the product of an intelligentsia, a team of politicians or a vanguard of CEOs. It is the slow realisation of what Neil Postman calls a technopoly, a world in which every aspect of human life is submitted to the rule of technique and technology.[22] Thus, in the modern world the solution to every problem — from marriage and family to geopolitics and global warming — is better technique and more technology. But, as argued above, there are limits to what technology can do. Most importantly, it cannot remove the root cause of human evil, sin.

---

21. Jacques Ellul, *The New Demons* (New York: Seasbury Press, 1975), 88–121.

22. Neil Postman, *Technopoly: the Surrender of Culture to Technology* (New York: Random House, 1992).

Therefore, taking a brief look at the present conditions of the modern world, one concludes that the Western world does not need a chaplain, the role society is happy for the church to fill, but a prophet. The only viable candidate for the job is the church. Even if other experts can diagnose the present ills of society and foresee the disaster ahead, the church alone has the gospel, the powerful message of God that heals the brokenness of the human condition and redirects the course of history.[23]

THE SALT TO PRESERVE AND THE LIGHT TO GUIDE

A final question must be faced. To some, the church described and defended above might be unrecognisable. It might appear to be the product of a wish-dream rather than a representation of what is real. But this disparity between the hope of the church and the struggle of the church is not a reason to give up on her but a motive to rediscover her mission and purpose. Chesterton memorably made the point in *What's Wrong with the Modern World* as follows: 'The Christian ideal has not been found tried and wanting, it has been found difficult and left untried'.[24]

Rather than settling for less, the modern world should listen to the teaching of Jesus and recognise the church for what she is, salt and light. The church alone is the salt that can preserve the West from moral and cultural decay and the church alone is the light that can guide humanity toward the kingdom of God.

I (still) believe in the church.

---

23. Anthony Giddens describes the modern world as a juggernaut, the Hindu cart carrying a god that destroys everything in its path. See Anthony Giddens, *The Consequences of Modernity* (Cambridge: Polity Press, 1990), 151–173.

24. The full text can be accessed: http://www.ccel.org/ccel/chesterton/whatwrong.i.i_1.html

8

WHY I (STILL) BELIEVE IN PREACHING

David J. Randall

More than fifty years ago W. E. Sangster opened his *The Craft of the Sermon* with the statement: 'Preaching is in the shadows. The world does not believe in it'.

Today it is not only the world that does not believe in preaching. Many within the church and even some preachers seem to have lost confidence in it. It might have been expected that evangelicals, who take a high view of Scripture, would be most convinced of the vital importance of preaching as God's means of telling forth the gospel message and building up His church, but this loss of confidence can be found in such circles also.

The back cover of *Feed My Sheep,*[1] a symposium on preaching, says, 'Biblical preaching is nearing extermination in our day. There is "sharing", "suggesting", plenty of storytelling, and lots of preaching to "felt needs". But the authoritative, expositional opening of the Word of God is more rare to find all the time'.

The downplaying of preaching is evidenced by (a) the shortening of sermons in many places (ostensibly on the grounds of modern

---

1.   Soli Deo Gloria Publications, 2002; the book is subtitled *A Passionate Plea for Preaching.*

attention spans), (b) the replacement of sermons with other forms of communication such as video presentations or discussion groups and (c) the demise of evening services.

This chapter is not being contributed by a 'famous' preacher, but by an ordinary pastor who has ministered the Word of God twice a Sunday (and on other occasions) for over forty years. We will consider some factors that may have contributed to a loss of confidence in preaching, look briefly at what the Bible says about preaching, and argue for renewed confidence in it as God's means of spreading the gospel and building up His people.

In one of his books, Martyn Lloyd-Jones wrote about what he regarded as the most urgent need in the Christian church today. If the manuscript had been damaged and the next part was missing, what would people guess would have come next? There could be many suggestions, but our contention here — MLJ's contention — is that the most urgent need in the Christian church is the preaching of God's Word. Nothing can be a substitute for it.

LOSS OF CONFIDENCE

There are several factors which may play their part in the loss of confidence in preaching.

There is the fact that preaching the eternal Word of God is a daunting task. It is such a high calling that we might say with Paul, 'Who is sufficient for these things?' (2 Cor. 2:16).

There is also the loss of old attitudes that held the office of the Christian minister in high regard. Perhaps especially in Scotland there was an attitude of respect for the preaching of God's Word, which could even morph into the kind of 'sermon-tasting' that viewed the sermon as an art form or a kind of entertainment. It need hardly be said that such attitudes have dwindled to nothing. One writer has gone so far as to suggest, 'It is hard to work in a role whose very existence is viewed as an epitome of archaic cultural redundancy'.[2] It may be akin to the contemporary trend against

---

2.   Josh Moody, *The God-Centred Life* (IVP, 2006), 148.

regarding anyone as having any kind of 'authority'. People today are reluctant to show deference to anyone.

Then there is the idea that people today cannot sit still listening for half an hour. We live in an age of 'sound bites'; camera angles only last a few seconds before switching to something else, and people are expected to give a response to big questions about political or ethical matters within a few seconds. People will happily sit still for several hours to watch a film or a tennis match, but we are told that, if we expect people to come to church, we must cut the length of sermons (or even cut them out altogether).

Another issue is the trend toward 'chatty' (not to say cosy) styles of speaking nowadays. Clearly there needs to be a rapport between preacher and listeners, but at least in the days before ubiquitous public address systems preachers needed to lift up their voices and speak in a strong way. The development of modern means of communication has been a huge blessing, but it carries its dangers also. There is the danger that 'Instead of proclaiming, warning and inviting, you will be sharing, musing and conjecturing'.[3]

A factor which may have affected some preachers is the idea which has been promulgated in some circles that a thirty minute sermon demands thirty hours of preparation. This would obviously seem a daunting prospect,[4] especially for people who are expected to preach twice a Sunday and on other occasions too. Good preparation and hard work are essential, but it is perhaps unhelpful to set out such unrealistic notions.

The preference of many for discussion or study groups may also have had a share in the downplaying of preaching. It is true that 'iron sharpens iron' and people can be greatly helped by listening to others discussing some aspect of biblical application, or by seeking to express their own convictions, but sadly in many minds such discussion has become a substitute for, rather than a supplement to, the preaching of the Word. Christopher Ash has expressed the

---

3.   Tim Keller, *Preaching* (Hodder & Stoughton, 2015), 33.

4.   Though it is somewhat better than the description I once saw of a resource for preachers which claimed to 'make it really easy to prepare biblical, life-changing sermons in almost no time at all'!

point: 'So often this is the objection we face: "There you are, six feet above contradiction, pulpiteering, setting yourself up as if you knew what to say, and expecting me to sit submissively while you rant on and on in your monotonous ministerial monologue"'.[5] It has even been asserted[6] that 'the sermon delivered to Christians had only a small part to play in the life of the primitive church and that much contemporary practice not only lacks a biblical foundation but is even injurious to the life of the Christian community'!

The very word 'preach' is sometimes used in a way that militates against true preaching. On the one hand we frequently hear media references to 'fundamentalist preachers', and at the everyday level anyone who expresses a point of view strongly may meet with the response, 'Don't preach at me'. This hardly encourages true preaching. There is also the pressure of the secularised culture in which we live and move and have our being. For example, pluralism reigns in society and there might be a nervousness about preaching truths such as that stated in Acts 4:12: 'there is salvation in no one else, for there is no other name under heaven given among men by which we must be saved'.

It is easy to be discouraged if there is little evidence of results from preaching (and if attendances are small). When attendees leave church with a mere 'I enjoyed the service today' or some such comment, it hardly encourages the person who stands there week by week, preaching his heart out. In some cases this may lead preachers to concentrate their attention on other things, even to the extent of becoming 'managers of religious organisations' seeking to cope with the demands of legislation and bureaucracy. Previous

---

5.   Christopher Ash, *The Priority of Preaching* (Christian Focus/Proclamation Trust, 2010), 54.

6.   David Norrington, *To Preach Or Not To Preach* (Paternoster, 1996), x. Derek Tidball (*Preacher, Keep Yourself From Idols* [IVP, 2011], 27) refers to Norrington's as 'The most systematic (and flawed) critique' of preaching. Norrington writes (p.75), 'By using the regular sermon the preacher proclaims each week, not in words, but in the clearest manner possible, that, be the congregation never so gifted, there is present, for that period, one who is more gifted and all must attend in silence upon him (less often her).' He says (p.96), 'There is no compelling reason to try to re-educate hearers to appreciate a popular method of yesterday'.

ages might have said that if preachers are too busy to preach, they are just too busy, but modern demands press in with urgency and insistence, so that the main thing can easily become a secondary thing.

Lastly, there may be a fear of running dry; people might feel, 'If I am supposed to preach twice a Sunday, maybe I'll run out of things to say'. Charles Spurgeon once read a newspaper article which expressed amazement that he could keep on year after year with 'such a narrow groove to travel in'. He reflected:

> My brethren, it is not so, our themes are infinite for number and fulness. Every text of Scripture is boundless in its meaning; we could preach from the Bible throughout eternity, and not exhaust it. ... Had we to speak of politics or philosophy, we should have run dry long ago; but when we have to preach the Saviour's everlasting love, the theme is always fresh, always new. The incarnate God, the atoning blood, the risen Lord, the coming glory, there are subjects which defy exhaustion.[7]

These are some factors that may lie behind the loss of confidence in preaching that has characterised recent times. If Derek Tidball's comment is true, that preaching is 'a significant barometer of the health of the church over the centuries',[8] it is clearly of great importance that there should be confidence in preaching on the part of Christians generally and preachers in particular.

PREACHING IN THE BIBLE

Scripture highlights the importance of preaching in many places.

Acts 6:2 tells of a complaint that arose in the early church — 'And the twelve summoned the full number of the disciples and said, "It is not right that we should give up preaching the word of God to serve tables"'. They proceeded to the appointment of seven deacons, so that the apostles would be able to concentrate on their responsibility

---

7.   Spurgeon, The Full Harvest (Banner of Truth, 2006 edition), 292.

8.   Tidball, 26.

for preaching the Word. There was nothing unworthy about serving tables, but the particular task of the apostles was to preach.

This ties in with the teaching of Ephesians 4:11-13, 'he gave the apostles, the prophets, the evangelists, the shepherds and teachers, to equip the saints for the work of ministry, for building up the body of Christ, until we all attain to the unity of the faith and of the knowledge of the Son of God, to mature manhood, to the measure of the stature of the fullness of Christ'. All Christians have a ministry and the task of the shepherd/teacher is to so minister the Word that believers are equipped for their ministry. Again, the importance of preaching the Word is commended.

In Romans 10:14 we find Paul rhetorically asking how people will hear the gospel 'without someone preaching?' And in 1 Corinthians 9:16 we find his strong sense of compulsion about preaching: 'necessity is laid upon me. Woe to me if I do not preach the gospel'.

Earlier in the same epistle — 1:21 — he writes, 'it pleased God through the folly of what we preach to save those who believe'. The A.V. translated it, 'by the foolishness of preaching', but the emphasis seems to be on the message rather than the medium. It is that message of the Cross which may seem foolish in the eyes of many, but it is God's means of salvation and the believer can say, 'far be it from me to boast except in the cross of our Lord Jesus Christ' (Gal. 6:14). The 'foolishness' may lie more in what is preached than in the preaching, but the text certainly also assumes the importance of preaching it.

In the pastoral epistles, we find Paul encouraging Timothy, 'preach the word' (2 Tim. 4:2). He uses the same word as Jesus used when He said, 'this gospel of the kingdom will be proclaimed throughout the whole world as a testimony to all nations' (Matt. 24:14), and in 1 Timothy 5:17 he refers to 'those who labour in preaching and teaching'. The reference to labouring reminds us of the preacher's responsibility to work hard in the study; it would be neither honouring to God nor responsible to the people to skimp on preparation, to allow other things to steal time that should be spent in studying the Word. As James Stewart said, 'Slovenly work, careless technique, faulty construction and inarticulate delivery have had their day: they will pass muster no longer'.[9]

Although there are over thirty Greek words for preaching, the two principal New Testament words are *kerusso* and *euangelizomai*. The first is found more than sixty times and the second more than fifty times in the New Testament. The first word signifies: proclaim as a herald, and we need to keep in mind the obvious fact that the New Testament world was a world without the means of communication which we take for granted now. The word for herald conjures up the image of the old town crier, a herald with a significant message which had been committed to him by someone else for him to pass on faithfully. The second word relates more to the content of the message with its root 'evangel', good news. Preaching is the heralding of the good news of what God in Christ has done, saving His people and building them up in their most holy faith (Jude 20).

In the case of Paul, the New Testament gives us both his example and his precept. His example is given in Acts 20:27 where he could say to the leaders of the church in Ephesus that he had declared to them 'the whole counsel of God'. From these words (and their context in Acts) we learn that his preaching was (a) forthright in its manner. He was not expressing an opinion or passing on some suggestions; he was declaring something that is true; (b) comprehensive in its scope. It was not just a simple ABC outline, but the whole body of doctrine; and (c) authoritative in its source, because it originated not with himself but with Almighty God. It is He who has breathed out all Scripture which is profitable for us (2 Tim. 3:16). Paul was not 'into' sharing a few thoughts, or expressing his own views or the convictions that had grown upon him. He proclaimed the whole counsel of God.

---

9. J. S. Stewart, *Preaching* (English Universities Press edition, 1955; originally published as *Heralds of God*), 91.

There are obviously other aspects of preaching; a sermon may be:

- apologetic — in seeking to answer difficulties and counter objections
- pastoral — in dealing with the real-life situations of the hearers
- educational — in teaching the story and doctrine of Scripture
- inspirational — in sending people away with a grander view of Christ and the gospel

But basically preaching is proclamation. In response to some who would replace sermons sometimes with discussion groups, it has been whimsically remarked that we do not read at the end of the Sermon on the Mount that Jesus said to the disciples, 'Get everyone to break up into small groups of seven or eight where they can discuss what they've just heard'! Actually it ends with the famous parable of the two builders, and 'Everyone then who hears these words of mine and does them will be like a wise man who built his house on the rock' (Matt. 7:24).

Afterwards, Matthew tells us, 'the crowds were astonished at his teaching, for he was teaching them as one who had authority' (Matt. 7:28–29). If it be said that no preacher today has the authority that Christ had, we must remember that we do not speak on our own authority. The only authority we have, and the only ground for anyone standing in a pulpit or at a lectern, is the delegated authority of Christ, recognised by the community of faith.

There is a place for other forms of communication in the church, including discussion and dialogue, but these should be supplements to the preaching of the Word, not substitutes for it. There is a need for a recovery of confidence in preaching — not because of any authority residing in the preacher but because of the authority that resides in the Word of God. A herald is not called to discuss the message with his hearers but to announce it.

RECOVERING CONFIDENCE

Far from apologising for it and losing confidence in it, the need is for more confidence in preaching as God's means of saving people

(1 Cor. 1:21). Paul wrote, 'Not that we are sufficient in ourselves to claim anything as coming from us, but our sufficiency is from God, who has made us sufficient to be ministers of a new covenant' (2 Cor. 3:5–6). Our mandate comes not from ourselves, nor even from the church, but from the Lord Himself. It is He who bids us proclaim the Word. Of course there must be the sense of calling to preach (for ministry is not 'just a job') and there needs to be a recognition of that calling by the church (for no one is meant to be a law unto himself), but undoubtedly the mandate comes from the Master.

It is true that the word 'dialogue' is found in the New Testament but it is important for us to see the sense in which that is true. It is not dialogue in the sense that I speak my part, somebody else speaks his, and by the process of synthesis we discover the truth. Dialogue is actually a Greek word used by Luke in Acts to describe Paul's preaching. It says he 'dialogued with them'. It means that he took the truth of the gospel and dialogued with their minds concerning it. He would ask questions, for example. He spoke to them in this way: 'Do you not know that your bodies are members of Christ himself?' (1 Cor. 6:15, NIV), 'Do you not realise that Christ Jesus is in you?' (2 Cor. 13:5, NIV), 'You were running well. Who hindered you?' (Gal. 5:7), 'Who has bewitched you?' (Gal. 3:1).[10]

Yes, I (still) believe in preaching, because it is of God's appointing. One of the New Testament texts most frequently quoted by evangelicals is 2 Timothy 3:16 in which Paul says that all Scripture is breathed out by God and profitable for various purposes. He then goes on immediately (with no chapter divisions in the original text), 'I charge you …: preach the word' (2 Tim. 4:1–2). It's *kerusso* again — sound it forth, announce it. Biblical preaching will address both the mind and the emotions; it is logic on fire, a rational message that calls us to respond with all of our heart, soul, mind and strength.

---

10. *What is Biblical Preaching?* (P&R Publishing, 2008), 29f.

EXPECT GREAT THINGS FROM GOD

This was the second part of William Carey's famous saying: 'Attempt great things for God; expect great things from God.' A discouraged young preacher once spoke to an older friend about seeing little fruit from his preaching. The older man asked, 'Do you really mean to say that you expect that when you speak people will be changed?' and the young man diffidently said, 'Well, I suppose not'. The other responded, 'Well, that's why nothing is happening'!

We are called to preach in expectation that God will honour His Word (Isa. 55:11). It is not merely a matter of filling a half-hour once, twice or thrice a week, as if it were some kind of ritual. God's Word is alive and active (Heb. 4:12) and so we may look for results from the proclamation of it. If people say that few people remember what they have heard over the weeks and years, we may remind them of the fact that we do not need to remember all the breakfasts, lunches or dinners we have eaten to benefit from them. We may not remember many but it is in the strength of these meals that we grow and thrive.

A different image was used by a preacher who was delivering the Warrack Lectures on preaching:

> We have every right to look for results; but we must also have faith to believe that they are there, even when we cannot see them. Take a trip to Loch Ard and gaze at the government-owned forest. Go back a month afterward and study it once more. Nothing seems to have changed. Yet experts say that in the interval it has added two million feet of new timber and grown in value by £22,000.[11]

I believe in preaching because it is God's means of enabling spiritual growth and vitality. Our confidence is not self-confidence but a reliance on God who is faithful to His Word. Why should anyone surrender the preaching of the wonderful message of Scripture? Why should it not be proclaimed with a boldness that is not our

---

11. Hamish McKenzie, *Preaching the Eternities* (Saint Andrew Press, 1963), 80.

own, an assurance that comes from on high and a confidence that is a million miles from the self-confidence of an orator. Our authority is from none other than Almighty God.

HOW OFTEN?

Another area in which there is the need for a recovery of confidence in preaching concerns evening services. Most *liberal* churches either never had an evening service or have given it up long ago. Today, however, some *evangelical* churches have given up evening worship and others are considering doing so.

Roger Ellsworth has asserted: 'We need more of the Bible', so 'Why are we cutting back on services that provide the preaching and teaching of God's Word? Would we approve of a doctor cutting back on essential care for his patients? The primary manifestation of the cutting back mentality ... is either the complete elimination of Sunday night services or the exchange of preaching on those nights for other activities'.[12]

Several justifications of this trend have been offered:
- people should spend time with their families instead of going to evening worship
- people are too tired to come out twice
- people can listen to messages on-line
- people should be free so that they can witness to friends and neighbours
- the lure of television
- the distraction of Sunday sports and entertainments

Sometimes, however, the discussion doesn't get much further than — 'Why do I *have to* go twice on a Sunday?' — which seems to imply that attendance would be some kind of penance or dreary duty. The asking of the question reveals the root problem that lies behind the potential demise of the evening service — namely the

---

12. *Evangelical Times*, July 2014, p. 31. Ellsworth also issues the hard-hitting challenge: 'If pastors would get into their studies earlier, reduce the amount of time they spend "surfing" the net, stop attending time-wasting meetings, lessen the amount of time they spend chatting with cronies and minimise their time on "Facebook", they might well find that they can produce more than one sermon a week. Pastors and church members are good these days at cluttering up their lives with unnecessary things and dignifying it all with the word "busy".'

lack of spiritual appetite. In the physical realm, loss of appetite is a sign that something is wrong, and the same is true in the spiritual realm. One of the signs of spiritual health is a keen desire to get as much teaching and fellowship as possible, as well as a keen desire to take every opportunity to worship the great God who has inspired the Scriptures and acted in Jesus Christ for our salvation. To ask 'do I have to ... ?' becomes an irrelevance; it is a sign of spiritual malaise rather than maturity.

Hebrews 10:25 famously tells Christians not to forsake the opportunities for fellowship — with the particular emphasis that any such neglect would have a discouraging effect on other people. It is not only for one's own spiritual growth in grace that attendance at the services is important. It is also an encouragement to other Christians, even as one's absence is a discouragement to the rest of the family.

In many parts of the world Christians would give a great deal to have the opportunities we enjoy. One reads of people in some countries who are so eager for the Word that they even encourage preachers to give them as much as possible. Such keenness is a rebuke to the lackadaisical attitude found among so many in the free world.

Do people really need to see the fulfilment of Amos 8:11 before they appreciate the privilege they have? Amos recorded the Lord's prophecy, 'the days are coming. . . when I will send a famine on the land — not a famine of bread, nor a thirst for water, but of hearing the words of the Lord'. This would be a dreadful state of affairs, and the very prophesying of it should be a wake-up call for slumbering Christians and people who regard evening worship as an unnecessary burden.

There are also certain obvious practical reasons why evening worship is important. It gives the opportunity of worship and fellowship to people who, for one reason or another, can't get to morning worship. This might apply to people on shift work, on call, parents taking it in turns to look after babies. Again, there ought to be provision for those who lead the church's own children's club, Sunday School (whatever name is used) during morning worship. These are people who work on behalf of the whole church and it is important that there should be an opportunity for them to worship and sit under the Word.

In some places alternative forms of Sunday evening meetings are held which do not include preaching — replacing the sermon, for example, with group discussion. No doubt all congregations should provide opportunity for people to meet together, relatively informally, to help one another in their biblical understanding and their spiritual walk. Such small group work, however, should be seen as a supplement to the preaching of the Word and not a substitute for it.

THE PREACHER

In this chapter we have considered preaching, and I conclude with a few words about the preacher. The first prerequisite is obviously a sense of calling to such a ministry. It is not a matter of whether one likes to speak in public, much less hear the sound of his own voice. There needs to be the sense of compulsion encapsulated in Jeremiah's testimony about having a burning fire in his bones that he couldn't keep within himself (Jer. 20:9). He also records the Lord's word, 'Let the prophet who has a dream tell the dream, but let him who has my word speak my word faithfully' (Jer. 23:28).

Given such a calling, I conclude with five assertions about preaching:

I believe in preaching **with conviction**. Since the message is not ours but God's, we have no need for diffidence or halfheartedness in preaching it. The story is told of someone's surprise on hearing that the sceptical David Hume was going to hear George Whitefield. The friend said, 'Surely you don't believe what Whitefield is preaching, do you?' David Hume answered, 'No, but Whitefield does'. May there always be that sense of conviction based on the truthfulness and authority of God and His Word.

I believe in preaching **with relevance**. There may be a timelessness about the message of Scripture, but the context in which we preach the Word is constantly changing. The preacher needs to keep abreast of our social and moral context in order to apply the Word to the situation in which people are called to follow Christ today. Love for our hearers demands sympathy, love and relevance.

I believe in preaching **with consistency of life**. No one is or will be perfect in this world, but there is no doubt that someone who stands to proclaim the truth of God must also seek to live under its authority. No one will have any time for the preacher whose life contradicts his message. The preacher's life should 'adorn the doctrine of God our Saviour' (Titus 2:10).

I believe in preaching **with faithfulness**, the faithfulness that says what Micaiah ben Imlah said long ago when he was urged to agree with the news that King Ahab wanted to hear — '"Let your word be like the word of one of them, and speak favourably". But Micaiah said, "What my God says, that will I speak"' (2 Chron. 18:12–13). There will always be pressures and temptations for preachers to say what is likely to be popular but God's calling is to faithfulness. In the 1930s when the Nazis were growing in popularity, the challenge for preachers was,

> ... to proclaim God's prophetic Word without compromise. Berliners were in the mood to hear sermons that made them feel better about their Fatherland but they were not always receptive to messages that made them feel bad about their sin. They wanted a religion that made them better Germans, not a religion that forced them to confront their inward need of a Saviour. But Dietrich never failed to give them the latter ...[13]

I believe in preaching **with humility**. The preacher is only a messenger. He is not called to reveal his own thoughts, ideas or cleverness,[14] but to expound and apply the Word of God, not primarily to speak about what we should do but about what God has done. We are 'ambassadors for Christ, God making his appeal through us' (2 Cor. 5:20), and our task is to emulate John the Baptist's attitude: 'He must increase, but I must decrease' (John 3:30).

I (still) believe in preaching.

---

13. M. Van Dyke, *Radical Integrity: the Story of Dietrich Bonhoeffer* (Barbour, 2001), 66.

14. James Denney famously said that no one can at one and the same time show that he himself is clever and that Jesus is mighty to save.

9

WHY I (STILL) BELIEVE IN PRAYER

Stefan Gustavsson

Prayer is essential in the Christian life, but not merely as a religious duty. It is one of the most wonderful consequences that flow from the truth of Christianity.

According to Christianity, in the beginning there was not silence but the Word (John 1:1–4). Even before the world existed, there was relationship and communication. Jesus spoke on several occasions about the relationship He had with the Father before creation. In His prayer on the night when He was arrested He spoke to the Father of 'the glory that I had with you before the world existed' and said, 'you loved me before the foundation of the world' (John 17:5, 24).

Communication existed not only *in* God, but also *from* God to humanity. The creation narratives show how God chose to relate to humanity by speaking. Using language and words that were comprehensible to the first humans, God commissioned them to be fruitful and multiply. He called them to subdue the earth and rule over all the animals. He gave instructions as to what they should eat to nourish their bodies and what the source of their knowledge of good and evil should be. Even when they ignored Him, He called for them in the garden, 'Where are you?' (Gen. 1:28-30; 2:17; 3:9)

Throughout human history, God has continued to seek contact with humanity, speaking to us and waiting for our response. In the Christian faith, prayer is the most foundational means for us to respond to the divine call and it is a proof of God's affirmation of humanity. We really matter to Him.

PRAYER IS NOT THERAPY

Naturalism — the view that the natural world is the only reality — is the dominant world view in our culture and stands in stark contrast to the Christian faith. According to this perspective, God and the supernatural do not exist at all. Therefore humanity is all alone and forgotten in a threatening existence. At most prayer can be viewed as a form of therapy. The whole point of prayer is to find an inner calm and increase one's sense of well-being. At its worst prayer is nothing more than self-deception. To turn to someone who doesn't exist and expect help is clearly meaningless. Rather than leading to well-being, it becomes an opiate that anaesthetises people and prevents them from taking responsibility for their lives.

Christian faith presents a radically different world view. Its starting point is the existence of a living and personal God who is the Author of all life. His plan for our world is that community should flourish — both on a human level between people and between Him as Creator and us as His creation. On this perspective prayer opens the door for humanity to enter into a relationship with the Creator. Prayer can obviously have therapeutic benefits like increased well-being, but this is a side effect. It is not the nature or purpose of prayer. Prayer is communication and fellowship with God.

Perhaps a personal example would be helpful at this point. In the early 1980s, I was part of a team of student evangelists. My teammate Peter and I were responsible for planning a camp. We needed to reserve the camp facilities, contact musicians and speakers, find people to be in charge of the kitchen, plan the programme, and much more. Towards the end of our planning Peter lost his voice and could not speak for several weeks. When we met I did all the talking while Peter jotted his comments on paper! Then a strange situation developed. We recognised that we would have to touch base a few days later to go over the brochure one last time before it was sent to the printers. We also knew it would be impossible to meet in person that day. Therefore we decided that I would call Peter even though he had stopped answering the phone since he lost his voice. We decided on a date and time and he promised to lift the receiver and listen.

That was the oddest phone call of my life. I dialled the number. The phone rang on the other end and I heard someone lift the receiver.

Silence.

'Hey Peter! This is Stefan. How's it going?'

Silence.

'I just wanted to let you know that…'

And I went through the whole list, point by point, with the information he needed.

Silence.

'Keep up the good work. Talk to you later.'

Silence.

When I hung up, it struck me that this phone call is an illustration of prayer in a Christian's life. Even though I didn't hear anything or sense any immediate response, I knew that Peter was on the other end. I knew that he was listening to what I said and that the course of future events would be impacted by what I said.

That's what prayer is like. God is a real Person who listens attentively and takes our sincere requests seriously.

PRAYER IS NOT MYSTICISM

In addition to naturalism, we find that there is also a growing interest in mysticism in our culture. Mysticism is built on the belief that there is more to our world than meets the eye; there is also a supernatural dimension to reality. There are many forms of mysticism, but they tend to share certain common presuppositions:

- Ultimate reality cannot be understood by propositional communication or logical thought; it can only be experienced beyond the rational.
- The road to spiritual experiences and contact with ultimate reality is one of silence and meditation.
- The direction of the spiritual journey is inward with unexplored springs and forgotten openings towards the divine that exists in us, not outwards towards a God who is separate from humanity.
- The goal is oneness with the divine, not fellowship and dialogue with someone who is distinct from humanity.

Christianity shares the mystic's conviction that there is a supernatural dimension to reality, but there are also important distinctions that need to be made.

a) First, our starting point is not an unknown reality, but a revealed God. He spoke 'at many times and in many ways ... to our fathers by the prophets' and now 'he has spoken to us by his Son' (Heb. 1:1–2). We don't know everything about God and don't have exhaustive knowledge about Him. But since He has revealed Himself, we can know something true about who He is, and relate to Him in both word and thought.

The prayers in the Bible presume a certain knowledge about God that is a foundation for our prayers of thanksgiving, confession and supplication. When Daniel prayed to God, his prayers were filled with words about God. 'O Lord, the great and awesome God, who keeps covenant and steadfast love ... To you, O Lord, belongs righteousness ... To the Lord our God belong mercy and forgiveness' (Dan. 9:4–9).

b) Second, the direction of the Christian's spiritual journey is not inward towards oneself, but outward towards God. It is not that God is far removed. 'Yet he is actually not far from each one of us', as Paul said on Mars Hill in Athens (Acts 17:27). But God is not to be equated with the depths of our subconscious. Prayer is about turning one's focus away from oneself and our preoccupations towards Someone else. We see this in the introduction to the prayer Jesus taught His disciples, 'Our Father who is in heaven' (Matt. 6:9, NASB).

According to Christianity humanity is not divine, nor shall we become gods. We will always remain human. When God became a man, it was not so that humans might become gods, as is sometimes claimed, but rather that humans and God could be friends again. When we read in 2 Peter 1:4 the curious expression that we may 'become partakers of the divine nature', it is not about some kind of reverse incarnation whereby humans become gods. No, Peter is using an expression from contemporary religious philosophy to express the conviction that Christians one day will share in Christ's glory.

c) Third, human language is an indispensable means of communication between God and humanity. God began to speak to people at the creation and continues to speak today. In the Bible we find verbal communication from God to us. If God speaks with human language, then people are invited to speak to God with human language.

d) Fourth, the goal is a personal fellowship between God and humanity, not a merging of the two. It is an I-Thou relationship (to use Martin Buber's term). It is an ongoing conversation where both speaking and listening have a natural place. The uniqueness that each person has should never be eradicated, but celebrated and expanded through fellowship with others.

It is not silence that builds fellowship between us humans, but language; we communicate through words and speech. Our relational problems almost always have their root in failed communication. We fail to express our thoughts, feelings and needs with words. Our relationships dry up in silence. But we have received a word from God and an invitation to respond — in prayer.

A SECRET REVEALED

We have good reason to look more closely at the New Testament word for mysticism. The Greek word *mysterion* occurs many times in the New Testament, where it is generally translated as mystery. But Paul gives the word a special meaning. It does not mean mysterious and unapproachable. On the contrary, Paul uses it to describe the revealed secret! He writes to the Colossians about 'the mystery hidden for ages and generations but now revealed to his saints'(Col. 1:26). In 1 Corinthians 2 he writes:

> But we impart a secret and hidden wisdom of God, which God decreed before the ages for our glory. None of the rulers of this age understood this, for if they had, they would not have crucified the Lord of glory. But, as it is written, 'What no eye has seen, nor ear heard, nor the heart of man imagined, what God has prepared for those who love him' — these things God has revealed to us through the Spirit. For the Spirit searches everything, even the depths of God (1 Cor. 2:7–10).

Notice the four claims about the gospel that Paul makes:
- the gospel is not a human innovation; it is God's secret
- it is not a temporary whim; its content was determined before the beginning of time
- it was unknown by humans and spirits alike for long expanses of time
- it has now been revealed by the Spirit to the apostles, who have made it known

In Ephesians, Paul returns to the theme of a secret revealed: 'When you read this, you can perceive my insight into the mystery of Christ, which was not made known to the sons of men in other generations as it has now been revealed to his holy apostles and prophets by the Spirit' (Eph. 3:4–5; cf 3:9–10). The secret is now public knowledge! Fellowship with God in prayer is not a mystic groping blindly in the dark. It is built upon a foundation of God's communication with us.

PRAYER IS NATURAL

We meet people every day who speak with each other, who eat and drink, laugh and read, who receive information and work. These are natural and important parts of what it means to be human. But we rarely see anyone pray. A day at work, window-shopping, watching television, a visit to a government office, sporting event or cultural happening — these activities all have one thing in common: the absence of prayer. We take it for granted that we ignore God in our public and collective actions.

Some of us freely pray silently when no one is watching or listening. And then there are special buildings — churches or chapels — where people can pray. But prayer has been sanitised from public life. One gets the impression that prayer is something people can have as an add-on, something odd rather than something natural.

From a Christian perspective, nothing could be more mistaken. Prayer is the most natural activity of all since we are created to be in a relationship with God. Not expressing oneself to God makes humans somewhat less human. It is essentially as unnatural as not communicating with other people. Communication is a foundational part of being human. We are not islands unto ourselves, even though our being bent or curved in towards ourselves can sometimes give that impression. No, we are created to reach out beyond ourselves towards other people and towards the One who gives us life.

When we reach towards God we overcome the basic problem with our human limitations. We are small and weak in a world full of overwhelming forces. Our limitations prevent us from having a clear view of the totality of life. We must constantly make decisions even when we cannot see the consequences of our choices. But if there is an infinitely powerful and wise God to whom we can relate our concerns, our limitations are no longer a problem. We are in relationship with Someone who has the insight and power we lack, and who can lead us and help us.

PRAYER ACCORDING TO JESUS

Prayer plays a central role in the teaching of Jesus. Time and again He encourages His friends to believe in the reality of prayer: there is a God who hears and answers!

> Ask, and it will be given to you (Matt. 7:7).

> Again I say to you, if two of you agree on earth about anything they ask, it will be done for them by my Father in heaven (Matt. 18:19).

> Ask, and you will receive, that your joy may be full (John 16:24).

Jesus not only encourages us to pray; He also teaches us how to pray.

a) In the first place, *we should pray in Jesus' name*. This is especially clear in the gospel of John, where prayer in Jesus' name is a recurring theme. 'Truly, truly, I say to you, whatever you ask of the Father in my name, he will give it to you' (John 16:23; cf John 14:13-14; 15:15; 16:24). Jesus' name opens the way to the heart of the Father.

Here it would be easy to mistake such prayer 'in Jesus' name' for some kind of magic formula, as if just speaking the name of Jesus means that things will happen. The name of Jesus is not a magic word! There is no inherent power in the word 'Jesus' or in the order of the letters in His name. Jesus Himself is clear that merely calling on His name is not enough. 'Not everyone who says to me, "Lord, Lord," will enter the kingdom of heaven, but the one who does the will of my Father who is in heaven' (Matt. 7:21). The promise that God will hear our prayers is not contingent upon the letters J-E-S-U-S. 'If you ask me anything in my name, I will do it' (John 14:14). Jesus is a Person who decides what He will do.

That's why He also dismisses prayers made as a shallow ritual. Notice what He says in the Sermon on the Mount:

And when you pray, you must not be like the hypocrites. For they love to stand and pray in the synagogues and at the street corners, that they may be seen by others. Truly, I say to you, they have received their reward. But when you pray, go into your room and shut the door and pray to your Father who is in secret. And your Father who sees in secret will reward you. And when you pray, do not heap up empty phrases as the Gentiles do, for they think that they will be heard for their many words. Do not be like them, for your Father knows what you need before you ask him (Matt. 6:5–8).

Praying in Jesus' name is not about the letters or the name in itself. It's all about the Person who bears the name. If we were to approach God in our own name, there would be many legitimate reasons for God to send us away. But by His death and resurrection, Jesus has opened the way for us to come to the Father. Therefore are we welcomed when we call upon Jesus' name.

b) Secondly, *we must pray in faith*. It's not enough simply to say the words; we must speak with confidence in the Lord. There is a clear parallel with the gospel message about salvation; it's not about merely saying the words. '[If] you confess with your mouth that Jesus is Lord and believe in your heart that God raised him from the dead, you will be saved' (Rom. 10:9). Paul sees a clear connection between a verbal confession and faith in one's heart. In the same way, prayer is about speaking in confidence to Jesus: we believe in Him as our Lord!

The promises about the prayer of faith are astounding. '[If] you have faith like a grain of mustard seed, you will say to this mountain, "Move from here to there", and it will move, and nothing will be impossible for you' (Matt. 17:20). A little later in the same gospel, Jesus says, 'Truly, I say to you, if you have faith and do not doubt, you will not only do what has been done to the fig tree, but even if you say to this mountain, "Be taken up and thrown into the sea", it will happen. And whatever you ask in prayer, you will receive, if you have faith' (Matt. 21:21–22).

Jesus strengthens our faltering faith: God is able; trust Him. Yet this promise cannot be divorced from the will and plan of God for the world. Jesus is not writing a blank cheque that can transform us into superheroes who can tap into supernatural powers for our own arbitrary purposes. No, we must understand these promises in their proper context. Consider John 15 as an example: 'If you abide in me, and my words abide in you, ask whatever you wish, and it will be done for you. By this my Father is glorified, that you bear much fruit and so prove to be my disciples' (John 15:7–8). Jesus gives both the conditions and the purpose of this promise: the precondition — fellowship with Jesus and faithfulness to His word; the purpose — that discipleship will deepen and the Father be glorified. It is against this background that He says to us, 'Ask, and it will be given to you'.

c) Thirdly, *we should persevere in prayer*. Our faith reveals its true nature through perseverance. Our true zeal can be seen in our prayer life.

Jesus told a fascinating parable about perseverance that should encourage us not to give up. The story is about a widow who nags an indifferent judge to review her case. Her perseverance finally leads the judge to say, 'because this widow keeps bothering me, I will give her justice, so that she will not beat me down by her continual coming'. Jesus then adds, 'Hear what the unrighteous judge says. And will not God give justice to his elect, who cry to him day and night? Will he delay long over them? I tell you, he will give justice to them speedily' (Luke 18:1–8).

PRAYER — AND WHAT *NOT* TO EXPECT

Jesus' promises to hear prayer are clear and we should be careful not to dilute them. At the same time, we must exercise care to understand them correctly. We obviously recognise that prayer cannot be divorced from who God is, and therefore we ought not to pray for things that are contrary to the nature of God or His revealed will. For example, we should not pray for evil and unjust plans to succeed, nor should prayer be divorced from God's choice in creation and salvation.

To start off with, *we should not expect that God would undo the workings of creation itself*; it is His own work. He has already chosen to create a world in which we are called to work to provide for ourselves. Thus we should not pray that God would give us our daily bread if we are unwilling to work. God certainly provided manna for the children of Israel during their wilderness wanderings, but once they had entered the Promised Land, there was no more manna and the people were expected to provide for themselves by working the land God had given them. In the same way, God can meet us in extraordinary situations and provide for our needs. But our continual prayer cannot be that the order God has established in creation would be rescinded. Our prayer should rather be that God would bless us when through work we take our rightful place in the scheme of creation.

Secondly, *we should not expect God to undo our human limitations*. He has created a world with the rhythm of day and night in which human beings need regular periods of rest and refreshment. Our limitations are a part of the goodness of God's creation. To pray for the ability to remain awake 24/7 for the rest of our lives would not be a good idea, as it would entail a rejection of the way God has created us. Instead, we should pray for help in using our waking hours wisely and also for good rest.

Thirdly, *we should not expect God to undo all the consequences of the Fall*. Through Jesus the kingdom of God is breaking through into our world and we can already taste 'the goodness of the word of God and the powers of the age to come' (Heb. 6:5), but the fallen world remains a stubborn fact of reality even for Christians. Many aspects of the Fall will not be revoked until Jesus comes again. Not the least of these is death itself. No one can escape death and we should not pray that we would be spared from dying.[1] However, we can pray that we may die well when the time comes.

---

1. The Old Testament recounts two incidents where a person was taken directly to heaven without dying first: Enoch in Genesis 5:24, and the prophet Elijah in 2 Kings 2:11. We are never given reason to believe that their cases should be regarded as normative for a believer.

There is an interesting example in Luke 4 that shows how Jesus Himself viewed the period between His first and second comings. When He came to the synagogue in Nazareth He was asked to read from the Scriptures. He read a passage from the prophet Isaiah: 'The Spirit of the Lord is upon me, because he has anointed me to proclaim good news to the poor. He has sent me to proclaim liberty to the captives and recovering of sight to the blind, to set at liberty those who are oppressed, to proclaim the year of the Lord's favour' (Luke 4:18–19).

Then, to everyone's surprise, He said that these words were being fulfilled before their very eyes. If we read the passage in its original context in Isaiah, we see that Jesus stopped in the middle of a sentence! Isaiah spoke in one breath about both 'the year of the Lord's favour' and 'the day of vengeance of our God' (Isa. 61:1–2). It is clear that Jesus did not mean that every promise was being fulfilled at that time; the day of vengeance, that is, the great Judgment Day, had not yet come. At His first Advent He proclaimed the year of the Lord's favour or grace and invited people to the kingdom of God. At His second coming He will first judge evil and then win the definitive victory over sin and death. At that time all the prophecies which Isaiah proclaimed will be fulfilled, including the promise that one day God will 'swallow up death forever' (Isa. 25:8).

PRAYER CHANGES HISTORY

Jesus taught His disciples to pray, 'your will be done'(Matt. 6:10). Yet He also encouraged them, 'ask whatever you wish' (John 15:7). We can pray for God's will to be done and yet also pray for things that we want; that is our privilege as sons and daughters of God. He invites us to come before Him and express who we are as well as our needs, desires and dreams! As we freely and fearlessly express what we want, we also bow to His sovereign will. He sees the big picture that we cannot see — and He knows what He is doing.

Because of His promises, we believe that God always gives an answer, even though it may not always come in the ways that we had hoped. The future history of the world will be impacted by the fact that we have spoken to the Lord, but not in a trivial way where our prayers dictate what God has to do. Anyone who has seen the film 'Bruce Almighty' understands the catastrophic results that would come about if God were forced to answer every selfish and naive prayer!

Billy Graham has written:

> I am sometimes amused when people tell me, 'God answered my prayer'. What they mean is that God gave them what they asked for. But if He had not granted their request, He would still have answered their prayer. We forget that 'No' and 'Wait' are answers, as well as 'Yes'. I have answered every request made by my children to me. The answer has not always been what they wanted, but it has always been in accordance with what I have thought was best for them at the time. God is the same way, except that His answers are always right and good and best, while mine may or may not have been. And remember, whether prayer changes our situation or not, one thing is certain: prayer will change us![2]

The future will always be different as a result of us having spoken to God about a situation. Whether short-term or long-range change, whether the situation we pray for or ourselves as people who pray — prayer always makes a difference! Prayer changes history. This is a conviction that permeates Jesus' teaching and which therefore should also permeate our lives.

Prayer is a *grand affirmation of humanity*. Our thoughts are not bound to the limits of our own heads or to our human relationships. We can lift them up to God. Our lives are tied together with the Creator of the universe and we are challenged to join Him as actors on the stage of human history.

For all these reasons, I (still) believe in prayer.

---

2.   Billy Graham, *Unto the Hills — a Daily Devotional* (Word Publishing, 1996), 9.

10

WHY I (STILL) BELIEVE IN FOLLOWING JESUS

Richard Lucas

I've seen many posters outside churches, with all sorts of messages, from 'The wages of sin is death' to 'Why not try church? It might just be your cup of tea'. But I've never seen one saying 'Christians are good people'.

The Humanist Society of Scotland, however, has no qualms about proclaiming the moral virtue of non-believers. A campaign they ran featured the slogan '2 million Scots are good without God'. How exactly they assess that all of the non-religious people in Scotland are 'good' I don't know, but the implication is clear: you don't need God for morality.

Well, in one sense they are right: people who do not believe in God can and do exhibit morally admirable behaviour. This is because a person's God-given conscience is not short-circuited the moment they cease to believe in God. So, not believing in God does not necessarily lead to immoral behaviour in an individual, but in a culture (in the long term at least) without belief in God, moral accountability decays, moral standards deteriorate, and the very concept of objective moral obligations is holed below the water line. Morality ultimately depends on God.

MORAL ACCOUNTABILITY

On an atheistic materialist view our brain is an electrochemical machine. Everything we think and do is determined by the laws of physics. Free will is an illusion and whatever we think or do, we could not have done otherwise. If we have no control over our actions, the concepts of moral accountability and responsibility are destroyed, and there is no rationale for deserving reward or punishment. Saying that a person is responsible for their actions becomes as irrational as saying that a computer is responsible for its actions.

In a court case, lawyers may defend people by claiming that they were not fully in control of their actions at the time of the crime because of mental illness or drug effects, and, if successful, these mitigating factors might reduce the punishment given as responsibility was diminished or even absolve the accused of guilt altogether. On an atheistic materialist view, everyone should be declared unable to control their actions, as our usual decision-making process is as much the product of inexorable forces of nature as mental illness and drug influence. Therefore everyone is 'not guilty'!

Leaving out a supernatural aspect to human life results in losing a key element of the concept of morality. Regardless of what people may argue in philosophical discussion, when it comes to real life crimes, people have a deep intuition that evil deserves punishment.

As a Christian, I believe that people are not just physical bodies, but also have a non-physical element, a soul, that exists outside the realm of natural cause and effect. Therefore, I can rationally justify why I hold myself and others morally responsible for their actions. Not only does my Christian world view allow for the existence of moral accountability, but it also introduces the One to whom we are accountable: God. Ultimately, there is no 'getting away with it' as God is all-seeing and all-knowing.

Is this sense of accountability to God an inferior reason to behave well and do the right thing? Many claim that it is. A common form of the objection is, 'I do the right thing because it is the right thing, not just to avoid the flames of Hell'. As a Christian, my standing with God is determined by my relationship with Him through Christ, not my moral worthiness, so 'the flames of Hell' do not lick at my imagination when I face a moral choice. However, my love, respect and gratitude towards God influence my behaviour. When I try to do the right thing in my marriage, it's not so that my wife doesn't leave me, but to share in and maintain a good relationship. My desire to please God through my actions is equally natural and positive.

If my relationship with God is not at stake through my moral choices, in what sense am I accountable to God? What are the consequences of immoral actions? The commendation of God is of great value to me — when I stand before Him I want to feel that I have lived my life for God. No earthly pleasure can outweigh the regret of having disappointed God.

Whatever other reasons anyone can give to act morally, account-ability to God can always be added as an extra one. Therefore the net result has got to be increased moral motivation, and surely all can agree that that's a good thing. Accountability to God can be a key factor in situations where there seems to be a good chance of getting away with it from a human perspective. Who's going to know about an omission on the tax form, a quick look at porn, or a quiet lie behind the scenes? God is.

Christianity underpins the very concept of moral accountability through belief in a supernatural soul, and it is to an all-seeing, all-knowing God that we are ultimately responsible.

MORAL CONTENT

What would happen if the government repealed all traffic laws, declaring the Highway Code obsolete, instead just urging all road users to be careful and try to avoid accidents? Chaos would ensue. One person might regard 150 mph as a perfectly sensible speed through your town. Some would feel safer driving on the right, some on the left and some straight down the middle. Traditionalists would stick to clockwise-round roundabouts, but others would prefer to take the most direct route to their exit.

Leaving people to make their own moral decisions without external authority is similarly perilous. Even the well-meaning may be unable to foresee the full consequences of their actions, and the scurrilous will be able to hide their self-justification under a veneer of moral flexibility.

Humans, to varying degrees, have the capacity to put together a convincing argument, and this ability can be turned to the construction of elaborate defences of immoral actions. I know that I can often argue convincingly with myself that a certain course of action would be beneficial, but my knowledge of God's revealed standard of morality restrains me. Many a man has convinced himself that abandoning his family for another woman was the 'loving' thing to do, best for everyone. Knowledge of the definite prohibition of adultery cuts through the fog of rationalisation and gives the man no room for self-justifying manoeuvring.

As a Christian, I believe that God has revealed many truths to us through the Bible. The fact that this was necessary indicates that we would not have worked them out unaided, or that we are prone to deviate from them. Without an external source of distinct moral authority, humans tend to slide into rationalising their own preferences at the expense of the well-being of family, friends and wider society, especially in the longer term.

Returning to my Highway Code analogy, there are some aspects of road use that require structure to prevent accidents. Drive on the left. It's not that driving on the left is inherently necessary to road safety, but the whole thing is going to work out best if everyone follows the same structure. Consider the biblical principle of one day of rest in every seven. Is that really inherently morally superior to one in six, or eight? Probably not, but society benefits from a uniform structure that preserves common family and leisure time for all.

Later in this chapter I'm going to look at some distinctive areas of biblical moral teaching and discuss how moral standards decline without them.

MORAL OBJECTIVITY

'Torturing innocent people for fun is OK.' I'm sure you agree that this statement is wrong, but in what way is it wrong? Is it wrong in the same way that '2 + 2 = 5' is wrong? A factual error? I believe that it is. Torturing innocent people for fun is wrong regardless of the prevailing view in your society or anyone else's society, regardless of your personal opinion or anyone else's, and regardless of the time you happen to live in. That's because the statement 'Torturing innocent people for fun is wrong' is a fact. 'Torturing innocent people for fun is wrong' is a truth claim, and it's true. That's what is meant by an objective moral standard. Morality is not a matter of subjective opinion. There are moral facts that are true for all people at all times.

When debating with atheists, things get really interesting from this point onwards. They never want to deny that torturing innocent people for fun is wrong, but they also don't want to concede that objective moral values exist, because they know that they struggle to account for them. Having fudged this issue, the atheist has just three possible explanations for the origin of moral obligations, and they all fail totally.

Explanation 1: Evolution

The story can sound very plausible. Developing humanity benefitted from a fortuitous emerging instinct to care for and cooperate with each other. Yielding an evolutionary advantage, this herd mentality has become hardwired into our brains.

I don't believe that evolutionary theory can account fully for the wonderful complexity and diversity of life on earth, but I have a particular suspicion of evolutionary psychology. It just seems too flexible. Why are we sometimes caring and kind? It had an evolutionary advantage. Why are we sometimes selfish? It had an evolutionary advantage. An evolutionary advantage can always be imagined for any and every human trait and its converse, from monogamy to promiscuity and even homosexuality.

But even if the evolutionary account is true, why are we obliged to follow our evolved instincts? 'Do what comes naturally' is not a moral principle. The right thing to do is often the thing that doesn't 'come naturally'. Similarly 'follow your psychological urges' is hardly a solid foundation for morality.

The evolutionary philosopher Michael Ruse is frank about this predicament, describing objective moral obligations as an 'illusion fobbed off on us by our genes'.[1] In other words, objective moral standards don't really exist, but our brain is wired to believe that they actually do, because we wouldn't obey them if we didn't. Needless to say, we have no ultimate obligation to obey illusory psychological phenomena.

So, evolution might explain why we sometimes behave morally, why we have moral intuitions, but it can't explain why we should live in accordance with them, and that's what morality is all about, knowing what we ought to do.

Never fear, says the atheist, I've got another explanation up my sleeve....

Explanation 2: Social convention

Morality is a social construct, it is claimed. People in a society arrive at a consensus about what's right and wrong and, *hey presto*, there you have it: a moral system. So to describe something as immoral amounts to saying, 'We don't approve of that in this society'.

There are two fatal flaws in this. Firstly, there is not a moral principle that states that we have a duty to conform to our society's moral standards. Society's moral standards can be wrong. What if your society has a flourishing and popular slave trade? Is it your moral duty to support it like everyone else? Of course not. We have

---

1   M. Ruse and E. O. Wilson, "The Evolution of Ethics", in *Religion and the Natural Sciences: The Range of Engagement*, ed. J. E. Hutchinson (Orlando: Harcourt & Brace, 1991), 310.

a duty to improve our society's moral standards. But improve them relative to what standard? An objective moral standard above any particular culture is needed.

Secondly, regarding morality as a social convention inevitably leads to sociocultural relativism. A society believing that torturing innocent people for fun is OK is not just different, but wrong — morally deficient. Some may plead that it's 'true for them', or strike back, 'But that's just you. What gives you the right to tell someone that torturing innocent people for fun is wrong?'

Once someone is reduced to arguing like this, it is clear that they actually have no foundation for moral objectivity at all. For all of the sophisticated philosophical mumbo-jumbo that is spoken about moral values being relative, everyone talks as though they are objective when addressing real issues.

Don't despair! The atheist has one last card to play....

Explanation 3: Human reason produces morality

Can't people work out what's right and wrong by thinking about it logically? There are lots of clever philosophers in university ethics departments. What are they doing if they are not using their intelligence to work out what's right and wrong? Are they not creating moral systems by reason, evidence and logic?

The answer is 'No, they are not'. They do not start with evidence, reason and logic, but with moral intuitions that cannot be justified rationally. They then systematise and distil the essence of these intuitions into ethical theory. But note where they start: intuition.

Statements such as 'don't hurt people unnecessarily' are obviously right, but why? Is it possible to produce a logical argument to support it? Let's have a try.

Don't hurt people unnecessarily because it hurts and people don't like it.

OK, so what, why does that mean I shouldn't do it?

Well, you wouldn't like it if someone did it to you.

Correct, but why does that mean I shouldn't do it to others?

Er....

We know it's true, but we can't explain why. Logical argument alone cannot lead to a moral position. It is not possible to argue to a moral 'ought' from any amount of non-moral information.

Now I know the most basic moral principles as well as you do: don't hurt or harm, human flourishing and happiness should be promoted, etc. But why do we believe them? The answer is that we just know. It is intuition.

But why should we trust these intuitions? How would an atheist respond to a Christian saying, 'I just feel there's a God', 'I just know', 'It's just intuition'? Would they be happy with that? Of course not. So why are they happy to accept their moral intuitions as authoritative without a rational foundation? From an atheistic perspective, there is no answer. In debates, atheists flit from one failed explanation to another, as though three failed arguments can somehow combine to produce one good one.

A moral system needs four components:
- a foundation accounting for the very existence of objective moral obligations,
- general principles that capture the essence of the morality,
- rules that give structure for the expression of these principles,
- application of these rules and principles to real cases.

Atheists like to skip over the first stage, the foundation, because they haven't got anything substantial to say, and then focus on the later stages. They are building on sand, with no foundation.

The atheist ethicist is like a magician pulling a rabbit out of a hat. The tricky part of this trick is not pulling out the unfortunate bunny by its ears, but sneaking the rabbit into the previously empty hat without anyone noticing. Moral principles such as 'act according to love', 'do not harm', 'maximise happiness', etc. are plucked out of thin air and then treated as a solid foundation for moral reasoning. With a sufficiently distracting glamorous assistant and dextrous sleight of hand, the majority of the audience might be fooled, but the philosophically aware will notice.

Explanation 4: God

We regard intuitive principles such as 'don't hurt people unnecessarily' as reliable and objective, and we are fully justified in doing so — if they originate in a God-given conscience that gives us perception of an objective moral realm that reflects God's morality. God Himself is the ultimate standard of goodness, and He gives us insight into morality through our conscience.

It's not just that some things are wrong because God says so. God's nature is perfectly loving, just and good, and we are obliged to Him, as our Creator, to live in accordance with His will, imitating His qualities.

If we reject God as the ground of objective morality, we cannot explain, for example, why it is a fact that hurting innocent people unnecessarily is wrong.

Without the concept of a supernatural soul, our understanding of moral accountability cannot be sustained. Belief in God gives us a stronger motivation to act morally. Without God's self-revelation through Jesus and in the Bible, the content of our morality would not be protected from selfish dilution and we would be ignorant of some moral truth. And, to cap it all, the very idea of objective moral obligations is holed below the waterline without belief in God.

Why do I still believe? Because my Christian faith makes sense of the world as I experience it. What's missing from secular ethics is a soul to account for free will and an ultimate source of moral truth. The Bible's teaching supplies both. Two thousand years later, no credible alternatives have been proposed.

GOD'S REVEALED MORAL STANDARDS

So far so good, but what if the content of God's morality seems flawed? What if Jesus' example seems misguided? Some religious teachings strike me as bizarre and pointless. While I must be humble and accept that God knows better than I do, I would hope that the Bible's moral teaching would be recognisable as the ultimate moral wisdom.

Because of our God-given conscience, there is much moral principle where our culture and society is in tune with biblical morality: rape, theft, murder, generosity, etc. However, I'm going to focus on areas where the biblical moral vision diverges from the many alternative views in our culture. If I find that the biblical is superior, I will be reassured that it is indeed a revelation from God. (A prime example of this superiority is the institution of marriage, but I'll leave that to Gordon Macdonald in Chapter 13.)

a) The Sanctity of Life

The Bible teaches that human life is a gift from God, created uniquely in His image, and inherently valuable. Its value does not depend on so-called quality of life or capabilities.

In contrast, Peter Singer, renowned ethicist and Australian humanist of the year 2004, said this: 'Human babies are not born self-aware or capable of grasping that they exist over time. They are not persons', therefore, 'the life of a newborn is of less value than the life of a pig or a dog'.

If you disagree with him, he'd call you a speciesist — having an irrational and sentimental bias towards one's own species.

The influence of biblical teaching on the unique value of human life is eroding. That's why abortion is accepted and infanticide (the killing of babies) is being countenanced at an academic level. We may recoil in horror at this, but other non-Christian cultures in history have practised infanticide and it is far from unknown in other cultures today. If a baby is only regarded as precious if it is wanted, then killing a baby becomes acceptable. An adult cat is more self-sufficient and able than a human baby, so if we base value on capabilities, the cat will be regarded as more precious and worthy of protection than the human baby.

My conscience screams to me that killing babies is wrong, and I'm glad that I can defend that view intellectually from my standpoint as a Christian.

The other area where the relativising of the value of human life is manifesting is euthanasia and assisted suicide.

Once we concede that some lives have no value, suicide becomes a rational option. The vestiges of Christian influence in Britain, and our consciences, mean that most people would baulk at a jump directly to promoting suicide generally. So, instead, campaigners start with the thin end of the wedge, but if assisted suicide is allowed for the terminally ill, why should it be denied to the merely ill? If it is available for the physically ill, why not the mentally ill? Why restrict it to the ill? What about the person who is just tired of life? What about the person unable to self-administer poison — should they be 'denied the right to die'? Why should children be denied this right? The logical end point of the slippery slope is euthanasia on demand, presenting suicide as a valid option at every stage of life. Other (more secular) countries are further down this road than we are.

Euthanasia on demand would result in a huge waste of life. Most people surviving a suicide attempt do not try again. In the well-established Werther Effect, awareness of suicides increases the incidence of suicide in a population. In the converse Papageno Effect, stories of people resisting the temptation to suicide and then leading fulfilled lives lower the incidence of suicide.

We now hear people committing suicide described as 'brave'. The corollary of this must be that some who choose to continue to live must be cowardly. We could easily reach a stage where we feel responsible to justify our decision to continue living, especially if we are needing expensive or burdensome care.

I want a society where everyone feels wanted and cared for, and the Bible's teaching allows me to defend that.

b) Debt

Personal debt, national debt, business debt, developing world debt: debt is a major problem in the world today. According to the Bible, debt is a profoundly moral issue. Interest on loans to the needy is banned, and caution is urged with all loans. Taking security on a loan is also questioned.

This contrasts with the more common view that debt is just a matter of supply and demand. Urging individuals and countries to borrow unnecessarily and at unfavourable terms is regarded as normal business practice and as politically mainstream. Individual lives are ruined by consumer debt. Poor countries are bound by crippling interest payments and rich ones feel they never have enough money to spend without effectively stealing it from future generations through national debt.

Appropriately, campaigners for the relief of developing world debt went under the 'Jubilee' banner, reflecting the biblical principle that debt must never be allowed to be a permanent millstone, keeping the poor poor indefinitely. The Bible recognises the cycle of poverty created by debt and helps us avoid it and break it.

Our economic context is very different, but we lack the wisdom in the Old Testament Law that restrains the negative consequences of debt.

c) Distribution of key resources

In Old Testament Israel, each family owned a parcel of land which couldn't be permanently sold. People were thus prevented from building up huge estates while others lacked the resource to provide for their family. This poverty-preventing law doesn't translate directly into our economic system as land ownership is no longer crucial to sustaining life, but the principle does. Many people now cannot afford a home to live in, and so have to rent instead — everyone needs a roof over their head. While renting, they enrich a landlord while they are being prevented from building up security in a capital investment for themselves.

In buying a property to let, landlords are often not providing the tenants with a service that they desire, but instead pricing them out of the market and then exploiting their need of accommodation. There is a place for letting a home while temporarily elsewhere, and renting is some people's preferred option in some circumstances. However, the business model of building a portfolio of homes to let is fraught with moral tension.

My biblically inspired view here is not commonly heard, but when I survey the housing market and the problems with it and listen to politicians' proposed solutions to it that don't get to the heart of the problem, I am reassured that biblical moral teaching reflects a higher wisdom than man's.

d) The Sabbath

The Bible proposes that one day a week be set aside for rest, worship and family time. The benefits in terms of maintaining structure and balance in individual lives, restraining workaholics and ensuring common family time are immense. Man's efforts to achieve the same ends are inferior. For example, the European Union working hours directive fails to encourage common family time.

In our individualistic culture, any proposal about structuring and synchronising society to achieve an overall benefit to well-being is likely to fall foul to objections about individual freedom — personal autonomy is paramount. God's pattern of structuring our working lives exhibits a wisdom that man seems unable to muster unaided.

e) Integrity

The Bible demands absolute integrity and honesty in personal and business dealings. This standard is currently eroding, with a double standard emerging. Politicians are held to very high standards, with even possibly innocent administrative slips being pounced on as grounds for resignation, while generally in our society lying is common and accepted. Dishonesty is often proposed as a solution to a problem or the way to attain a goal. Society pays the price when we can't trust each other, and the warning is stark from areas where integrity has decayed to an alarming extent and corruption cripples nations. A recent study showed a correlation between corruption in a nation and the willingness of individuals to cheat in a simple dice game. Acceptance of lying opens the door to many behaviours that would be ruled out if lying to cover them up were not an option. Adultery is a classic example of this.

Left to work it out for themselves, many arrive at the conclusion that a bit of tactical dishonesty is fair game to achieve their goals. The Bible draws the line where it needs to be, ruling out self-justified dishonesty and protecting relationships from the personal, through to the corporate and the political.

f) Alcohol

Alcohol causes massive problems in Scotland. Half of Scottish adult prisoners and seventy-seven per cent of young offenders were drunk at the time of their offence, and alcohol is implicated in seventy per cent of assaults, sixty-one per cent of murder accusations and an estimated fifty road deaths per year. Add to this the toll of alcoholism, domestic abuse and damaged health, and it is easy to see why Scotland's politicians keep returning to this issue. They will try anything, it seems: minimum price controls, new safe consumption advice, exhortations to use taxis after drinking, campaigns against domestic violence, education, etc.

The one thing they won't say, though, is what the Bible teaches: don't get drunk. Drunkenness is inherently irresponsible as it entails losing control of one's actions and thus risking people getting hurt. The damage can be to the self, others and one's family, often leading to significant cost to the state as well. Society recognises the sickness but refuses the cure.

We constantly hear that Scotland needs a 'new attitude to alcohol', but it seems we can't quite decide what it should be. So ingrained is the social acceptability of excessive drinking that politicians would fear to contradict it, even if they held to the biblical standard themselves.

Acceptance of the Bible's instruction to refrain from drunkenness would solve a multitude of problems and save lives.

g) Care for the poor, sick, refugees and orphans.

A responsibility to look after those in need is clear throughout the Bible. In the Old Testament Law, a system was instituted whereby farmers deliberately left some crops around the edge of a field so that those in need could take them. Alongside this, we have Jesus' exhortations to personal generosity.

There is a wonderful balance in the Bible's teaching. We can't delegate our responsibility in this area. When we see need, we must respond to it personally and immediately. On the other hand, we should also seek to structure society to help the most vulnerable.

Perhaps our society overemphasises the latter at the expense of the former, feeling virtuous by wanting the government to be more generous with other people's money, while not really engaging in sacrificial personal giving. Our culture of personal charitable contribution is also distorted from the biblical ideal. The giant cheque photo opportunity and high profile sponsored event contrast with Jesus' commendation of secret sacrificial giving.

In the Bible's teaching, I find a balanced and challenging approach to helping those in material need that doesn't allow us to pass the buck, precludes self-righteous grandstanding and encourages good systems to ensure care for all.

h) Forgiveness

Forgiveness is a paradoxical and philosophically perplexing concept, but the Bible clearly encourages us to mirror God's forgiveness in our human affairs. A willingness to forgive enables reconciliation, rehabilitation and restoration in relationships on every scale, from marriage to the international stage. In our society, it is regarded as quite acceptable to say 'I'll never forgive him' and such like, and an explicit decision to harden one's heart towards someone will usually go unchallenged.

How many marriages would be saved if couples understood Jesus' instruction to forgive? How many work places would be refreshed as a poisonous atmosphere is dissipated? How many international tensions could be diffused? How many people would face up to their own failings if they felt compelled to let go of their unforgiveness towards others?

The grim satisfaction of embittered resentment is a poor exchange for the freedom of forgiveness, but, without the Bible's influence, people often don't seem able to work that out for themselves.

i) Backbiting

Jesus is clear: if you have a grievance against someone, go to that person and try to sort it out. It is often much easier to discuss with a sympathetic and unchallenging friend instead of taking steps to actually deal with the issue. This neglected principle is crucial to a positive working environment. Instead of resolving, we poison others' reputations and turn one against another, inviting them to share in a grievance instead of forgiving and seeking reconciliation. There is a certain comfort in bringing people over to your own side, turning them against your enemy, and it takes clear instruction to guard against it. Jesus gives just such guidance.

j) The Heart

Jesus placed a special emphasis on our thought world as well as our actions. External rules are inadequate: we must properly order our mental life if we are to act morally. Thoughts of lust, vengeance, greed, etc. lead to immoral actions. Only a pure heart will lead to right actions.

Many believe that it is possible to let their conscious thoughts run riot, while controlling their actions and speech as they should. It doesn't work. As the proverb says, out of the overflow of the heart, the mouth speaks.

Purity of heart is not exactly a hot topic of discussion in twenty-first-century Scotland, but Jesus knows that only change at the core of our soul can lead us to follow His example and teaching in our lives.

MORAL GUIDANCE IS LESS THAN HALF OF THE STORY

Looking over these ten moral spheres, I am convinced that God's wisdom is superior to man's. My thesis that God's revelation is needed to protect and maintain the best standards of morality is affirmed.

However, moral guidance is not enough. When a person asks for God's forgiveness and enters into His family through Jesus' atoning death, a process begins. Christians do not struggle to live as God wants in their own strength, but God works in their character to change them from the inside out. The core of our motivations is progressively manipulated back into alignment with God's character. The Bible doesn't just present the ultimate in moral wisdom; it presents the means to gain the power to live as God desires.

Christians are often coy about this phenomenon. Let's leave it to the humanists to proclaim their moral virtue. We Christians are self-confessed sinners redeemed by a gracious God. For all of the Holy Spirit's work in our hearts, we remain imperfect, to say the least. So should we shy away from talking about this outside the privacy of our churches?

I don't think so. I have experienced God's transforming power in my life. Frankly, I am a better person than I would be without it. People who know me might marvel that this could be the case, but I know that it is. I have found church communities to be different than other groups of people, partly because of an understanding of the sort of teaching I have outlined, but also, I believe, because of characters being formed through God's moulding. If you doubt me, get involved in a Christian community and see what you find for yourself.

CONCLUSION

As an intellectual edifice, my faith rests on many supports, from the wonders of creation to my personal experience of encountering God. Within these reasons to believe are the ones I've discussed here.

Moral accountability is only possible if we have a supernatural element like the Christian concept of the soul. The very existence of the objective moral obligations that we all take for granted depends on God's existence. When I compare my culture's attempt to generate its own moral code with God's revealed moral will, I am repeatedly struck by the superiority of biblical teaching. The progressive change of heart needed to live more in accord with

God's character is brought about by God. I'm experiencing this myself, and I see it collectively in the church.

There are many visions of morality in the contemporary marketplace of ideas, but none compares to this.

That's why I (still) believe in following Jesus.

11

WHY I (STILL) BELIEVE IN HUMANITY

DAVID ROBERTSON

As G. K. Chesterton once quipped, when we lose our belief in God, it is not just God we lose but humanity. There are those who say they don't believe in God because they believe in humanity, but what I want to suggest to you is precisely the opposite. Without belief in God humanity is at stake.

For many people in our culture the big picture is the narrative that twenty-first-century liberal humanism teaches. This is the narrative that is predominant in education at all levels, in the secular media and amongst most politicians. It is taught as fact, although in reality it is a big picture story that does not really fit the facts.

In contemporary Western society, secular humanism is the default religion. It is one that assumes it is just superior to every other philosophy and that it alone has the correct understanding of humanity. Through the glasses of secular humanism, the whole of humanity — who we are, our history and our present — is reinterpreted.

Let me give one example. Diarmid MacCulloch recently had a three-part series on BBC2 entitled *On Sex and the Church*. He said that he thinks religion has got everything appallingly wrong and has been terrible for us in sexual terms. The basic resume of his position is: *before Christianity came on the scene, sex was a pleasure that people enjoyed in the Greco-Roman pagan paradise. But then along came Christianity, and especially St Paul and then Augustine, and lo and behold sexual repression entered into Western society. It has taken many hundreds of years, but now finally after the Enlightenment we are returning to those wonderful golden days. The only barrier remaining in the way is repressive religion, especially that of the Calvinists and the Catholics. In our brave new world people should be free to sleep with whoever they want, whenever they want. After all sex is just an appetite like eating. What's wrong with having a smorgasbord of love? As long as we don't harm anyone what's the problem?*

But there is another big picture — one which, for the moment, we are still allowed to teach, one upon which the whole of our society has been based. We are currently in the process of rejecting that picture, but maybe we should stop and consider. Maybe we are not heading to a secular sexual nirvana? Maybe we are heading into the pit of hell? Maybe, having exchanged the truth of God for a lie, we have been given over to every kind of depravity?

WHAT IS HUMANITY?

Psalm 8:4 asks the question: 'what is mankind that you are mindful of them, human beings that you care for them?' (NIV)

'What is man?' is the title of an essay by Martin Luther King published in 1959 in which he argues that humanity is more than an animal and less than God. It is the basic understanding of humanity that has prevailed in Europe and the West for most of the past two thousand years. It is an understanding of humanity that is, ironically, being destroyed by our secular humanists.

When we cease to believe in God, it is not just that we lose the sense of the divine — we also lose the sense of the human. That is why the ultimate in humanitarianism, or humanism, is to enable people to know God. In fact, without the divine we are missing an essential part of what it is to be human.

The Shorter Catechism (Question 10) sums up the biblical teaching nicely. 'How did God create man? God created man male and female, after his own image, in knowledge, righteousness, and holiness, with dominion over the creatures.'[1]

This involves:

- Gender — we are created male and female
- Identity — our identity is found in God
- Marriage — we are created for one another
- Society — we serve God and one another by following the Maker's instructions

But then things go wrong. The Fall of humanity described in Genesis has an enormous impact. The fallout is considerable — it affects the environment, society, and how we relate to one another and to God. It disturbs, disrupts and destroys our most basic relationships.

The basic difference between humanity before the Fall and humanity after, is that before the Fall we lived to do the will of God; after the Fall we are autonomous and seek to be as God. We do it our way. We go our own way. We are as gods — determining our own right and wrong. At least that was the promise of the devil. Autonomy is at the root of all our troubles. And autonomy is what our society demands and celebrates:

> *And now, the end is near*
> *And so I face the final curtain*
> *My friend, I'll say it clear*
> *I'll state my case, of which I'm certain*
> *I've lived a life that's full*
> *I've travelled each and every highway*
> *But more, much more than this*
> *I did it my way.*[2]

Sin is rebellion against God and an assertion of our own sovereignty and authority. No Christian with any biblical understanding would ever say — it's my body and I'll do with it what I want!

---

1   *The Westminster Shorter Catechism*, (Edinburgh: W. Blackwood & Sons Ltd., 1979), 116

2.   Song written by Paul Anka and popularised in 1969 by Frank Sinatra.

The secular humanist world view takes what humanists would like to be true today and interprets the past through that limited and fanciful view. The Christian world view interprets the present through the eyes of the past. Nowhere is this seen more clearly than in the areas of sex, sexuality and gender, to which we now turn.

SEXUALITY

In answer to the age-old question, 'Who am I?', our children today are being taught that sexuality is a key part, if not the key part, of our identity. Media, schools and the big corporations are pushing this as a given. And yet the notion of sexuality as identity is a relatively new one stemming from the late nineteenth century and especially from the work of Freud in the early twentieth.

Among the arguments in the church about sexuality one has stood out as the most powerful. It's what I call the Lady Gaga theory — *Born This Way.*

The initial reason for accepting the idea of an innate sexuality as normative came about because people argued — *what could be wrong if God made me this way?* But such a question betrays shallowness in understanding — of what humanity is, who God is and how the Fall has affected us. In more recent years the notion of a fixed sexuality is now being challenged by those who once argued that it was the very basis for accepting gay rights. Rather than 'God made me this way' we are now coming to a position where people get to choose their own sexuality. It becomes a question of self-identity. Fixed sexuality is becoming fluid sexuality. That's why in Britain today, although only around one per cent of young people will claim to be homosexual, two per cent will claim to be bisexual.

Recent studies have demonstrated:

> The understanding of sexual orientation as an innate, biologically fixed property of human beings — the idea that people are 'born that way' — is not supported by scientific evidence.

While there is evidence that biological factors such as genes and hormones are associated with sexual behaviours and attractions, there are no compelling causal biological explanations for human sexual orientation. While minor differences in the brain structures and brain activity between homosexual and heterosexual individuals have been identified by researchers, such neuro-biological findings do not demonstrate whether these differences are innate or are the result of environmental and psychological factors.

Longitudinal studies of adolescents suggest that sexual orientation may be quite fluid over the life course of some people, with one study estimating that as many as eighty per cent of male adolescents who report same-sex attraction no longer do so as adults (although the extent to which this figure reflects actual changes in same-sex attraction and not just artefacts of the survey process has been contested by some researchers). [3]

In this highly significant quote the gay rights activist Peter Tatchell argues for the end of homosexuality and heterosexuality altogether:

Overcoming homophobia will result in more people having gay sex but fewer people claiming gay identity. The medieval Catholic Church, despite all its obscurantism and intolerance, got one thing right. Homosexuality is not, it suggested, the special sin of a unique class of people but a temptation to which any mortal might succumb. [4]

He goes on to argue that anyone can and will sleep with whomever they want, not on the basis of sexuality but just simply on the basis of lust, if not 'love'.

Tatchell is winning the argument. In a recent survey more than half of young people in Britain said they saw sexuality as fluid. A *Daily Telegraph* article once stated that there were *no* women in Britain who were exclusively heterosexual. Yes — this is the mad world that we create when we seek to remake humanity in our own image rather than God's!

---

3. *New Atlantis* journal, 23.8.16.

4   http://www.petertatchell.net/lgbt_rights/queer_theory/goodbye_to_gay.htm;   accessed 26.8.17

One positive thing about this is the recognition that sexuality can actually change, although our liberal elites are a little confused on this one. On the one hand they want to ban reparative therapy, claiming that it is harmful because it goes against a person's innate sexuality; on the other hand, they are now teaching that we can choose our sexuality. I think that from a Christian perspective we can recognise that our sexualities can be confused and messed up and that in a fallen world, genetic, environmental and historical factors can each play their own role.

I am greatly impressed with those Christians who have come to terms with the fact that they are attracted to people of the same sex and yet refuse to self-define as homosexual. They prefer the more accurate term 'same sex attracted'. The *Living Out* website is a superb resource, designed as it is by people who 'experience same-sex attraction and yet are committed to what the Bible clearly says, and what the church has always taught, about marriage and sex'.[5]

Let's now move on to that most crucial of relationships — marriage and the family.

I am an IKEA Christian! I don't have a practical bone in my body so when I go to IKEA (as little as I can possibly manage!), I take home the packaged chair, open it up, count the screws, lay out the material and proceed to build. I follow the maker's instructions. For me that is what we need to do as humans in order to function and flourish — follow the Maker's instructions.

Marriage has been under attack for some time in other ways — through serial monogamy, easy divorce and pornography. In the past few decades queer theory activists like Peter Tatchell have sought to destroy marriage from a different angle. Just over a decade ago

---

5.   http://www.livingout.org/ The website was set up, it says, 'to articulate a perspective that is not often heard – that of men and women who are honest and open about their same-sex attraction, but who have discovered that obedience to Jesus in this area of life is fulfilling, healthy and authentic. We want people who experience same-sex attraction, those who self-identify as lesbian, gay, bisexual or transsexual (LGBT) or who are just questioning; their family and friends; their churches and pastors; and those investigating Christianity, to find here a plausible way of living out what Christians have consistently believed about marriage and sex.' Accessed 6.7.17.

he even wrote an article attacking homosexuals who wanted same-sex marriage, because he wanted to destroy marriage, not embrace it. He has now embraced same-sex marriage but I don't think his opinion has really changed. All that changed were the tactics. He knows that in order to destroy marriage all that had to happen was people like David Cameron, Barack Obama and others agreeing to 'redefine' marriage.

Those who thought that the redefinition of sexuality as an identity choice, followed by the redefinition of marriage, would be the end of the re-imaging of humanity, have already been proved wrong. Now we have moved on to the destruction of gender. Most people today have been brought up in a world where we were just male and female (aka Genesis). We no more got to choose our identity in terms of gender than we did in terms of skin colour or height. But this is now all changing.

The destruction of gender has come about through the adoption of the transgender movement as the *cause celebre* of the metro elites. It used to be the case that transgender was seen as a psychological disorder known as gender dysphoria. Now this has been removed and replaced with the politicised view that transgender has nothing to do with biology or medical process, but is rather just a matter of self-identity. In the Western societies that accept and impose this philosophy, it all becomes a matter of whatever anyone feels. You are, you can be, whatever you feel. Self-declaration is enough.

Why does this matter? All the evidence shows that transgender people are far more likely to self-harm, attempt suicide and have poor mental health. Some want to argue that this is because of the stigmatisation and all we need to do is change attitudes. But whilst that can clearly be a factor, it's not by any means clear that it is the only or even main reason.

If we all have the right to choose our gender, then gender really becomes meaningless — not least because gender is not, in this theory, limited to two. Now you can have your fifty-eight genders if you wish. In fact one activist told me that there are as many genders as there are people. You realise of course what is happening when you get to that stage? You're getting rid of gender altogether — that crucial part of being human.

The practical effects of this are phenomenal. For a start, it kills all women's sports. It will also put to an end the government's plans to have gender quotas in terms of politics and business. It's how you end up with the great restroom row in the United States.

The Scottish government is going to change the law to allow for non-binary gender — that is neither male nor female. In a recent article the *New York Times* celebrated the fact that Scotland has now become the most homosexual and transgender-friendly society in the world! They cited Bob Orr, the owner of Edinburgh's first LGBT bookshop: 'It's extraordinary: we have started a conversation about a genderless society. The boundaries are going. And that was always the point — that sexuality ceases to matter'.

Again what is happening here is that gender is moving from identity to self-identity. One aspect of this is the use of non-binary pronouns of which there are many! In New York there are now thirty-one protected gender identities (Facebook offers you fifty-eight, including, for example, androgyne, non-binary, pangender). You can be fined if you refuse to use the preferred pronoun. It is not just that speech is being confused; it is that freedom of speech is being taken away. In our attempt to become as God we are creating a new tower of Babel, enforced by the State.

But again we ask — where's the harm in gender fluidity? Apart from the mass confusion? For me the main thing about what is happening is that it is a form of child abuse. Let me explain.

It has long been recognised that the best context in which to bring up a child from birth to adulthood is within the context of a family, and that family has normally been understood as being a man and a woman and whatever offspring they may have. Much research on children in same-sex households shows that normal households with a mum and a dad are by far the better context in which to bring up kids. It should not be surprising to those of us who follow the maxim, 'follow the Maker's instructions', that children do better with mum and dad. For couples with children, the dissolution rate for same-sex couples is more than double that of heterosexual couples.

Children are a special case when addressing transgender issues. It is important to realise that only a minority of children who experience cross-gender identification will continue to do so into adolescence or adulthood. Eighty-four per cent of those who identify as transgender in childhood revert to their biological sex in adulthood.

I think that transgender people need help. It is a genuine psychological condition. But there is a world of difference between realising that a small group of people need help and support and thinking that this justifies attempting to change the whole way we view ourselves and bring up children.

Let us ask the question again — Where's the harm? The American College of Paediatricians has stated:

> Conditioning children into believing a lifetime of chemical and surgical impersonation of the opposite sex is normal and healthful is child abuse. Endorsing gender discordance as normal via public education and legal policies will confuse children and parents, leading more children to present to 'gender clinics' where they will be given puberty-blocking drugs. This, in turn, virtually ensures that they will 'choose' a lifetime of carcinogenic and otherwise toxic cross-sex hormones, and likely consider unnecessary surgical mutilation of their healthy body parts as young adults.[6]

Let me put it very simply and quite straightforwardly. When the Scottish government says that it is going to enforce and promote a radical culture that says that children can choose their own gender, it is engaging in organised, systematic, state-enforced child abuse. And in case you think this is some kind of fanciful horror story from the future — let me tell you about a seven-year-old girl who came home from school the other week and told her parents that she had been taught in school she could choose whether she wanted to be a boy or a girl. This is happening now.

---

6 Matt Barber in Worldnetdaily.com, 18.3.16; http://www.wnd.com/2016/03/transgender-conditioning-is-child-abuse/; accessed 26.8.17.

It is important to understand that in our post-truth society the promotion of transgender and gender fluidity has nothing to do with facts or truth. It is political and sexual ideology being imposed on the rest of us by those who regard themselves as the cultural and social elites. Their position is 'right' and anyone who dares question it is obviously an idiot, a homophobe or a transphobe — and probably all three! The BBC for example is now proposing to indoctrinate children into this ideology through its children's channel.

This gender fluid/gender identity revolution will have a tremendous impact upon society. There is a price to be paid for the enforcement of this ideology.

a) There is a cost in terms of **political freedom and democracy**. One of the key issues here is that we are moving from a Christian liberal democracy based upon the understanding that all human beings are made equally in the image of God, to a human rights democracy where human rights are treated like a religion and where these human rights are defined by the elites, and, moreover, are constantly changing. What is happening is that democracy is being done away with. The new ideology will be enforced by the legal system and the police. We now have 'protected beliefs' — even if you do not agree with them, it would be illegal to refuse to promote them.

b) The same thing happens in **the media and general culture**. The Dundee Book Prize was recently won by an American author whose book was a coming-out story about a trans teenager. The BBC has had a series of documentaries and news items about trans subjects. I remember one news item I was involved in, where they sent a film crew to record my thoughts and broadcast twenty seconds of it in an item lasting almost five minutes. Most of the rest of the time was taken up with a sympathetic story portrayal of a transgender couple. Nice narrative versus short nasty religious sound-bite. It was propaganda at its worst. And it never stops. And all this for less than 0.1% of the population. This narrative is now being taught through our media, soap operas and social media. Woe betide anyone who dares challenge it.

This new sexual philosophy of humanity is being reinforced in our politics through government-sponsored lobbying agencies to ensure that everyone has to stay on track with their new philosophy of humanity.

c) And above all it has become the focus of **our education system**. There is a massive experiment in social engineering that is beginning at the school near you soon, if it has not already begun. We are told that the police should come into schools and talk about homophobic and transphobic crimes. I know of a primary school that was setting up (unknown to the parents) a children's LGBT committee to ensure right attitudes — why does this remind me of Chairman Mao's little Red Brigades? And the signposts saying 'boys' and 'girls' were being removed from the toilets. A government-funded agency has given another group £200,000 to spread their propaganda, which amongst other things promotes puberty blockers for pre-teens and urges teachers not to use the terms boy/girl/he/she! This is not the future — this is happening now.

d) There is a cost in terms of **economics**. It costs around £40-£50,000 per year for each child refugee taken into care. These children are refugees from war and poverty. And in my view it is correct that a wealthy nation like ours does all we can to help. There are hundreds of such children. But there are hundreds of thousands of children who are refugees and victims from the war on marriage, the attack on humanity, coming because of humanity's pride and arrogance in seeking to go against the Maker's instructions. Who is counting the cost of the social disintegration that is occurring because of the foolish attempt not only to reinvent the family, but also to reimage humanity?

WHERE ARE WE GOING?

If we take away humanity made in the image of God, if we try to reimage according to our own imaginations, then we will continue to go down this road to hell. C. S. Lewis saw this decades ago. The third part of his sci-fi trilogy, *That Hideous Strength,* described with eerie precision where we are going.

What's the next *cause celebre* for those who are seeking to unmake humanity? I suspect it will be transhuman. In terms of the continuing attack on marriage it will be polyamory[7] and polygamy. I also suspect that incest will become increasing acceptable, with sympathetic depictions in the media being followed by some celebrity cases and justified by the 'love means love' tag.

A while ago I spoke at a debate in Aberdeen. The older people present, including a gay couple with whom I got on really well, agreed with my statement that polygamy and incest would be a step too far. But what astounded me was that a significant number of the under thirties could not see a problem. And indeed given the criteria for SSM (why stop people who love one another from marrying), there is actually no logical reason to prevent that.

What about paedophilia? This is different. This is the big one. For some reason after the 1970s paedophilia became the great sin — only to be overtaken in recent years by homophobia. I thought this would remain the case but I have now changed my mind. In my view within the next decade some forms of paedophilia will become acceptable. Already the first steps are being made.

It's a sexuality. In July 2010 the Harvard Mental Health Letter stated that 'paedophilia is a sexual orientation and unlikely to change. Treatment aims to enable someone to resist acting on his sexual urges'.

In 2015 the American Psychiatric Association classified paedophilia as a sexual orientation. Several years ago, at the end of a debate on gay adoption, I was accosted by some supporters of Peter Tatchell. Much to the horror of my opponent they told me

---

7. The practice of or desire for intimate relationships with more than one partner, with the knowledge of all partners.

that if they babysat my children (then aged seven and eight), they would teach them to 'experiment sexually' because that was good for children.

While addressing the paedophile North American Man/Boy Love Association, or NAM/BLA, a prominent gay rights activist said the following:

> It seems to me that in the gay community the people who should be running interference for NAM/BLA are the parents and friends of gays. Because if the parents and friends of gays are truly friends of gays, they would know from their gay kids that the relationship with an older man is precisely what 13-, 14-, and 15-year-old kids need more than anything else in the world. And they would be welcoming this, and welcoming the opportunity for young gay kids to have the kind of experience that they would need.[8]

Not only polygamy and paedophilia but also increased acceptance of pornography and prostitution (what is now classed as 'sex work', as though selling your body were somehow a job) are regarded as acceptable. Because we no longer believe in God, we no longer believe in humanity and thus the boundaries which recognise our humanity are slowly being removed. Because of this I also believe that we will end up with increased abortion and with euthanasia. Why? Because children in the womb who are unwanted become inconvenient, as do older people who are unproductive.

Our rejection of God means that we are also rejecting:

a) Rationality, logic and truth. We were made logos in the image of the Logos. We were made in knowledge, righteousness and holiness. When we reject the source we also will ultimately lose the fruits. So we are moving from a world where rationality, logic and truth are presupposed to one where irrationality, confusion and lies are the predominating factors. What we feel is true matters far more than what is true. In this crazy mixed up world it means that if I feel that I am a five-foot Chinese woman, then I am a five-foot Chinese woman. This is what the post-truth world is.

---

8. Speaker at North American MBL Association meeting in 1983.

b) Family, church and society. These will be replaced by individuality, corporation and disintegration.

c) Love, peace and goodness will be replaced by hatred, strife and immorality.

> *Yeah, my blood's so mad, feels like coagulatin',*
> *I'm sittin' here, just contemplatin',*
> *I can't twist the truth, it knows no regulation,*
> *Handful of Senators don't pass legislation,*
> *And marches alone can't bring integration,*
> *When human respect is disintegratin',*
> *This whole crazy world is just too frustratin',*
> *And you tell me over and over and over again my friend,*
> *Ah, you don't believe we're on the eve of destruction.*[9]

CONCLUSION

I believe in God because I believe in humanity. I believe in humanity because I believe in God. Perhaps it's better to say that I am more concerned about individual human beings than 'humanity' in general. Even as I have been writing this I have been thinking of individual stories of those who are affected by these issues: the student who had been raped, the confused transgender teenager, the transgender lecturer and transgender lawyer I met some twenty-five years ago. I often speak with those who face homosexual temptations or those who have committed adultery. There are people who are trapped in internet porn, those who are victims of child sexual abuse and those who think they have to prostitute themselves to make a living. Each of them is a human being made in the image of God.

As well as the individual stories there are what I call 'the middle stories', the cultural trends — one year it's sexuality, another

---

9.   *Eve of Destruction, song written by P. F. Sloan in 1964 and recorded by Barry McGuire in July 1965 (Dunhill Records).*

it's trans. What will it be next year? We don't counter this by Christendom, by British values or American values or Scottish values. We need to go to the real big story.

The big story is of course the gospel, the good news of the God who so loved the world that He gave His only begotten Son. It is the good news of the God who first of all created humanity and saw it spoiled by sin and evil, and now is recreating humanity in His image. Because I believe in this God who is the Saviour of the world, I know that humanity has real hope.

All you need is love. There is so much ugliness in this world, so much brokenness and much of that is expressed in, and increased by, human brokenness and relational and sexual dysfunction. Can the lost be redeemed, the ugly made beautiful? Yes, there is the ultimate makeover. God is love. And His way is the way of love. The way of Christ is the way of beauty.

This has been the message of the good news since the New Testament and it remains our message today. It is summed up by the African church leader, Augustine:[10]

> Let us love, because he first loved us. For how should we love, except he had first loved us? By loving we became friends: but he loved us as enemies, that we might be made friends. He first loved us, and gave us the gift of loving him. We did not yet love him: by loving we are beautiful ... But our soul, my brothers, is unlovely because of iniquity: by loving God it becomes lovely. What a love it must be that makes the lover beautiful! But God is always lovely, never unlovely, never changeable. He who is always lovely first loved us; and what were we when he loved us but foul and unlovely? But he did not leave us foul; no, but he changed us, and out of the unlovely makes us lovely. How shall we become lovely? By loving him who was always lovely. As the love increases anew, so the loveliness increases: for love is itself the beauty of the soul ... How do we find Jesus beautiful?

---

10.   In his *Homily Nine* on 1 John.

Secular humanism will lead to the destruction of humanity; Christianity leads to its recreation.

That is why I (still) believe in God — because I am a real humanist.

12

WHY I (STILL) BELIEVE IN LIFE

NOLA LEACH

'Christian love is a way of saying to another it is good that you exist, it is good that you are in the world.'[1] Each human life is of inestimable value. Life is precious.

But increasingly today life is cheap and the most dangerous place for a baby is in the mother's womb.

For other people judgments are being made about whether their life remains of value. These are sensitive issues to address and we must be mindful of the emotions involved. For example, what does it say to a woman contemplating the painful decision — and usually it is painful — of whether or not to have an abortion if we stridently condemn her with the words 'abortion kills'? Our response must be more nuanced. Similarly we know that there are many with experiences of inadequate end-of-life care and family and friends who have been torn apart watching loved ones suffer.

How do we hold to Christian truth that all life is precious against the voices saying that this is out of date and just plain wrong? In this chapter I want to argue that we have a God who wants good for

---

1.   Josef Pieper: *About Love*, trans. Richard and Clara Winston (Chicago Franciscan Herald Press, 1974), 19.

us. Moreover we are called to work for the good of society. Jesus came to bring life in all its fullness.

God's ways are just and if we follow them we will flourish. It is not, therefore, surprising that, despite voices to the contrary, many in society today, believers and unbelievers, are arguing for life.

In an age of individualism, to assert that my life is valuable is seemingly a good thing. Yet today's culture has taken this truth and distorted it. Nowhere is this clearer than in the abortion debate. 'What I want is all that matters; it is my body and my right to choose. I am autonomous', the argument runs. In an age of consumerism I say 'I want' and in an age of relativism I can say 'why not?' In a technological age we can fix it. There is no doubt that societal and cultural views have shifted and freedom to choose one's own destiny has become all. Therefore to hold any contrary view is out of date, wrong and uncaring.

However, as the German philosopher, Josef Pieper, says, existence is good and for both biblical and societal reasons this contrary view is more important than ever.

THE BEGINNING OF LIFE

Let us look at beginning of life issues first.

The figures are staggering. While exact statistics are difficult to obtain, there were 185,122 abortions recorded in England and Wales in 2012.[2] It is fair to say we are probably talking about 200,000 a year now. In recent years, ninety-seven per cent of all legal abortions have been carried out for social reasons.[3] It has been estimated that more human beings have been killed by abortion in forty years than in all the wars in recorded human history.[4]

There are those who would have us believe that the foetus is just a bunch of cells, yet technology is challenging this. The ability to

---

2. Department of Health: *Abortion Statistics, England and Wales: 2012.*

3. *Ibid.*

4. Society for the Protection of the Unborn Child 2015: http://spuc-director.blogspot. it/2015/10/more-human-beings-killed-by-abortion-in.html Accessed 5.7.17.

photograph the development of the embryo week by week means women are seeing the developing form of a baby. This is clear by the language that women, and men, use. A pregnant woman says, 'I am having a baby', not 'this is a cluster of cells'.

Staggeringly at the size of a poppy seed at five weeks the tiny heart begins beating, at six weeks the intestines and brain are beginning to develop, by nine weeks basic physiology is in place, and by eleven the baby is almost fully formed. By the time of the twelve week scan reflexes kick in and it begins to open its fingers, curl its toes and the mouth makes sucking movements.

Moreover, pregnant women's actions change. Counsellors tell us that even women seeking abortions are not eating certain foods in case it damages the baby and they often find themselves looking at baby clothes. Recently, and rightly, there has been an outcry, sometimes from the most unlikely places, against abortion on the grounds of gender, but if it is wrong to abort a female because she is female why is it not wrong to abort a male because he is a male?

One of the most notable changes in direction has recently come from the liberal scientific think tank of the Netherlands where Liberal writer Charlotte Lockefeer-Maas, the editor of *Liberaal Reveil,* concludes that the current abortion law is against the liberal principle that 'every life has value'.[5] This includes the life of the baby below twenty-four weeks. She writes, 'Terminating a pregnancy is killing a living human life.' The mother's self-determination is not sustainable. Even after rape this is the case. One cannot justify evil with another evil. She goes on to say that one must recognise that life begins at conception; 'the smallest embryo is valuable in itself', she amazingly says.

Over the years we have failed women. Abortion is not good for women. There is a growing body of evidence that women who have abortions may be at an increased risk of mental health disorders, even when there is no history of mental health problems,[6] and

---

5   http://www.refdag.nl/nieuws/politiek/liberale_publiciste_abortus_botst_met_liberale_ principes_1_964027 Accessed 5.7.17.

6.   Fergusson, Horwood, Boden, *Abortion and mental health disorders: evidence from 30-year longitudinal study* (British Journal of Psychiatry, November 2008. Vol. 193), 6.

strong evidence points to a link with subsequent preterm birth.[7] There is even evidence of increased susceptibility to breast cancer. Stories of inadequate counselling and even the pre-signing of forms by doctors are emerging. A recent newspaper article highlighted sixty-seven doctors doing just this and possible prosecutions are pending.[8]

Of course there will be the arguments over when life actually begins, but this is to miss the point. God calls all life into existence. This is an amazing mystery. Psalm 139:13 proclaims God's sovereign knowledge of us individually: 'you formed my inward parts; you knitted me together in my mother's womb'. We are indeed 'fearfully and wonderfully made'. God knew us when He called us into being. Jeremiah reminds us that God says, 'Before I formed you in the womb I knew you' (Jer. 1:5). We have to hold together the immaterial and the material, the already and the not yet. The human embryo is in the process of becoming what it already is; it is an embryonic human. Our creation was intentional.

Moreover, Genesis reminds us that we are image-bearers of God, made in His image, a reflection of His character and being. We derive our meaning from outside ourselves, made of the dust (Gen. 2:7), made into a family (Gen. 5). As John Stott has written, 'It is God's grace which confers on the unborn child, from the moment of its conception, both the unique status which it already enjoys and the unique destiny which it will later inherit. It is grace which holds together the duality of the actual and the potential, the already and the not yet'.[9]

The Christian faith teaches that in the person of Jesus we see God's final vote of confidence in the original human model. When God breaks into human history He comes as an original and unique human being. When Mary visits Elizabeth, Elizabeth sees Mary

---

7. Hardy, Benjamin, Adenhaim, *Effect of induced abortions on early preterm births and adverse perinatal outcomes* (Journal of Obstetrics and Gynaecology Canada 2013 Vol 35), 2.

8. http://www.telegraph.co.uk/news/uknews/law-and-order/10795793/MPs-demand-police-inquiry-over-pre-signed-abortion-forms.html. Accessed 5.7.17.

9. John Stott: *Issues Facing Christians Today*, 4th Edition (Zondervan), 403.

as 'the mother of my Lord' (Luke 1:43, NIV), and in turn her baby leaps in her womb as he recognises God's Son.

The Bible repeatedly emphasises the preciousness of life and says that we should do all we can to protect the vulnerable, weak, poor and needy.

Threats to this preciousness can also be seen in attempts to legalise Physician Assisted Suicide and Euthanasia.

END OF LIFE

In recent years the campaign for the right to end one's life if it is unbearable has grown exponentially. If the safeguards are there, what is the problem? However, even the arch proponent of physician-assisted dying, Lord Falconer, has admitted that there can never be fully effective safeguards. Indeed, it remains those closest to the dying who are most strongly against a change in the law — doctors, palliative care practitioners — not to mention disability groups.

We need to be clear what we are in fact talking about, as Professor John Wyatt reminds us in his book *A Right to Die?* Language frequently precedes and accompanies a change in ethical behaviour. Euthanasia is the intentional killing, by act or omission, of a person whose life is thought not to be worth living. This can be voluntary (the patient requests it) or involuntary (without the patient's consent) — a doctor administering a lethal injection. Doctor-assisted suicide is also intentional medical killing, but the final act is performed by the patient. 'Assisted Dying' is a disingenuous euphemism variously defined but includes both.

In the UK both of these are illegal, but the argument to change the law is generally gaining ground in society.

The main arguments are on the basis of compassion and autonomy.

THE ARGUMENT FROM COMPASSION

If someone is in considerable pain they need to have their suffering ended — it is the loving thing to do. This resonates with the man and woman in the street and at one level is a powerful argument, which even those within the church have espoused. God calls us to love those who are suffering; this is love in action.

Former Archbishop of Canterbury, George Carey, has written:

> When suffering is so great that some patients, already knowing that they are at the end of their life make repeated pleas to die, it seems a denial of that loving compassion which is the hallmark of Christianity to refuse to allow them to fulfil their own clearly stated request after of course a proper process of safeguards has been observed. If we truly love our neighbours as ourselves, how can we deny them the death that we would wish for ourselves in such a condition?[10]

In 2014 Desmond Tutu argued that laws to prevent people from ending their lives were an affront to those affected and their families. Many, like Lord Joffee who introduced an Assisted Dying Bill in 2006 at Westminster, did so out of concern for those who are suffering, but as H. L. Mencken wrote 'There's always an easy solution to every human problem — neat, plausible and wrong'.[11]

THE ARGUMENT FROM AUTONOMY

This argument claims that every person has the right to choose the manner and timing of their death. From the Enlightenment onwards in one's private life and in morality the individual is sovereign. In liberal thought it is the choice which is good in itself regardless of what that choice is. Indeed the word autonomy itself means self-rule. The English author of fantasy novels, Terry Pratchett, argued that everyone had the right to determine the time and manner of their death, but this is not as simple as it sounds. John Wyatt reflects:

---

10. Lord Carey of Clifton: Assisted Dying Bill second reading debate; House of Lords, 18th July 2014.

11. H. L. Mencken: *A Mencken Chrestomathy* (Vintage Books, 1949), 443.

What kind of society would it be that assisted people to kill themselves for any reason whatsoever? A society that provided lethal medications for depressed individuals with suicidal thoughts, that provided humane alternative methods of self destruction for people threatening to throw themselves off a cliff or in front of a train, that made suicide an easy process for the lonely, elderly, disabled, or despairing people. Is this the kind of society that is being proposed and is this a society that we would honestly wish to belong to?[12]

RIGHT TO DIE

This self-rule is a desire to be more like the Creator than the created.

We do not have this autonomy. There is no provision in Scripture for compassionate killing even at a person's request. All human life belongs to God. 'The earth is the LORD's and everything in it' (Ps. 24:1; NIV). 'The LORD brings death and makes alive; he brings down to the grave and raises up' (1 Sam. 2:6; NIV). 'My times are in your hands' (Ps. 31:15; NIV). My life is not mine to do with as I please; it is God who determines its beginning and its end. Life is a gift from Him.

As Gilbert Meilaender wrote, 'We are most ourselves, not when we seek to direct and control our destiny, but when we recognise and admit that our life is grounded in and sustained by God'. [13]

We are not defined by our genetic makeup. This does not explain who we are. Our ultimate identity comes from outside of ourselves, from God (Gen. 1:26). As we have already seen, human life is not just a gift of God's grace, amazing as this fact is, but it is a reflection of His very being. To destroy a human life is therefore a profound insult to the being and character of God Himself. That is why there is a taboo against the shedding of blood; it is linked to the indwelling image of God.

---

12. John Wyatt, *Right to Die?* (IVP, 2015), 85.

13. *Bioethics. A Primer for Christians* (Wm. B. Eerdmans Publishing, 2013), Chapter 1 – Christian Vision.

Euthanasia, being the intentional killing of another human being, contravenes the profound moral order of the structure of the created universe which is written on our hearts. It is therefore morally wrong; it is also dangerous.

'SAFEGUARDS'

Let us return briefly to the so-called safeguards often proposed to illustrate this.

In the 2015 attempt to change the law in Westminster it was suggested that the individual should be terminally ill with only six months to live and must enter into the process voluntarily.

However, the process of determining exactly how long an individual will live is extremely difficult. In Oregon, often held up as the model to be followed, one in four doctors said they would not be confident to determine a six-month life expectancy.[14] Some patients who had been prescribed lethal medication and chose not to take the drugs subsequently went on to live for up to another thirty two months — their very lifespan demonstrates the challenge of accurate prognosis and the weakness of this 'safeguard'.

It is also likely that a doctor would be under a positive obligation to suggest this course of action if it becomes regarded as medical treatment. Two doctors — a consultant and an independent doctor — should agree the patient is eligible. This poses problems, as the second doctor would not necessarily know the patient or even have the expertise required and so called 'doctor shopping' could result. If we are saying one doctor cannot make an accurate prediction, then neither can two or four or ten.

Moreover, the process completely changes the doctor/patient relationship. It is the duty of a doctor to help the sick and never to injure or harm them.

A safeguard has been suggested that a doctor cannot suggest assisted dying to a patient but in reality in preparing a patient for

---

14. Ganzini L, Nelson HD, Lee MA et al, *Oregon Physicians' Attitudes About and Experiences with End-of-Life Care Since Passage of the Death with Dignity Act* (in Journal of the American Medical Association 285, 2001), 2363.

death he would at the very least be saying this was an option. In Oregon, Physician Assisted Suicide (PAS) has been integrated into medical practice to the extent that 'a patient was refused chemotherapy but offered assisted suicide because it was covered under her insurance plan'.[15] This story highlights the most dramatic shift that the legalisation of PAS would entail — doctors are no longer employed to sustain life as long as possible. The doctor/patient contract is therefore permanently altered. The trust between doctor and patient is threatened. Who is making the judgment on whose life is worth living and whose not?

No longer are doctors always trusted to sustain life but they are given the power to take it away. If a patient seeking PAS is turned down by one doctor, there is nothing stopping them approaching another doctor — the medical service effectively becomes PAS 'on demand'.

It is proposed that the patient must have mental capacity to make the decision, but depression can affect one's judgment. Often terminally ill patients swing from hope to depression and back again. According to the Royal College of Psychiatrists many doctors do not know how to diagnose depression. How many of those surviving suicide attempts later regret their actions when seen from outside the cloud of depression? How serious then that doctors could be allowed to act on what could be a patient's depressive thought. Even a safeguard requiring a 'cooling off' period between the request for assistance being formally accepted and the life-ending prescription being issued does not take seriously the danger of long-term depression.

Real concerns exist regarding transparency and monitoring. Doctors have to be the people to report data to the state, but they are a self-selecting group and some may not report their actions. In the Netherlands as of 2005 an estimated twenty per cent[16] of cases were not reported and an advocate of the Oregon law has argued

---

15. *Death Drugs Cause Uproar in Oregon*: ABC News 2008; http://abcnews.go.com/Health/story?id=5517492&page=1. Accessed 5.7.17.

16. Van Der Heide A, et al, *End-of-Life Practices in the Netherlands under the Euthanasia Act* (New England Journal of Medicine, May 2007, Volume 365), 19.

that other US States should not have 'the needless and intrusive burden of government reporting'.[17]

The argument from autonomy poses the view that it is only the patient concerned who is affected. This is not the case. A cursory look at the safeguards illustrates the truth that the medical profession is affected. The Hippocratic Oath was a groundbreaking shift in practice. Until then in the primitive world the sorcerer and the doctor were often one and the same with the power to kill and to cure. With the Greeks the profession was dedicated to life under all circumstances. This would change and it is still the case that the majority of medical practitioners working with patients at the end of their lives do not want the responsibility which would come with this change.

In cases of Physician Assisted Suicide, patients take the lethal dose of barbiturates themselves. The doctor is not present, but what happens if it does not work? Based on the figures from Oregon and applied to the UK, forty-seven people would regurgitate the medication every year and thirteen regain consciousness.[18] Medical staff would have to step in which would be very traumatic.

Behind the fear of losing control is a false individualism. We are not a series of isolated individuals, but persons in relation to persons. As we have already seen we are born into families. Family members are always affected. Talking of his desire to end his own life, the late Terry Pratchett said that his wife did not want him to end his life; she wanted to care for him. Anecdotally doctors tell of subsequent depression in family members who have witnessed a loved one visiting Dignitas.[19]

Assisted suicide is never a private act. Nobody chooses it in isolation. Euthanasia and assisted suicide are matters of public

---

17. *What we know from Oregon's 'Death with Dignity' Experiment* (Huffington Post 9th October 2011).

18. *Oregon's Death with Dignity Act Report 2013*. This is based on the known data set of what has occurred in 510 of the 752 deaths in Oregon. This includes 6 who have regained consciousness. 4% have regurgitated. 1% has regained consciousness.

19. A Swiss clinic that provides assisted/accompanied suicide to people who suffer from terminal illness and/or severe physical and/or mental illnesses.

concern because they involve one person facilitating the death of another. Journalist George Pitcher wrote of the 'profound adverse effects on the social fabric of our society, on our attitudes towards each people's deaths and illnesses, on our attitudes towards those who are ill and have disabilities'.[20]

Cynically, but I would argue, realistically, economics will inevitably come into play. In 2008 Baroness Mary Warnock stated, 'If you're demented, you're wasting people's lives — your families' lives, and you're wasting the resources of the National Health Service'.[21] By the year 2030 it is estimated that there will be 15.5 million elderly people in the UK.[22] Currently there are three million over eighty years old. One in four people will be over sixty-five by 2050. Physician-assisted suicide would save money that could be put to better use.

I remember talking with a Consultant in palliative care shocked at the stories she told of unscrupulous relatives in these situations. Many sick and older people feel a burden emotionally and economically on their families. To end their life would release that burden.

The same Consultant wrote of the moving story of her mother's experience. Nearing the end of her life, she felt the quality of life was no longer there; she wanted to die. Thankfully, conversations with a wise hospital chaplain gradually made her feel of worth again. She lived for another four years, experiencing the joys of family life, seeing grandchildren born, enjoying outings. If the law to enable physician-assisted suicide had been there, she would have taken that option. Instead, the Consultant wrote, 'I am so glad she didn't and, what is more, so was she'.

The ultimate argument from autonomy states that we can control the dangers. We cannot. One only has to look at the slippery slope in Europe where in the Netherlands legalising assisted suicide led to

---

20. On Radio 4, 3rd June 2009.

21. *Dementia sufferers may have a 'duty to die'* (The Telegraph, 18th September 2008).

22. *Older, healthier and working: Britons say no to retirement* (The Guardian, 24th August 2013).

213

the widespread killing of the sick. In thirty years they have moved from euthanasia for the terminally ill to euthanasia of those who are chronically ill; from euthanasia for physical illness to euthanasia for mental illness; from mental illness to psychological distress or mental suffering; and now simply to the person over seventy who is 'tired of living'. Professor Theo Boer, a former supporter of assisted suicide, told Parliament that the practice changed from being a last resort to normal procedure. Assisted deaths increased by about fifteen per cent every year since 2008.[23] Twelve per cent of all deaths in the Netherlands are now at the hands of doctors.[24] In Belgium there was a twenty-seven per cent surge in numbers of these deaths in one year when Belgium legalised euthanasia, and between 2002 and 2012 there was a five-hundred per cent increase in euthanasia deaths and it is now even legal for children to be euthanised.[25]

Very soon consciences are dulled and medical professionals cope because it is part of their job. As one medical practitioner recalled, 'The first time I had to euthanize a patient it was terrible, I agonised over it. The second time it was easier and the third time it was a piece of cake'.

A POSITIVE MESSAGE

This culture of death is so far removed from what the Bible teaches. 'Give justice to the weak and the fatherless; maintain the right of the afflicted and the destitute. Rescue the weak and the needy', says Psalm 82:3-4. Paul urges us, 'Bear one another's burdens, and so fulfil the law of Christ' (Gal. 6:2).

We may well understand that someone does not want to be a burden on others, but we are designed to be part of others, caring for each other. Dependence is the essence of love. This is a biblical principle. Joseph Pieper talks of love as a way of affirming the

---

23. *Euthanasia in the Netherlands in Out of Control* (Life Site News 25th September 2015).

24. *Number of mentally ill patients killed by euthanasia in Holland trebles in a year as doctors warn assisted suicide is 'out of control'* (The Daily Mail, 13th October 2014).

25. *Ibid.*

value of someone's life. If we kill them we are in effect saying their life is worthless.

John Donne's famous words, 'No man is an island, entire of itself ... any man's death diminishes me because I am involved in Mankind',[26] ring true, and Christianity teaches a much better way. Yes, suffering and old age are real challenges, but there is no situation, however awful and apparently meaningless, which cannot in some sense be transformed by God's grace and power. God is redeeming suffering, bringing blessing and healing out of evil and pain.

A large number of people have found richness and purpose despite pain and hardship. I recall the wonderful witness of a dear friend of mine suffering from motor neurone disease. She was a nurse and so knew well what a terrible death she might face; yet as she lost more and more control of her body her faith became stronger. Her husband said that he never heard her complain. Her nurses spoke of the radiance of her faith and, right up until the day she died, she was blessing people.

Or who can forget Matthew Hampson, the young rugby player who, after collapsing in a scrum, was left paralysed from the neck down, requiring a ventilator to breathe, who then divided his time between raising money for spinal care, coaching youngsters at local schools, and writing columns for magazines.

This is the celebration of life created by God for His glory. When we care for the person affected by disease or dementia with genuine respect, sacrificial love and compassion we are pointing to a future hope. We care for people not in the light of what they once were but what they will become. This life is not the end of the story. There is a new creation.

John Wyatt has written of the Christian hope:

Our resurrection bodies will put us in right relationships with one another and with the cosmos. To be embodied is to be in relationship and that remains the case with our resurrection bodies. In the new heaven and the new earth there will be no sickness that

26. John Donne, 1624; extract from Meditation 17.

needs healing, and no tears that need comforting, But there will be greeting and blessing, laughter and love, joy and peace. Our relationships with others will be healed and redeemed.[27]

The duty of the law is to protect. It is right therefore that those who believe in the value of life should do all they can to defeat attempts to change the law. As Tim Keller powerfully reminds us in his book *Generous Justice,* the God of Scripture is a God of justice as well as salvation.

Throughout Scripture the inestimable worth of each individual called into being by God, His image-bearer, made a little lower than God Himself (Psalm 8), means we have no option but to believe in life now and always. Rather than lead people to an untimely death, as Christians we should nurture life, love and hope.

For all of these reasons, I (still) believe in life.

---

27.   John Wyatt, *Right to Die?* (IVP, 2015).

13

WHY I (STILL) BELIEVE IN MARRIAGE

Gordon Macdonald

There are three reasons why I (still) believe in marriage as a relationship which is exclusively between a man and woman with a lifelong commitment and which has a public dimension:

- First, as someone with an interest in history, the Christian tradition and teaching on marriage is important and should not be lightly discarded.
- Second, I have come to realise the extent to which marriage reveals the character and nature of God to creation.
- Third, marriage is good for community stability, and marital breakdown is detrimental to the well-being of human society.

THE CHALLENGE FOR THE CHURCH

Faced with the challenges of high levels of cohabitation, family breakdown and the redefinition of marriage in the civil law to include same-sex relationships, Christians face increasing pressure to accommodate a diversity of expressions of sexuality and sexual relationships within the life and practice of our churches. Many church ministers for pastoral reasons find it difficult to refuse to marry a couple if one of the parties has previously been divorced. Similar pressures are already emerging in relation to the 'marriage' of same-sex couples, with some Christian denominations indicating their willingness to 'marry' same-sex couples.[1] In order to be equipped to resist this pressure, it is necessary to return to first principles derived from the creation narrative contained in the Bible.

SCRIPTURAL FOUNDATIONS

The biblical creation narrative tells us that life originates from the spoken word of God, that the earth did not come into existence by chance or create itself, and that human beings are created in God's image. We understand also that humans are spiritual as well as physical beings. We are created distinct from animals, have responsibility to be stewards of the earth, and are instructed to make use of its resources so that human life may flourish. We understand that the creation of two sexes is an objective fact, that as a species we should marry and procreate in obedience to our Creator, and that God's intent is to have fellowship with human beings. These principles are essential to the Christian understanding of what makes for human flourishing and societal well-being. They are principles which have shaped human societies over the millennia.

The Christian understanding of marriage and its role in society has its roots in the Old Testament and early Judaism. Specifically,

---

1.　These include the Rheinische Evangelische Kirche and the Scottish Episcopal Church. See www.christiantoday.com/article/german.evangelical.church.votes.for.same.sex. marriage/76974.htm Accessed 4.7.17. On 8th June 2017, the General Synod of the Scottish Episcopal Church 'voted in favour of altering the church's Canon on Marriage to remove the definition that marriage is between a man and a woman and add a new section that acknowledges that there are different understandings of marriage which now allows clergy to solemnise marriage between same sex couples as well as couples of the opposite sex. The revised canon also stipulates that no member of clergy will be required to solemnise a marriage against their conscience.' Quoted from http://www.scotland. anglican.org/church-votes-allow-equal-marriage Accessed 4.7.17. Also, on 25th May 2017 the General Assembly of the Church of Scotland approved a report which could pave the way to allow ministers to conduct same-sex marriages in the future. http:// www.churchofscotland.org.uk/news_and_events/news/recent/church_a_step_closer_ to_conducting_same_sex_marriages Accessed 4.7.17.

the Israelites saw marriage within the context of procreation, preserving the future of the nation and imparting faith in the one true God to the next generation.[2] Marriage was viewed positively and as a duty in response to God's command to 'Be fruitful and multiply and fill the earth and subdue it' (Gen. 1:28). An Israelite's sense of self was rooted in his/her national identity and the relationship that existed between God and His people.[3]

Within Israelite society, two perspectives on the creation narrative and its implications for marriage developed. The first saw marriage as being primarily about protecting male progeny. The second interpreted the law and prophetic writings to argue in favour of a more equal relationship between, and with distinct roles for, husband and wife. This was based on the conclusion that the image of God was reflected in both Adam and Eve and that the latter's creation indicated that man was not to 'stand alone' or to be divinised.[4] In ancient Israel, therefore, there was an awareness of the prophetic nature of marriage as a witness to the relationship between God and the Jewish nation. There was also the understanding that marriage reminds human beings that we are created and are not divine.

The covenant relationship established between God and Abraham in Genesis 15, later reiterated in the giving of the Law to Israel at Mount Sinai, reflects the marital analogy. The key characteristic of a covenant is that it is a permanent legal agreement. As the covenant between God and Abraham is everlasting, so the marriage covenant is lifelong.

The marital analogy recurs throughout the Old Testament. Often the references are to the breakdown of the relationship, owing to the idolatrous practices of the Israelites. Such practices were accompanied by sexual immorality, often in the form of both male and female cult prostitution. The ultimate fulfilment of God's

---

2.   Coleman, P.; *Christian Attitudes to Marriage: From Ancient Times to the Third Millennium* (London, SCM Press, 2004) 2.

3.   Haughton R., *The Theology of Marriage* (Cork, The Mercier Press, 1971), 27.

4.   *Ibid,* 82–83.

covenant with Abraham is found in the life, death and resurrection of Jesus Christ and His eternal relationship with His Church — consisting of both believing Jews and Gentiles.

One result of the sin of Adam and Eve was the corruption of the relationship between the sexes. Genesis 2:18 describes Eve as the 'helper' of Adam. This verse has been misused to justify a misogynistic attitude which gives women an inferior status.[5] However, that perspective misses the point. The Hebrew concept contained in this verse means to be like but opposite. It is a concept of the difference and complementarity of the two sexes which are brought together in marriage. Eve was like Adam in being created in God's image, but was created to complement him rather than replicate him. She was a companion for Adam, with whom he could dwell in true fellowship. Together they had the potential to procreate and fulfil the command of God to populate the earth. They were created with equal worth and value, but with different roles, temperaments, skills and gifting. The headship of Adam was to reflect the authority and self-giving nature of God. Eve's submission to Adam's authority was not intended to entail her subjugation, but rather recognition of God's authority as expressed in His created image and within the context of a mutually self-sacrificial and loving relationship.

The Fall of Adam and Eve led to the corruption of all human relationships, including marriage. By the time that the Law was given to the Israelites, Moses found it necessary to codify the circumstances in which divorce could occur within the civil legal framework as is recorded in Deuteronomy 24. Over the following centuries, this administrative measure was subject to debate regarding the circumstances in which it would apply. One school of thought argued that a man could divorce his wife if she displeased him in almost any way. This view reflected the view of marriage which saw the wife as the property of the husband with an inferior social and legal status. Another school of thought held that divorce was only permissible on the grounds of adultery. This view reflected

---

5.   *Op. Cit.*, 4.

the strand within Israelite society which emphasised the equality of husband and wife and their joint reflection of the image of God.[6]

THE TEACHING OF JESUS

It was within this cultural and religious context that the ministry of Jesus occurred. In the Sermon on the Mount, Jesus emphasised the internalised nature of adultery and introduced a more profound understanding of the Law which applies to the heart as well as to external behaviour (Matt. 5:31–32). He excluded the legitimacy of divorce except in the circumstances of sexual immorality. Asked by the Pharisees about the correct interpretation of the Mosaic Law on divorce, He robustly defended the Law and the sanctity of marriage (Matt. 19:1–12). Jesus began His answer by referring to the creation narrative. He reminded His questioners of the fact that God created only two sexes and that it is in the coming together of male and female in marriage that 'one flesh' is formed. He highlighted that it is God who joins people together in marriage and that humans should not seek to undo this divine work. Questioned further by His disciples, Jesus goes on to discuss those who do not marry either because they are eunuchs by birth, owing to the intervention of others or because they choose celibacy in order to pursue God's vocation for their lives. He adopts a strong line on divorce.

Although His comments were initiated by a question relating to the law on divorce, many Christians believe that the Lord also gave a clear indication in this passage that polygamy and homosexual relationships are incompatible with God's intent for human sexual relations. Certainly it is evident that Jesus endorsed the view that celibacy is God's plan for those who do not get married to someone of the opposite sex.

The Christian understanding of marriage is derived also from the general teaching of Jesus with regard to love for God and

---

6. This dispute was between those who followed the teachings of Rabbi Shammai and Rabbi Hillel. The former argued that a man could divorce his wife only on grounds of adultery and the latter for a much broader range of reasons, such as displeasing him in some matter relating to domestic affairs.

neighbour, His prioritisation of the Kingdom of God, and His resolute commitment to the mission He received from the Father. His call on the disciples to take up their cross reveals the absolute commitment and self-sacrifice which is demanded of Christians. In such a context, it is inconceivable that any self-gratifying agendas would be tolerated and temporal marital relationships are relativised in the light of the coming kingdom of God (Luke 20:34–36). Moreover, on a number of occasions during His earthly ministry Jesus uses the imagery of marriage to refer to the divine kingdom (Matt. 9:14–15; Matt. 22:1–14; Matt. 25:1–13). The implication is that marriage finds its ultimate fulfilment in the kingdom of God, but Jesus also states that marriage is a temporal institution of this present age (Matt. 22:30). The imagery of the Church as the bride of Christ features in the book of Revelation, suggesting a high vocation in marriage, but also relativising it as a temporal arrangement which will be superseded by full communion with God (Rev. 22:17).

THE TEACHING OF THE APOSTLES

The apostle Paul tells us, 'be imitators of God … And walk in love, as Christ loved us and gave himself up for us, a fragrant offering and sacrifice to God' (Eph. 5:1–2). Paul goes on to discuss marriage and instructs husbands, 'love your wives, as Christ loved the church and gave himself up for her…' (Eph. 5:25). The ordered nature of God and His relationship with His people is evident. So wives are instructed, 'submit to your own husbands, as to the Lord' and Paul draws the parallel between Christ's headship of the church and a husband's headship of his wife (Eph. 5:22–24). This structured relationship does not permit domestic abuse. The husband is not to treat his wife as a commodity but rather is expected to sacrifice himself in order to promote her well-being.

The apostle Peter endorses this view of marriage by encouraging Christian wives to have a gentle and quiet spirit. He links beauty of character on the part of Christian women with effective witness to the gospel. The respect given by Christian men to their wives facilitates communion with God and solicits a receptive response to prayer (1 Pet. 3:1–7). Peter's point is that, in Christ, the relationship between husband and wife is redeemed and the curse which befell relations between the sexes after the Fall is undone (Gen. 3:16; Rev. 22:3). No longer need wives fear domination by their husbands, as was common in the ancient pagan world and remains the case in some societies today. Nor is death to be feared. Her husband must respect her as someone who is equal in possessing human dignity and a joint heir with him of eternal life. Both men and women can know God and have a relationship with Him. This teaching on marriage contrasts with and challenges the strident nature of much of the modern feminist movement, but also rebukes misogyny and the objectification of women.

Paul encourages husbands and wives to meet the need for sexual intimacy of their spouse in order to counter the temptation to sexual immorality (1 Cor. 7:1–5). The principle which underpins this injunction is that by entering into a marriage a degree of autonomy is sacrificed, reflecting the 'one flesh' nature of the relationship. Neither party is completely independent from the other nor has absolute ownership over his or her body. There is both unity and diversity within the relationship. It is a relationship of mutual love in which two people sacrifice their own preferences in order to exist as one unit.[7] So the relationship within the Godhead is one of both unity and diversity and is characterised by love and self-giving.

Marriage reveals God's relational nature and His purpose for creation. That purpose is to call to Himself a people who will dwell and commune with Him eternally. As marriage is intended to be permanent until death causes it to end, it provides an analogy of God's eternal relationship with His people. This explains the strong line which Jesus takes on divorce (Mark 10:1–12).

In the Old Testament, Israel's worship of the gods of the surrounding pagan peoples is compared to an act of adultery.[8]

---

7. Paul's teaching does not justify marital rape as the consent and decision-making of both husband and wife are needed.

8. This is exemplified in the book of Hosea. Gomer, Hosea's adulterous wife, is analogous

In the New Testament, the church is presented as the faithful bride of Christ (Rev. 21:1–4). Moreover, we are told that God will dwell with His people. The original relationship which existed between God and mankind is restored and will last for eternity. God has made a covenant to love and redeem His people. Like marriage, it is a relationship which is permanent. God is faithful. It is the essence of His nature (Rom. 3:3–4; 1 Cor. 1:9; 2 Tim. 2:12). He will remain committed to the church forever.

The established Christian tradition considers lifelong monogamous marriage as God's ideal for human sexual relationship. Marriage is viewed as the cornerstone of interpersonal relationships, societal well-being and the appropriate context for raising children. Moreover, it reveals the Creator to humanity, is an analogy of Christ's relationship with the Church, and prophetic of the eternal kingdom of God. Marriage is established upon the foundation of the two sexes as an objective fact of, and reflecting the image of God in, creation.

Our understanding of the institution of marriage, therefore, is not a secondary matter upon which Christians can legitimately disagree, but rather it is a 'plumb line' issue in terms of Christian orthodoxy. Those Christians who seek to redefine marriage in order to accommodate the cultural norms of the age and to present a more 'inclusive' form of church are at risk of falling into the sin of heresy. By seeking to accommodate other types of relationship, they fail in their duty to faithfully represent God and to proclaim His truth to the world. Like Aaron at Mount Sinai, they are fashioning an idol and raising it up to be worshipped by the people of God.

THE BIBLE AND HOMOSEXUALITY

Karl Barth claimed that homosexual activity is motivated by a refusal to acknowledge and submit to God. It involves succumbing to the temptations of transcendence and/or autonomy and making

---

to the nation's unfaithfulness. The relationship breaks down, but subsequently Hosea is reconciled with Gomer. In a parallel with his personal life, God uses Hosea to pronounce judgment upon the Israelites but also to declare a promise of future restoration.

a claim for the power of God by seeking to overturn the created order.[9] Rather than being content to exemplify the image of God, we seek to rise above our creaturely nature and fall into the sin of idolatry. It is accompanied by a disregard for human beings. An ideal of masculinity and/or femininity free from relations with the opposite sex is accompanied by a desire to substitute someone of the same sex for the despised partner of the opposite sex which is motivated by a desire for autonomy, self-sufficiency and self-gratification.[10]

Robert Gagnon expresses a similar view, arguing that the complementarity of the two sexes is the key to understanding the biblical prohibition on homosexual relationships.[11] He suggests that such relationships are 'an inexcusable rebellion against God'.[12] Moreover, he views them as an attack on the true self which is created in the divine image.[13] He concludes that the writers of Scripture consistently viewed same-sex relationships as being contrary to nature.[14] Those biblical passages which refer to homosexual relationships paint a picture of an outright ban on all such activity, whether consensual or not. Particular condemnation is reserved for cases of homosexual rape or attempted rape, but also for shrine prostitution. Although there was no uniform approval or disapproval of homosexuality in the ancient world, shrine prostitution was the most acceptable form of such activity. Hence the biblical condemnation of such practices can be seen as an absolute rejection of homosexual activity.[15]

If marriage is a reflection of God in creation and human pride lies at the heart of homosexual behaviour, this suggests that on no account should Christians ascribe moral equivalence to these two

---

9. Barth K., *Church Dogmatics* Vol III, Part IV (Edinburgh, T&T Clark, 1961), 154.

10. *Ibid*, 165–166.

11. Gagnon R. *The Bible and Homosexual Practice: Texts and Hermeneutics* (Nashville, Abingdon Pres, 2001), 37.

12. *Ibid*, 40.

13. *Ibid*, 31–32.

14. *Ibid*, 61.

15. *Ibid*, 131.

distinct types of relationship. Rather same-sex relationships should be seen as an idolatrous parody of marriage in which the image of God is distorted by an attempt to be a god and to define the moral law for ourselves. The view that idolatry of self is at the heart of same-sex relationships is supported by a variety of scriptural references. Paul advises that the idolatry of the ancient pagan world was directly associated with homosexual conduct (Rom. 1:18–27). It was rejection of the revelation of God in nature, His law and the divinely sanctioned created order which underpinned this idolatry.[16] Other adverse social traits were associated also with Gentile idolatry. Pride, social injustice, sexual immorality, exploitation of the poor, oppression of the vulnerable, and humiliation of people of other nationalities were also characteristic of these societies (Isa. 1:7–17, Ezek. 16:48–49).[17] God, in an act of judgment, gave the Gentiles over to the inevitable outcome of their rebellion through the supplanting of natural relations, based on the complementarity of male and female, by same-sex relationships.

Some Christians reject the argument that Paul refers to consensual and exclusive same-sex relationships between adults. This view is in danger of ignoring the wider context of idolatry and its impact upon sexual morality. In twenty-first-century Britain people do not routinely attend a pagan temple and engage in sex with male and female cult prostitutes, nor consciously worship fertility gods. Nevertheless, the increase in premarital sex since the 1960s with an associated decline of commitment to marriage and increase in cohabitation, high levels of relationship breakdown and divorce, and overt same-sex relationships all have their root in a self-serving consumerist mindset and the worship of self.

Peter Jones argues that the sexual revolution which started during the 1960s, and has permeated Western societies ever since, is associated with the importation of Eastern spirituality and the rise

---

16.   *Ibid*, 79–86.

17.   References to Israel as Sodom refer to the adoption by the Israelites of idolatrous practices common to the surrounding Gentile nations.

of neo-paganism.[18] Specifically, he argues that pagan spirituality has always been associated with androgyny and the blurring of distinction between the sexes. The spiritual root of this is the denial of the distinction between Creator and creation, a denial which results in the worship of the creation as the means of sustaining life. Jones argues that the USA (and by implication other Western societies) in recent decades have changed religions, rejecting the Christian sexual ethic. In its place, a neo-pagan spirituality has been adopted which is associated with sexual promiscuity, homosexual behaviour and transgender identity.[19]

Jones's argument is very interesting. If we consider the attitude of the pagan Roman world towards marriage and compare it with modern secular society, some interesting similarities can be observed. In Roman society marriage was viewed as a private civil contract and divorce by mutual consent was allowed. Similarly, in modern secular Western societies marriage is increasingly being considered as a private matter between consenting adults. Although it is solemnised in, and recognised by, the civil law, increasingly society has moved to accept the view that people can define marriage for themselves, that divorce proceedings are largely a matter for the couple concerned, and that the public interest in maintaining marriages is irrelevant or non-existent. We have accepted no-fault divorce and reduced waiting periods prior to divorces being granted. Marriage has been redefined in law in order to accommodate the demands of same-sex couples for legal recognition.

REDEFINING MARRIAGE?

If marriage can be redefined by the state to suit the subjective experiences of one group in society, can it not be redefined further

---

18. He refers to this as 'Oneism' — the belief that creation is a single self-sustaining entity and that there is no distinctive Creator who sits outside of the creation and maintains it. He refers to the Judaeo-Christian world view as 'Twoism' — the belief that there is a distinction between the Creator and the creation.

19. Jones, P., *Androgyny: The Pagan Sexual Ideal*, Journal of the Evangelical Theology Society, Vol. 43/3, Sept. 2000, 443-469, available at www.etsjets.org/files/JETS-PDFs/43/43-3/43-3-pp443-469_JETS.pdf. Accessed 4.7.17.

to include other relationships? Once the objective definition of marriage as a relationship between one man and one woman and for life is compromised, what is to stop polygamy, three-person homosexual or bisexual relationships or even incestuous relationships being incorporated into the definition of marriage if sufficient demand exists?

The Christian understanding of marriage is that it has a public dimension with a public interest in its success. Its definition is not a subjective construct, but rather an objective fact which is derived from nature and creation. While the majority of the population identified as Christian and the churches maintained a powerful influence in national life, public attitudes to marriage remained fairly stable.

Over the last five decades, however, there has been a huge decline in active Christian commitment as expressed in regular church attendance.[20] As a consequence the largely Christian morality which was prevalent until the 1950s and 1960s has been incrementally substituted by one in which marriage, although still an aspiration of the majority, is viewed as an ideal but no longer a precondition for sexual relations or the procreation of children. The consequence of this sexual revolution has been the catastrophic undermining of family stability and social cohesion. For example, the number of couples in the UK who cohabited prior to marriage increased from roughly ten per cent during the late 1970s to approximately eighty per cent by the early twenty-first-century. Moreover, there was a decline of around 44% in the number of marriages that occurred per annum between 1972 and 2007.[21] Divorces increased from 56,000 in 1969 to over 140,000 in 2007 in the UK (excluding Northern Ireland), with forty per cent of marriages now ending in divorce.[22] Over fifty per cent of babies now being born in Scotland are the children of unmarried parents.

---

20. Evangelical Alliance, *Faith & Nation: Report of a commission of Inquiry to the UK Evangelical Alliance*, 36.

21. The Centre for Social Justice, *Every Family Matters: An in-depth review of family law in Britain* (London, 2010), 50.

22. The figure for England and Wales was 129,000 divorces in 2007. Added to this figure are the over 10,000 divorces a year in Scotland. *Ibid*, 51–52.

Marital breakdown has adverse consequences for society in terms of an increase in dysfunctional families, poverty, welfare dependency, crime, costs of elderly care and housing supply.[23] It may also be argued to cause psychological damage to children leading to a vicious cycle of insecurity and relationship breakdown. It may even increase the occurrence of homosexual relationships as a result of the psychological impact of absent fathers on boys.[24] Moreover, the increase in cohabitation adds to family instability with those in cohabiting relationships being much more likely than married couples to experience relationship breakdown. It is estimated, for example, that forty-three per cent of cohabiting couples split up by their child's fifth birthday in comparison to only eight per cent of married couples.[25] Yet sociological evidence is pointing to the benefits of marriage in terms of educational and health outcomes for children.[26] Overall there has been a catastrophic decline in interpersonal relational competence, with this phenomenon being particularly evident in poorer communities.

It is within the context of this decline in marriage that the demand of the lesbian, homosexual, bisexual, transgender and intersex communities (LGBTI) for legal recognition of their relationships has occurred. At the core of the LGBTI rights agenda is the desire to redefine the family, to undermine marriage as a social norm, to elevate same-sex relationships to a morally equivalent status with marriage, and to transcend the limitations of biology and creation by challenging the view that there are just two sexes.[27]

Government policies have come under increasing pressure to recognise same-sex relationships and to marginalise marriage.[28] The UK Government no longer refers to marriage in official forms,

---

23. Social Justice Policy Group, *Breakdown Britain* (London, 2006), 32–34.

24. Moberly E. R., *Homosexuality: A New Christian Ethic (Cambridge*, James Clarke, 1983), 2.

25. The Centre for Social Justice, *Every Family Matters*, 55.

26. *Ibid*, 57.

27. Morgan P., *Children as Trophies?: Examining the evidence on same-sex parenting* (Newcastle-upon-Tyne, The Christian Institute, 2002), 27.

28. *Ibid*, 28.

married couples are severely penalised in the tax and benefits system in comparison to single parents and there is an unwillingness to publicly recognise the benefits of marriage for fear of upsetting those in alternative family structures.[29] Legislative and policy trends, especially the ease of divorce, add to the pressures towards marital breakdown and social disintegration.[30] The uniqueness of marriage as a contributor to the common good is denied and the legal protections offered to it are extended to include other types of relationships. For example, in the UK most of the legal rights of marriage were granted to same-sex couples through civil partnership legislation in 2004. In 2014 the law was changed to allow same-sex couples in the UK (except in Northern Ireland) to get 'married'. The next stage of this social revolution will be to redefine gender, moving away from official recognition of there being only two sexes and giving societal acceptance and approval to a plethora of gender identities and giving legal recognition to 'non-binary' gender identity.

THE SECULAR STATE

These social changes and legislative developments are symptoms of a much deeper spiritual malaise. As Western societies have sought to grapple with the social changes which have arisen from the demise of Christendom, there has been an increasing centralisation of power in, and optimised expectations of, the state. The state presents itself as the ultimate guardian of moral law and, in effect, claims authority which resides in God alone. Increasingly subjective human rights constitute the basis of moral decision-making with those that are most persistent in articulating their demands able to define the parameters of the new moral code. Equality of outcome becomes the pre-eminent criterion by which justice is defined and the scriptural linkage between justice and righteousness is neglected by the institutions of the state.

---

29. The Centre for Social Justice, *Why is the Government anti-Marriage?* (London, 2009).

30. The Centre for Social Justice, *Every Family Matters*, 66.

In the secular ideology of the British state, Christianity is increasingly considered to be a private and subjective matter while equality and human rights are viewed as objective facts. However, it is those human rights that are subjectively interpreted while Christianity is based on objective truth. Where the choice is made to favour same-sex relationships over marriage, to change the sex on the birth certificates of transsexuals or to introduce a third category of gender on official forms, the subjective desires of individuals are prioritised over the objective reality of the created order.

The difficulty encountered by modern democratic states is that they may be drawn into a tyrannous relationship with society in which marriage is marginalised and religious liberty placed under undue restriction. The agenda pursued by LGBTI advocacy groups is not limited to demands for legal rights, but seeks also to obtain moral approval by society of same-sex relationships and to completely revolutionise societal norms with regard to sexuality and gender. Those voicing opposition to this ideological crusade suffer marginalisation and are often excluded from positions of influence in public life.

The state assumes an idolatrous position by seeking to redefine the moral law. Belief in the absolute sovereignty of human beings is combined with a failure to comprehend objective truth as revealed through creation and Scripture. The revelation of the Creator in nature is rejected and we worship an idol of our own making. The consequence is that God, in an act of judgment, gives us up to become slaves to our passions. Loss of interpersonal integration and social cohesion, including increased practice of same-sex relationships and gender confusion, are expressions of this judgment.

Marriage is an objective right as evidenced by its procreative purpose, social benefits and prophetic character. Its subversion by a subjective rights agenda runs contrary to divine and natural law upon which are based all truly valid laws. It is a creation ordinance which predates the founding of the modern state, supports the common good of humanity, and is intrinsic to the divine image in human beings.

The modern secular state does not have the authority to redefine marriage. For the state to seek to do so is an expression of idolatry. It is God who defines marriage, instituting it for all human history as a witness to His nature and intent for creation and for the good of society. The state may choose to fulfil its God-given mandate and voluntarily submit to Christ's authority or assert an idolatrous claim to ultimate sovereignty. The state and the church should both uphold marriage as a unique and praiseworthy institution which is due support and to be protected. No other sexual relationship should be elevated to the same level, as doing so will demote marriage from its rightful position and result in the breakdown of interpersonal integration in society.

The fate of Sodom remains a warning for every idolatrous political society which rejects the revelation of God, exalts itself, disregards marriage, promotes homosexual behaviour, and indulges in injustice and oppression of the poor and vulnerable (Ezek. 16:48–49). In a warning about false teachers within the church, Jude tells us that the fate of Sodom is a type for the final judgment of those who reject Christ (Jude 7). As in the case of Sodom, the idolisation of self leads ultimately to death, whereas the narrow path to life is found through faith in Jesus Christ and submission to His will.

This applies not only in relation to the spiritual life of individuals and churches but also to the communal life of societies. Yet when speaking of those who reject the gospel message as preached by His disciples, Jesus commented that it will be more bearable for the people of Sodom than for those people on the last day. Speaking of the Galilean towns where much of His ministry occurred, He said that the pagan people of Tyre and Sidon would have repented if the miracles Jesus did had been performed in those towns (Luke 10:10–15). The Lord's message is that those who hear the truth and reject it stand in danger of a more devastating judgment that that which befell Sodom. With our strong Christian heritage but also rapidly secularising society, that is the warning to which we should pay attention.

MARRIAGE AND THE COMING KINGDOM

The UK's Christian heritage and our national settlement on the roles of the church and the state were largely shaped by the sixteenth-century Reformation. The Reformers viewed marriage as an intrinsic good, arguing that God intended men and women to come together in order equally to procreate and for reasons of companionship. By serving God through the bond of marriage, parents raised and passed on the Christian faith to their children. God's blessing on marriage was acknowledged and reflected in the analogy of marriage with the relationship between Christ and the Church. Grace was imparted through faith alone rather than through marriage which was no longer considered to be a sacrament. The regulation of marriage was considered to lie within the jurisdiction of the civil authorities, who were expected to act as ministers of God in restraining evil and promoting the common good of society.[31]

We should not lightly throw off the wisdom passed down to us by our forefathers. Marriage remains a valid societal norm which contributes to the common good of humanity. It is a creation ordinance which has proved to be beneficial throughout history. Its purpose is to meet the need of human beings for intimacy and companionship, whilst providing a stable context for procreation and the raising of children.

It cannot be arbitrarily redefined by human governments because its definition rests upon God's authority and is written into the laws of nature. In contrast, postmodern political society emphasises the prioritisation of self-actualisation. It is characterised by a radical view of the equality of the sexes, which includes gender reassignment, the redefinition and undermining of marriage, and the promotion of diversity in family structures and sexual lifestyle choices. It seeks to displace the image of God in human beings by the idolisation of self. Its emphasis on sexual lifestyle choice presents a utopian vision based on human self-expression. Revelation of God in creation is denied, a new moral order is substituted

---

31. Coleman, *Christian Attitudes to Marriage*, 188.

for the law of God, and a false eschatology is promoted. This new order denies original sin and repudiates the command of God that 'all people everywhere [should] repent' (Acts 17:30).

Both the church and state are called to be witnesses to the eternal kingdom and the ultimate judgment of God. The godly king and the faithful high priest remain instruments of divine mission in the world. The two witnesses of Revelation 11 represent Moses and Elijah who respectively provided the law and spoke the words of God to Israel. They may be seen to represent the law-making function of human government and the teaching ministry of the church, imagery which refers also to the two olive trees mentioned by Zechariah (Rev. 11:1–12; Zech. 4:11–14; 6:9–15).

Marriage is prophetic of the coming kingdom of God. Denial of the true nature of marriage and the promotion of an idolatrous parody in its place constitutes a rebellion against the authority of God. If the church and the state engage in such actions, they fail to fulfil their respective missions to represent God to the world and they endorse a pagan world view. If our society does so, we can only expect that the Lord will remove His Spirit from our denominational and civic structures and that societal demise will not be long in following. To love God is to obey His commands (John 14:15). Where a remnant of faithful people does so and remains true to God's Word, the Lord's grace and mercy may be found. The promise of God remains for those who keep His law through the grace of Christ.

For thus says the LORD: 'To the eunuchs who keep my Sabbaths, who choose the things that please me and hold fast my covenant, I will give in my house and within my walls a monument and a name, better than sons and daughters; I will give them an everlasting name that shall not be cut off' (Isa. 56:4–6).

I am coming soon. Hold fast what you have, so that no one may seize your crown. The one who conquers, I will make him a pillar in the temple of my God. Never shall he go out of it, and I will write on him the name of my God, and the name of the city of my

God, the new Jerusalem, which comes down from my God out of heaven, and my own new name (Rev. 3:11–12).

Hallelujah! For the Lord our God the Almighty reigns. Let us rejoice and exult and give him the glory, for the marriage of the Lamb has come, and his Bride has made herself ready. … Blessed are those who are invited to the marriage supper of the Lamb (Rev. 19:6–7, 9).

For these reasons, I (still) believe in marriage.

WHY I (STILL) BELIEVE IN PUBLIC CHRISTIANITY

Gordon Wilson

This chapter is addressed to people who believe in God and the Lord Jesus Christ but feel at a loss or are dispirited because Christianity in the Western world appears to be in retreat.

The mention of the Western world — Europe and the United States of America — is deliberate. In other parts of the world the picture is different. To put things into perspective, it is worthwhile reminding ourselves of the international position. According to figures in the CIA Fact Book 2012, there are some 2.3 billion Christians in the world. Christianity is the fastest growing faith by conversion and natural growth so that every year there are an additional 25 million new Christians (World Christian Encyclopaedia). In proportionate terms there are 33.39% Christians, 22.74% Muslims, 13.8% Hindus and 8.77% Buddhists — to specify only the major faiths.

Given the 'noise' created by the atheists and secularists of today, it is salutary to note that there were only 9.66% non-religious and 2.01% atheists (estimated as at 2010). For most of the world, God is recognised and Christianity is holding its own. Indeed much of the surge in support for Islam comes from population growth in Islamic states rather than by conversion — even enforced conversion!

This does not mean that all is well in many countries outside the West. Save in the relatively liberal Gulf countries with their large expatriate populations, faiths other than Islam cannot be practised. In the Middle East, the rise of fundamentalist Islam has led to persecution, martyrdom and the expulsion of Christians. In Eritrea, Ethiopia and Egypt, with their deeply rooted Coptic faiths, Christians find themselves marginalised and attacked. There is interfaith conflict in Sahel Africa with many adherents being attacked and killed by Islamic militias. The tolerance of centuries has dissipated. In Iraq and Syria, Christians have suffered especially and many have fled to other countries or languish in refugee camps. Areas in Turkey and Syria which saw the earliest expansion of the Christian faith under the apostle Paul are now without churches. In China, to worship in an unauthorised church is to risk prison.

Despite this, the Christian faith has grown and is growing. The Lord Jesus never pretended that the way would be easy. From the beginning Christians were persecuted. Stephen, the first martyr, was stoned to death in Jerusalem, with Paul (or Saul as he was known then before his conversion) holding the coats of the killers in full approval of their actions. Many of the apostles including Paul met their own deaths as martyrs. In more recent times, death or exile was the fate of many Christians in the atheist Soviet Union or in the concentration camps of the cesspit of evil that was Nazi Germany.

Set against the sufferings of many men and women for their faith, our problems of the decline in religious observance in Europe are trivial. No one is going to attack us physically, let alone kill us.

But we are under attack. The year 1955 saw the highest church attendances in Scotland. Since then it has been downhill all the way for the established churches. The Christian churches have been marginalised and divorced from society. Many churches have been hollowed out with dwindling, ageing congregations. The number of ministers and priests has dropped and soon with retirements it will no longer be possible to have a church active in every community.

And yet, and yet! The position is not all black. In the United Kingdom, between 2008 and 2013, the total number of churches has risen from 49,727 (itself a significant figure) to 50,660. As the establishment churches have lost members and churches, there has been a staggering growth in Pentecostal and other smaller churches.

The traditional churches feeling the pain most are the Anglican, Methodist, Presbyterian and Baptist Churches. Yet Edinburgh Theological Seminary (formerly the Free Church of Scotland College) had a student intake of twenty-six in 2015,[1] and the Church of Scotland in the same year saw twenty-seven new students for the ministry.[2] This is evidence that there is an unsatisfied spiritual need in the UK today. It should also be noted that some of the growth can be attributed to immigrants who have brought with them a greater devotion and a more lively expression of worship than is sometimes found in indigenous churches.

Even in Victorian times, the churches found it difficult to increase attendance although nearly one hundred per cent of the population would have regarded themselves as Christian — which was where the Salvation Army and gospel reformers came to help fill the gap. Nominalism was rife and at various times there would be waves of revival.

So, for much of urban society there has been little change, except that a sizable proportion would no longer pay lip service to the existence of God or the moral duties associated with Christianity. Why this has happened is a question for social historians but there is little doubt that there has been a revolution in social attitudes since the 1950s when the churches were last at their zenith. The sexual liberation of the 1960s following upon the discovery and use of the contraceptive pill made the commandment for continence inconvenient when the penalty of pregnancy had been eliminated. The taking of drugs became acceptable. Hedonism was the *leitmotif* of the age. Set against this revolution in values, it is hardly surprising that the disciplines of biblical Christianity became countercultural, seemingly oppressive, and scarcely relevant to the needs of the

---

1. Of whom seven are candidates for ministry in the Free Church; the others are preparing for other ministries.

2. www.churchofscotland.org.uk/news_and_events/news/recent/church_welcomes_surge_in_new_trainee_ministers_as_hundreds_reach_retirement_age. Accessed 4.7.17.

twentieth century. And so apathy set in, bringing with it the stable-mate of ignorance.

If this were not bad enough, there was the huge upsurge in global capitalism which led to large-scale unemployment for some and wealth for many, to the attitude that society was for the strong to do well at the expense of the weak, and to a departure from the standards of Judeo-Christianity. Narcissism and worship of self became more important than society as a whole or the needs of others. Self-being became more important than care for others, fidelity went out of the window — another inconvenient instruction from the Bible — and so the former roots of society were undermined.

There is also the incongruity of humanism — the worship of humanity when the truth is that humankind is faulty. The human race may be technologically advanced, but by its addiction to violence it remains emotionally primitive, and yet humanity persists in its mistaken belief that, apart from cosmic disaster, it is master of its own destiny. Evidence of war and the pollution of the atmosphere shows that we are authors of the problems of the world; can there be any greater degree of hubris than this kind of arrogance?

For the West in the twilight of moral ascendancy, there is also an argument that in the broad expanse of time, greater economic forces were at work. Western society had been responsible for the spread of Christianity to Africa, South America and Asia. Now Western power is well past its peak. European countries no longer have empires or the same influence in the world. Rising powers such as China and India are far more important and the old certainties of Western civilisation have gone.

It is almost as if the West is facing the same decline, if not decadence, as brought about the fall of the Roman Empire. And with the loss of power, there has come a moral and ethical blindness in which sporadic military adventurism and international play-acting are replacements for the exercise of responsible leadership. When belief goes, then all is at risk.

In recent years, the pressures have intensified. Society is more intolerant of diversity. Political and cultural correctness surfaced.

With it, militant secularism appeared. Before, there was mutual respect between people of faith and those who had none — 'live and let live' was the theme.

Now, political correctness dominates and promotes the view that religion was a bad thing and ought to be extirpated. It has led attacks against the concept of faith. It wanted to proscribe the teaching of religion in schools including intelligent design. Some of the attacks were led by Richard Dawkins and intellectually by the late Christopher Hitchens. Others came from small militant groups of writers of articles and letters to the press. Their weapon of choice was the Equality Act, hitched to gay rights. Midwives who did not wish to perform abortions were faced with struggles of conscience or dismissal from their jobs. Those who did not conform to the demands of the state for equality at the expense of conscience were sued or coerced.

That is the world in which UK Christians now live. The state rules and must be obeyed. There is no room for individual conscience. Strangely, after the passage of two thousand years, it is not much different, except in degree and punishment, from the challenge that faced Peter, Paul and other early Christians. If they did not worship Caesar as a god, the Roman state would condemn them to imprisonment or worse. So when latter-day Christians feel despondent about the disrespect offered to their religion or worried about the anti-religious views of society, they have no reason to whine. We get it easy compared to practitioners of our religion through the ages. But we do need a whiff of their courage!

A WIND OF CHANGE?

Every now and then, there are revolutions in attitudes. There is a long, flat S-curve. We have now seen fifty years of licence and neo-liberalism. There is the beginning of a perception of the damage caused by unrestrained behaviour. Drug addiction, alcoholism, insecurity for children engendered by lack of respect for marriage, the rise of single parent families and in particular those relationships producing children from casual encounters, are evident. Feminists are aghast that the woman's right to choose means in some societies that the families opt for male children. Young women complain that pornography means that some males look upon them as the equivalent of sex toys to the exclusion of deeper relationships.

If my intuitions are correct, society is beginning to react against the prevalent philosophies of the past half century. But if so, it will take time to effect significant change even in these days of swift worldwide communication, and probably not until two or more 'baby-booming' generations pass on.

All very well, you may complain, but what about now? God has all the time of the universe but we do not. We are anxious for positive movement now. If that's how you think, you are going to be disappointed.

Let's put it into another contemporary frame. The impact of a small group of committed people can be illustrated from my experience. I joined the Scottish National Party in 1959. I believed in Scottish independence and was prepared to work for it more in hope than expectation. The SNP then was a tiny organisation of around two thousand members (probably exaggerated), few branches and no members of parliament. Let me put it this way: it was not seen as a good prospect for an ambitious young man!

And yet through the dedicated, organised work of a few activists it made progress over the decades, even if that progress was slow and often wracked by failure, gloom and defeat. After the 2015 UK general election, fifty-six of Scotland's fifty-nine Westminster Members of Parliament represented the SNP, although this was reduced to thirty-five in the 2017 Election, and in the Scottish Parliament sixty-three of the one hundred and twenty-eight Members represent the SNP. The Party came within a stone's throw of winning an independence referendum in 2014. Who could have seen those outcomes sixty years ago — but they happened!

There is a lesson here. The few SNP activists did not bring about this momentous change on the basis of their own blood and sweat. What they did over decades was to change attitudes and identities within this ancient nation so that being British receded and being Scottish marched onwards — aided and abetted by the tumultuous changes in society emerging from decline of empire, industrial decline, the impact of emigration and the gradual emergence of a new feeling of self-confidence, summed up in the first election slogan of President Barack Obama — 'Yes we can'.

However, it is reckless to pin any case to politics. Causes and personalities can detract from the arguments. Emotion and prejudice not infrequently unbalance judgment. Also, the vocation or trade of politics is not ranked highly these days. This is unfair. Parliaments are microcosms of people, with a distribution of the principled and the unprincipled, virtuous people and rogues. Perhaps it is self-selecting and certainly not for the shy or the humble, but within all political parties in all parliaments, there are many who are genuine servants of the people. It is equally true if parliaments reflect the populace, there will be many Christians. Those of us who are not atheists expect them to have the courage to speak up in public or in parliament to defend the faith and the values of that faith.

CHRISTIAN INFLUENCE

If it is right that we are on the cusp of societal change, how can we as Christians advance the cause of Jesus Christ?

Firstly, we have the blueprint laid out in the Bible. The early Christians were a threat to the consensual establishment. Just read the Acts of the Apostles for a taste of how the adherents of Judaism regarded Christianity as both blasphemous and sacrilegious, and how later the might of the Roman Empire was deployed against this troublesome sect. Yet the Great Commission handed down by the Lord Jesus was to spread the gospel of forgiveness and salvation to all peoples. This Great Commission still stands as our battle orders but we should not expect an easy time of it.

Evidence shows that amongst the more traditional churches, the ones that are escaping the worst effects of retreat are those of evangelical persuasion — that is, those which base their message on the Bible and are not prepared to go with the flow of a dissolute, unbelieving society. Of greater damage to Christianity than the revolution of the 1960s has been the softness of the established churches, unwilling to preach an unflinching message. Instead there is the heresy that since God is love He will forgive all behaviour regardless of the lack of repentance, thus reducing the Creator of the universe to an impotent idol.

And then we have *le trahison des clerc,*[3] the willingness of some clergy to pick and choose from the Bible those parts which suit the 'neo-liberal' tendency to go with the flow. If you give people 'pap', it is no wonder that attendances fall off. The message is not worth listening to! They forget that, given the nature of humankind, the Christian message is truly countercultural. It is the radical content that holds the appeal and increasingly will do so to a new generation seeking fresh inspiration.

Every now and then, there is a need for reformation in our religion as happened through the work of Luther and Calvin. This brought a reappraisal of man's relationship to God, and it is evidence that determined inspiration and work by the few can give the leverage that in due course of time moves the mores of the earth.

A NEW REFORMATION

A new reformation of the church will take the work of exceptional men and women whose genius will slowly percolate through Western civilisation and change the outlook of influential leaders and many of the people. Given the power of modern communications, such changes would also extend to Europe. There is, of course, no guarantee that any change will come from the top down. This then raises the problem of endeavouring to induce change at congregational and pastoral levels and how it can be achieved.

Here is an example. In 2007, my wife and I were attracted to St Peter's Free Church of Scotland in Dundee. Its pastor, David Robertson, had never been shy of expressing a muscular and vocal

---

3.   The betrayal of the intellectuals.

Christianity in the press, and his book, *The Dawkins' Letters*[4] (a response to the militant atheism of Richard Dawkins) made us want to hear more. We were brought to a deeper experience of the Christian faith.

Was it coincidence or grace that brought two entirely different people together and sparked a new approach? Who can be sure! David was beginning to gain a reputation as an evangelist. He was also a visionary. He sensed that after years of apathy and ignorance there was the wakening of new interest. By contrast, I had been a lawyer and politician, equipped with the practical skills of the former and the intuition of the latter. In my political career, I had been SNP Member of Parliament for Dundee East and for eleven years Party leader. All of this, with retirement, lay behind me, but it is difficult to cast off the experiences and skills of a lifetime.

So, after many discussions with David, and being aware that he was trying to do too much evangelistic work on top of his pastoral duties, it became clear to me that he needed an organisational platform to expand his work. Out of this came the formation of Solas (Centre for Public Christianity) — firstly informally with trustees and then as a charitable company.

The organisation operated under the brand name of Solas (the Gaelic word for light), but its purpose is better expressed through the longer title of *Centre for Public Christianity,* for this encapsulated the very real difficulty of projecting an unfashionable message to a secular world which was hostile to it. It is all very well to talk of going into the public market-place of old as did the apostle Paul, but what could you do if the modern version of the market-place, namely the media — press, radio and television — exercised the censorship of non-access?

The intention of the *Centre for Public Christianity* was to interconnect with modern society in imaginative ways, to penetrate the silence and through that get Jesus' message into public awareness. Solas uses social media for messaging, cafes as neutral places to engage those unlikely to darken the doors of churches,

---

4.   Christian Focus Publications, 2007.

and music. It does not act alone but seeks to train church leaders to encourage fellow Christians to assert the relevance of Christ in the modern world. Its activities have ranged from training in the UK to bringing evangelists from Europe for intensive courses.

This is a template for positive action by others elsewhere. And there is a more positive case to be advanced. Dogged by Darwinism for over one hundred and fifty years, science through molecular biology is revealing that the theory that Natural Selection was behind the creation of life and its development, the assertion that a chain of accidental mutations was responsible for life, is false. Such are the sophistications of DNA and molecular constructs that the odds against casual change exhaust the probabilities of accident and leave only the concept of intelligent design. Of course, for many people, an aversion to God means that they are more likely to believe in alien intervention — an advanced version of fairies at the bottom of the garden! Those who do not want to believe will stubbornly refuse to believe.

But it is not only in the sphere of life sciences that the existence of a universal Creator can be established. Professor John Lennox of Oxford University has asserted that the order of creation of the earth follows that of Genesis.[5] The Universe from the time of the 'big bang' operates to a system of physical laws without which nothing would have gelled.

Intriguingly, the cosmologist Professor Stephen Hawking, Research Director at Cambridge University's Department of Applied Mathematics and Theoretical Physics, was not very sanguine about the future of mankind when he declared in response to a question at the end of the BBC Reith Lectures on 7 January 2016:

> We face a number of threats to our survival from nuclear war, catastrophic global warming and genetically engineered viruses. The number is likely to increase in the future, with the development of new technologies, and new ways things can go wrong. Although

---

5.   *Seven Days that Divide the World* (Zondervan, 2011).

the chance of a disaster to planet Earth in a given year may be quite low, it adds up over time and becomes a near certainty in the next 1,000 or 10,000 years. By that time we should have spread out into space, and to other stars, so a disaster on Earth would not be the end of the human race.

Here is a clear admission of the dangers that the human race faces without support from the Creator, given that stellar travel may exist only in the imagination of science fiction.

The message of intelligent design is there to see. How do we get it over to unbelievers? Firstly, the apathy of the last few decades including the drift from the formalised setting of churches combined with shallow or non-existent knowledge of the Bible is leading, however gradually, to curiosity. It is that void or (dare I use the word) market to which we should direct attention.

Great intellects essential for another reformation cannot be ordered up online with the click of a mouse. There are some there but more are needed. For ordinary souls, there are some basic steps.

Initially, we need to expunge the defensive mentality that religion is on the way out. Far from it. It is on the way back.

Secondly, we have to sharpen our approach and make it suitable for all intellects. Many years ago, I exchanged canvassing techniques with a Mormon missionary. He had a copy of the Book of Mormon for those seriously interested, but he also had a folder putting the case of his church in a fashion that suited the intellect of the subject, progressively simpler and culminating in comic form. It catered for every taste. The essence was that it had a simple message to impart — the theology would come later!

With a more assertive Christian message, the next step is through training to give members of church congregations the knowledge to engage in debate, answer questions and above all have the confidence to speak out. This will provide activity at a grass roots level which is essential to gain momentum and roll back the atheism and secularism that is currently in the ascendancy and on the attack. It is not rocket science. Political parties carry out this sort of training all the time.

We must also make a better pitch for the young, making sure that our schools do not become proselytisers for the atheist world view. Christian education is essential and more thought has to be given to this critical element. One way would be to produce a series of films on the problems faced by Jesus in His ministry, the adventures of the apostles as they wrestled with the dangers of life in Jerusalem and elsewhere after Jesus' death; if you really want an exciting serial drama where better to look for plots than in Acts of the Apostles as they follow the trials and tribulations of Paul as he brought the gospel to audiences in life-threatening circumstances? Previously there would be no market in the commercial cinemas but now with the spread of streaming, there are opportunities for access to a broader audience.

Obviously, even if some costs could be recouped, it would be extraordinarily expensive. But why not have a pilot — and, given the vast amount of money expended on crumbling church buildings housing dwindling and ageing congregations, it would be worth the effort provided it was done professionally. Then there are videos for YouTube and other social media. The world of entertainment has moved in a revolutionary manner with this digital age. Can we really say the Christian movement (I prefer this broader definition than 'churches') has risen to the challenges of the twenty-first-century?

I (still) believe in public Christianity.

'Always be prepared to give an answer to everyone who asks you to give the reason for the hope that you have, but do this with gentleness and respect.' This admonition was given through Peter who, on a famous occasion (Mark 14:66-72), was rather unprepared to stand up for Jesus. But he was ransomed, healed, restored and forgiven, and he became a powerful witness and evangelist. Through his words, God calls His people to be prepared to share the good news that centres on the life, death and resurrection of Jesus Christ.

The ministry of **SOLAS – Centre for Public Christianity** is to give expression to the good news of that gospel in the public realm and to encourage and equip Christians to make open and public profession of their faith within the context of twenty-first-century European culture.

In response to those who seek to exclude Christianity from public life, SOLAS believes in the truth and contemporary relevance of the gospel. We believe that Europe was founded upon and largely owes its culture to Christianity, and that the current retreat from Christianity is leading to the breakdown of society and the collapse of family life. Secularism represents a backward step, and all the time Jesus offers fullness of life (John 10:10). We aim to enable people to reclaim this Christian heritage.

This involves vigorous public engagement on a number of fronts. SOLAS has been involved in public debates and conferences. We intend to provide good-quality training and resources, such as the Solas magazine (solasmagazine.com), Short Answers (solas-cpc.org/wp/shortanswers) and The Solas Papers (solas-cpc.org/wp/solas-resources/solas-papers). We will encourage Christians and churches to use the arts, philosophy, music, history, society, media, medicine, science, theology and the community of the church to express and teach the Christian faith, as given to us in the Bible.

Our vision is for church-based persuasive evangelism, particularly focusing on sceptics, cultural influencers and critical thinkers. We want to engage in positive apologetics, addressing current issues and the intellectual struggles related to those concerns, as well as the humanitarian needs of those at risk within society.

Our goal is the spread of the gospel and the extension of Christ's kingdom.

Also available from Christian Focus...

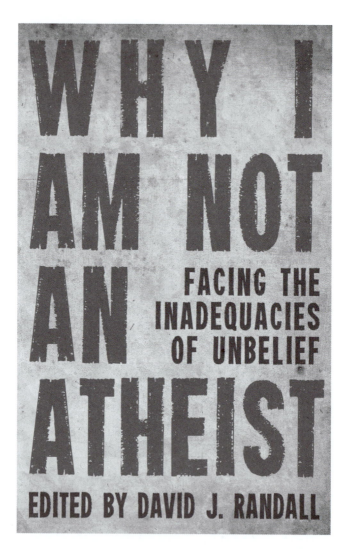

ISBN 978-1781-91270-6

WHY I AM NOT AN ATHEIST

Edited by DAVID J. RANDALL

Eleven Christians — including a biologist, a psychiatrist, a journalist, and a debater — travelled on eleven diverse paths to faith in Jesus Christ. This book is the compilation of their answers and experiences written in response to Bertrand Russell's *Why I Am Not A Christian*.

Contributors include Donald Bruce, Alistair Donald, Henk Drost, Elaine Duncan, Alex MacDonald, Pablo Martinez, David J. Randall, David Robertson, Chris Sinkinson, Heather Tomlinson and Ravi Zacharias.

Each of the contributors bring a warmth and rigor that is both personal and fully engaged with the questions our world — and our hearts — ask. This book will help your heart rejoice in the God who is Lord over every square inch of his creation, and whose word is trustworthy and true.

Mark Ellis
Pastor of Grace Church,
Dundee

For the many honest, open-minded sceptics who do want to reasonably weigh all the evidence, this book will be thought-provoking, stimulating and perhaps even life-changing.

William Philip
Minister of The Tron Church,
Glasgow

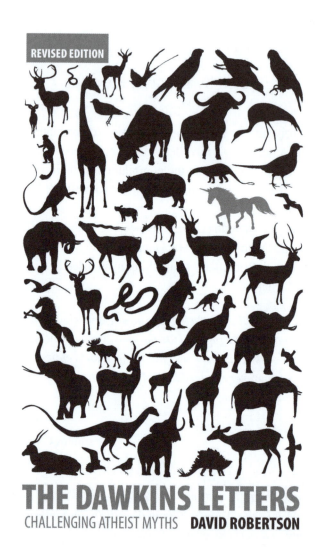

REVISED EDITION

THE DAWKINS LETTERS
CHALLENGING ATHEIST MYTHS   **DAVID ROBERTSON**

ISBN 978-1845-50597-4

THE DAWKINS LETTERS

David Robertson

When Richard Dawkins published *The God Delusion*, David Robertson wanted an intelligent Christian response — and so he wrote it. This honest book draws on Robertson's experience as a debater, letter writer, pastor and author to clarify the questions and the answers for thinkers and seekers, and to respond to Dawkins in a gentle spirit.

This book is a more than useful contribution to the 'Dawkins Debate' and one which has helped me to understand more about the flawed arguments contained within The God Delusion ... *Robertson is clearly well-read and marshals his arguments in a balanced and intellectually sound way. But this is not an inaccessible academic treatise; he writes clearly and understandably in such a way that most people will be able to grasp the arguments easily. He avoids the temptation to 'rubbish' Dawkins, just dismantles and challenges his arguments frankly and cohesively.*

Christian Marketplace
Resourcing retailers and suppliers

The book does a particularly good job of pointing out the unending contradictions between what Dawkins wants to believe and what he must actually believe.

Tim Challies
Blogger at www.challies.com

Christian Focus Publications

Our mission statement –

STAYING FAITHFUL
In dependence upon God we seek to impact the world through literature faithful to His infallible Word, the Bible. Our aim is to ensure that the Lord Jesus Christ is presented as the only hope to obtain forgiveness of sin, live a useful life and look forward to heaven with Him.

Our Books are published in four imprints:

CHRISTIAN FOCUS

popular works including biographies, commentaries, basic doctrine and Christian living.

CHRISTIAN HERITAGE

books representing some of the best material from the rich heritage of the church.

MENTOR

books written at a level suitable for Bible College and seminary students, pastors, and other serious readers. The imprint includes commentaries, doctrinal studies, examination of current issues and church history.

CF4•K

children's books for quality Bible teaching and for all age groups: Sunday school curriculum, puzzle and activity books; personal and family devotional titles, biographies and inspirational stories – Because you are never too young to know Jesus!

Christian Focus Publications Ltd,
Geanies House, Fearn, Ross-shire,
IV20 1TW, Scotland, United Kingdom.
www.christianfocus.com